The Making of
Totalitarian Thought

The Making of Totalitarian Thought

Josep R. Llobera

Oxford • New York

First published in 2003 by
Berg
Editorial offices:
1st Floor, Angel Court, 81 St Clements Street, Oxford, OX4 1AW, UK
838 Broadway, Third Floor, New York, NY 10003-4812, USA

Berg is an imprint of Oxford International Publishers Ltd.

Library of Congress Cataloging-in-Publication Data
Llobera, Josep R.
    The making of totalitarian thought / Josep R. Llobera.
    p. cm.
    ISBN 1-85973-790-0 (Cloth) – ISBN 1-85973-795-1 (Paper)
    1. Totalitarianism–History. 2. Race discrimination–History. 3. Social
Darwinism–History. 4. Eugenics–History. 5. History, Modern. I. Title.

    JC480.L596 2003
    320.53–dc21

                                                                003006207

British Library Cataloguing-in-Publication Data
A catalogue record for this book is available from the British Library.

ISBN 1 85973 790 0 (Cloth)
      1 85973 795 1 (Paper)

Typeset by JS Typesetting Ltd, Wellingborough, Northants.
Printed in the United Kingdom by Biddles Ltd, Guildford and King's Lynn.

www.bergpublishers.com

Contents

Introduction   1

1 Prelude to Modernity   7

2 Theorising the 'Other': The Emergence of a Discourse on Race
    in Sixteenth-Century Spain   17

3 Genealogies of Race   27

4 The French Revolution and Early Critics of Modernity: The
    Legacy of Maistre   41

5 Racial Theories of History: The Legacy of Gobineau   57

6 Darwinism and Social Darwinism: The Legacy of Galton   73

7 Crowd Theories: The Legacy of Le Bon   85

8 The New Science of Anthroposociology and Eugenics: The Legacy
    of Vacher de Lapouge   103

9 The Idea of Revolutionary Violence: The Legacy of Sorel   121

10 The Origins of Nazi Ideology   135

Bibliography   145

Index   167

Introduction

That material civilization does not ensure moral progress was the central proposition forcefully set forth by Rousseau in his *First Discourse*. It was a simple but disturbing truth that has been an anathema to the spirit of modernity that has dominated the world until the horrors of the very 'civilized' twentieth century (wars, genocides, tortures, famines, and so forth) convinced even the most sceptical of its fundamental actuality.

The twentieth century, which only began in 1914, ran its natural course by 1989. The preaching of new gospels has already commenced in earnest. Radical conservatives tell us that if mankind can survive its own militaristic foolishness, the true millennium is heralded in the astonishing technological revolution of the present in the context of a revitalized free market. On the other hand, for the postmodernists, the time of reckoning with past masters who failed in their predictions is in full swing; it is part of the normal process of intellectual purification required to enter the new promised land – a world characterized by the atomization of the socio-political and the distrust of legitimizing grand narratives. From the end of the era it is now safe to pass judgement on those thinkers of modernity – and they are legion – who prophesized, for the twentieth century, a bourgeois or a socialist heavenly kingdom based on industrialism.

What is extraordinary is not so much that we should have remained faithful to the creed of modernity for such a long time – after all material progress has an obnubilating effect – but rather that we should have ignored and muffled those voices who by the late nineteenth century were expressing serious doubts about the blessings of Western industrial civilization. Furthermore, these voices were not only critical of the pretensions of modernity; they were also clarifying, articulating and analysing the mytho-ideological elements required to understand (and even to make possible) the totalitarian movements of the century. In doing that, they were also throwing light on some uncomfortable principles of human nature and of social life.

The failure of the twentieth century to deliver its promises lies squarely in the inability of human beings to foster a sense of community at the national and, more importantly, at the international level. The irony of it all is that the bloodiest of struggles and confrontations have been fought by classes and states in the name of cultural values that were presented to people as communitarian in character, while hiding, in fact, the most naked egotistic interests of a few individuals or of a small elite.

The first three chapters of the book deal with issue of race in Western civilization. In Chapter 1 the Greco-Roman and the medieval world are briefly considered. It is a long and ambiguous period concerning race, although certain issues emerge slowly. The sixteenth century is, however, decisive in so far as, with the discovery of America, the appearance of a different race is widely challenging the existing social order. This happened essentially in the Spanish realm, where a vivid theological discussion on the American Indians took place. Chapter 2 explores the issue of whether the American natives were humans or non-humans. This was the crucial question, which was vigorously discussed over the years. On the other hand, the Spanish kingdom developed an ideology that viewed the Jews as a practically unchangeable race, and not a purely religious group. In this respect, race was an emerging element of the Spanish configuration.

Chapter 3 explores the early modern period in Western Europe. The myth of race, as the belief that mankind is divided into biologically different groups that can be classified hierarchically on an intellectual and moral basis, is very much a product of the expansion of Europe at the world level. The continuing process of political domination and of the economic success of the West bred a feeling of European superiority, which translated itself into a racial theory. Authors like Linnaeus, Buffon and Cuvier are considered.

With Chapter 4 we enter into the first major negative reaction to modernity. France was not only the nation in which there was a vigorous discussion between class and race, but more importantly, and as a specific reaction against the French Revolution, there was the appearance of Joseph de Maistre who, in the words of Isaiah Berlin, was a proto-fascist.

I believe that the major socio-political developments of the twentieth century are best understood by reference to at least four fundamental myths, which are articulated around the ideas of race, of the crowd, of revolutionary violence and of eugenics. What matters above all about these notions is their mystifying character, although they may also be perversions of scientific or pseudoscientific concepts. Their irrational appeal and the mystique that surrounds them, when properly manipulated, explain the fact that they should be endowed with such great social power.

These myths are not casual inventions or disembodied realities; neither are they free-floating ideas ready to be picked up by otiose intellectuals. In fact, they only make sense as part of the wider human experience of Western civilization. The myth of race, as the belief that mankind is divided into biologically different groups that can be classified hierarchically on an intellectual and moral basis, is very much a product of the expansion of Europe at a world level. The continuing process of political domination and of economic success of the West bred a feeling of European superiority, which translated itself into a racial theory.

In Chapter 5 the development of racial issues is focused on the appearance of Gobineau's *Essai sur l'inégalité des races humaines*, which was the first treatise to integrate disparate elements about races into a systematic and powerful philosophy of history. His theory tried to explain the rise and fall of civilizations in terms of racial miscegenation between a superior race (the Aryans), and the other races. Gobineau wrote his major racial treatise in 1853–5.

One important factor of the second half of the nineteenth century was the appearance of Charles Darwin. The impact of his work was remarkable, revolutionizing the place of man in biological evolution. A long-term polemical and pretended dimension of his work has generated the idea of social Darwinism, which is presented as a dangerous vision of society. Was Darwin a social Darwinist? There is not a straightforward answer to the question, as different arguments suggest. Eugenics or the notion that human society should be improved through biological manipulation, was one of the major themes of social Darwinism. This concept was specifically initiated by Darwin's nephew, Francis Galton – an author whom we will also consider.

There are three late nineteenth-century authors who are central to the shaping of twentieth-century totalitarianism. Their names are Gustave Le Bon, Georges Vacher de Lapouge and Georges Sorel. The work by these authors that we shall consider here was published between 1895 and 1906. Le Bon wrote on the crowd, Vacher de Lapouge on eugenics and Sorel on revolutionary violence. These authors were French and the period that we are talking about corresponds to the flourishing of the leading French social scientist Emile Durkheim. An attempt is made to show how he and his school approached this group of revolutionary and/or dangerous thinkers.

Chapter 7 deals with the myth of the crowd. The topic is more complex. because one should start with the notion of society as a social whole, irreducible and different from its parts. The organic metaphor of society was extremely popular in the late nineteenth century, and it helps to understand a variety of associated ideas (nation, national character, people, state, class, mass, mob, and so forth). That many of these notions were seen as the precipitate of the capitalist order, may assist in explaining their centrality. If I have focused specifically on the modern crowd it is because of its key role in the social movements and revolutions since 1789.

In his book *La Foule*, Le Bon defined the crowd as an assemblage of human beings considered as a psychological and social unit, and with a specific character and behaviour. By focusing on a variety of attributes of the crowd (unanimity, emotionality, credulity), Le Bon opened up a new avenue for research (he is the founder of social psychology), while giving powerful weapons to the manipulators of society. In the context of the late nineteenth century there was a close connection between crowd and race, and the latter was not often clearly differentiated from nation or people (as the common expression 'English race' testifies). For Le Bon, race – in the sense of 'national character structure' (Merton) – was a first-rank factor in determining the opinions and beliefs of the crowds.

Until now we have looked at two concepts – race and crowd – that had to do with the way of perceiving the social order. The two other myths – violence and eugenics – belong in a different categorical order; they are dynamic principles aimed at subverting such order.

In chapter 8 we look into eugenics or the notion that human society should be improved through biological manipulation, was one of the major themes of social Darwinism. As such it was closely related to Galton's idea of eugenics. In Vacher de Lapouge's *Les selections sociales*, the idea of eugenics (selectionism) acquires a multi-layered dimension in which the negative effects of social selections in history would hopefully be offset by a consciousness of systematic biological manipulation aimed at improving mankind. As the founder of the new discipline of anthropo-sociology, Vacher seems to be the author who took more seriously the possible social implications of Darwin's biological discoveries. He combined social Darwinism with Gobineau's racial theories of history but in the modified context of craniological studies.

The last author to be considered is Georges Sorel in Chapter 9. The notion that social change can be best achieved through revolutionary violence is very much an offshoot of the French Revolution and of its socialist heirs. Sorel's *Reflections sur la violence* took up an uncomfortable and hushed up subject and made it the centre of a strategy destined to overthrow the bourgeois order. At a time when the Marxists of the Second International were pussy-footing about the desirability of a revolution, Sorel took the uncompromising step of affirming its necessity and put forward a number of ideas to bring it about. He insisted on the political centrality of myths as psychological tools to encourage morality, creativity and action.

The final chapter deals with the making of totalitarianism in Germany. It is a rather modest attempt to indicate from the making of the racial and social-Darwinistic world-vision in Germany, through the work of H. S. Chamberlain, Ludwig Schemann, Otto Ammon, Ludwig Woltmann and H. F. K. Gunther, to the theory and practice of totalitarianism in Germany through the figure of Alfred Rosenberg who was the chief ideologist of the Nazi Party. What all these German ideologists owed to the four French thinkers considered here is also referred to.

The fact that most of the authors considered were French is no coincidence: it demonstrates the fact that France translated better, in intellectual terms, a generalized crisis that was European in dimension. However, in all fairness, though the French were the initiators, each of the major European countries produced a constellation of thinkers, of lesser or greater brightness, who articulated the same myths more or less at the same time.

I have associated each of the second half of the nineteenth-century French chosen authors with having adumbrated, if not actually discovered and analysed, the tremendous social potential of one of the key twentieth-century myths. But what really matters for the understanding of the twentieth century are not the myths in isolation, but their special blending in a homogenized ideological package, of which Nazi Germany was the classical case. The dreams of the Enlightenment, of liberalism, of socialism and of positivism produced twentieth-century monsters, and the clue to unravelling this mystery lie in the work of Gobineau, Le Bon, Sorel and Vacher de Lapouge. They were keen observers of both society and human nature, as well as unwelcome prophets of a new order. Their anti-bourgeois, elitist and anti-progressivist attitudes formed a peculiar combination that set them worlds apart from the dominant liberal-democratic or socialist positions; and yet their standpoint can only be understood as an attempt to find a way out of the crisis of modernity. They can be said to have ferreted out the dark aspects of human nature. In so far as they talked about them, studied them and even toyed with their social potential, these authors have often been blamed for the ills of the twentieth century. Their pessimism about human nature radically contrasts with the unbound optimism of the heirs of the Enlightenment. Their names have frequently been invoked as a way of exorcising the history of the twentieth century from all evil.

It is not surprising that the names of Gobineau, Le Bon, Sorel and Vacher de Lapouge have always been kept in the penumbra of the social scientific world. On the whole, the professionals of the social and human sciences have failed to recognize the role of these authors as social analysts. As prophets of doom, however, they have an assured place in the history of infamy of the twentieth century. Their alibi would have been to say that there was no crime in announcing the death of Western civilization. Because they were, and still are, intellectually unacceptable and politically explosive, they have suffered the worst possible fate: they have been ignored by social scientists, blamed by all for the social diseases of the twentieth century and their ideas have been insidiously ransacked by right and left of the political spectrum alike.

Another way of looking at my endeavour in this project is to see it as a quest for what went wrong with our nineteenth-century 'illusions of progress'. If I have called upon four more or less obscure prophets of doom it is because their sense of understanding of the socio-political reality and its directionality was often more accurate than that exhibited by the highly praised social thinkers of approximately the same period. In the end it would appear as if nineteenth-century political thought was fundamentally utopian in character in spite of its positivist pretensions, while an aptly appropriate label for Gobineau, Sorel, Le Bon and Vacher de Lapouge would perhaps be that of neomachiavellians. The myths that they untapped, although very different in nature, became social forces of the first magnitude, particularly when controlled by the modern state. These myths are mental constructions in which individuals strongly represent their common socio-political choices and objectives. The twentieth century has shown that human beings, even in the most civilized of countries, can be induced into a permanent state of exaltation in which they will kill and die for these myths. The great merit of our four gospel chanters is that they discovered the potential of these myths, though it was up to others (practico-political men) to exploit the discovery.

The end of the second millennium generated a choir of voices that predicted the repetition of history in the form of the return of totalitarianism, but under a different guise. It would appear as if the politics of violent conflict, racism, chauvinism and xenophobia are on the increase; that populist leadership and mass media manipulation are back in earnest; that biotechnology has given eugenics an acceptable face; that perhaps an unholy and explosive alliance between communism and fascism is on the making – a potent combination that seems to appeal to an increasing number of people all over Europe and elsewhere. All the more important to account for the roots of the 'dark side of modernity'.

One point should be absolutely clear. This book does not make the claim that the totalitarian regimes of the twentieth century can be accounted for in terms of the doctrines of a few thinkers. Sociological problems require sociological treatment. There is no substitute for a multilevel historical sociology when dealing with complex societal developments. The only pretence of this text is to provide a verisimilar picture of a specific configuration of thought that provided the foundations for totalitarianism, and more specifically of its Nazi variant.

–1–

Prelude to Modernity

Introduction

At first sight, what is most striking about the use of the word 'race' is its amazing diversity both in time and in space. Expressions such as 'human race', 'white race', 'Latin race', 'Jewish race', 'Slavic race', 'English race', 'degenerate race', 'inferior race' are still of common use or have occurred until recently in the popular parlance, as well as in cultured or scientific literature. What this shows is that, in its history, the idea of race has been intertwined with the ideas of nation, of ethnic group, of people, of class, and so forth. Hence all attempts to force a clear distinction between these concepts is practically impossible, and can only be achieved by imposing presentist criteria that distort the past.

What all these terms – race, class, nation, people, ethnic group, and so on – have in common is that they are all reflections of the importance of boundaries in human society. That these boundaries delimit groups that are defined by a variety of criteria (such as biological, environmental, historical and other criteria) and that are endowed with powerful symbolic associations, is hardly a great discovery. We could say, paraphrasing Lévi-Strauss, that boundaries are good for thinking about human beings, but we should add that they are also good for manipulating them, dominating them and exploiting them. Racial boundaries are extremely malleable mental maps of the human continuum: in fact, even the most manifest morphological features (such as skin colour, shape of skull, colour of hair) are only perceived and made use of under given cultural conditions and circumstances.

The notion of race has had its heyday. It began with the publication of Gobineau's *Essai sur l'inegalité des races humaines* and it ended with the Final Solution. For a century, the West was mesmerised by a concept that the Darwinian revolution and the new discipline of anthropology gave a scientific appearance. It is true that the scientific establishment was not unanimous in accepting the value of such a concept, and that particularly after the First World War a growing number of social and biological scientists expressed serious doubts about its scientific status and were concerned about its social dangers. Yet the concept remained, and to a certain extent it still remains extremely popular among large masses of the population.

The suggestion that the notion of race is a modern phenomenon, though correct as a general statement, should not be taken at face value. Indeed, it is possible to find thinking about race and racial attitudes in earlier periods of history and in a variety of cultures. Even more simplistic is the assumption that there is a lineal causality between the development of capitalism and the emergence of racial thinking. This proposition can only be true at a tautological level, that is, if the concept of capitalism is seen as a self-generating and comprehensive reality encompassing everything that is modern – racial thinking included. However, if the proposition is meant to signify that the upsurge of racial ideas can be accounted for in terms of economic factors (particularly colonial exploitation), as is usually the case, then the explanation is at best partial and certainly insufficient.

The complexity and ubiquity of racial ideas seems to indicate that, although that in their present form they are a modern phenomenon – and this is of course a truism – they actually belong in a wider category of facts deeply ingrained in human society. Building on the basic, innate defence mechanisms that human beings exhibit against anything that threatens them – and being different may be construed as a danger – all human groups have in one form or another defended themselves against 'Others'. We may call this attitude ethnocentrism to indicate the idea that each group strongly believes that its ways of living – its culture – is to be preferred to those of others. Some 'primitive societies' carry this attitude further bestow the native term for 'human being' unto themselves and nobody else. Some groups take these attitudes to the extremes that we refer to as 'xenophobia', that is, the hatred of all that is alien, foreign, different.

Now the word 'race' is relatively recent in the European languages. An Arabic ancestry for the term – *ras* meaning origin – as was suggested in the past, is etymologically unlikely. More probable is the hypothesis that it derives from the Latin *ratio*, in the sense of species. The word first appeared in south-western European languages (Italian, Catalan, Portuguese, Spanish) towards the end of the Middle Ages, though it was not used until the sixteenth and seventeenth centuries in other European countries (France, England). In Germany the term was restricted to the animal realm until the late eighteenth century. In its original sense, race referred to a group of persons (but also of animals or plants) with common descent. It was a word that was closely related to, if not synonymous with, terms such as 'caste', 'parentage', 'stock', 'lineage', and so on. That behind the idea of race there was, from the very beginning, an assumption of biological unity whichever way that might be conceived, is obvious if one considers the expression 'purity of blood' as it was used in the Iberian peninsula as early as the late fifteenth century. This expression was an odd mixture of religious and biological beliefs. It was used to differentiate between *old* and *new* Christians, in the sense that the latter were the descendants of Jews or Moors who had converted to Christianity a few generations before. A doctrine was developed that assumed that these people were morally tainted as a result of their ancestors having belonged to another, non-Christian religion. In early modern Spain, the statutes of purity of blood were socially important because being labelled new Christian meant, at best, the automatic barring from a number of professions, residential segregation, and so on, and, at worst, if accused of recanting, you could be burnt at the stake. Was this, as Poliakov has propounded, the first legalized form of racism in Europe?

In the twentieth century, 'racism' has been an extremely emotive word, particularly since the Nazi regime came into existence. It covers a great variety of situations in which the superiority of one race over another is affirmed. Because of the extremely negative moral associations that the term elicits at present, 'racism' is a term of abuse and should be used with caution, especially in the context of historical research. It serves no scientific purpose, and only very spurious and partisan political interests, to pass an overall judgement on Western civilization by branding it as racist. This kind of attitude, which we could label philosophizing from moral heights, can only be justified from a blind presentism that insists on applying to the past the same criteria that are applied to the present.

For those who believe in fairy tales, there is a clear anti-Semitic continuity between, say, Luther and Hitler via Herder, Hegel and Nietzsche. This intellectual lineage is presented as a proof that the manifest destiny of Germany was to stamp out the Jews.

Historical Background to Racial Theories and Racism

The Greco-Roman World

If it is appropriate to start the story of the idea of race in Ancient Greece, then the moment must be around the year 500 BC and the occasion the confrontation between the Greeks and the Persians. The first racial theory did not take the form of an attempt to show, à la Gobineau, that one race was superior to the others, but to put forward the idea that racial differences could be accounted for in environmental terms (Von Fritz 1973: 500). Who the author of that theory might be we do not know, but it is usually attributed to Hippocrates. In a nutshell, it suggests that geographical variations in both individual characteristics and political institutions are the result of climatic differences. Three majors areas are compared: mainland Greece, Asia Minor and northern Europe. The climate of Greece being basically varied, it has the effect of producing energetic and self-reliant people, who are destined to rule themselves in accordance with self-generated regulations. The people from Asia Minor live in a temperate climate, with few seasonal variations, and this makes them soft and hence prey to despotic rule. Finally, in northern Europe the extreme variations of temperature make people violent, aggressive and savage; because they cannot control themselves, they need leadership, but they choose their kings for that purpose. This theory may be seen as a rationalization of the democratic institutions of the Greeks, and yet the contrasts established in such a classification of races/peoples had a lasting effect on the history of ideas. At a time when the West felt in a position comparable to that of Ancient Greece, Montesquieu would put forward a scheme that reminded us of that of an obscure author of two-and-a-half millennia ago.

Because in Western civilization there was a close association between racism and slavery (Davis 1988), there is always the danger of positing a causal connection between slavery and racism. Eric Williams's statement that 'slavery was not born of racism, rather racism was the consequence of slavery' (Williams 1944: 7) cannot be applied to Ancient Greece. The evidence that we have does not permit such an assumption; ancient slavery was very much a fix feature of social life, which was not affected by racial issues except in a theoretical way. Slavery was not justified in terms of biological inferiority (though in Aristotle, as we shall see, it came very close to that), rather it was seen as a natural result of the existence of domination in society. Greek philosophers did not challenge the institution of slavery; they only argued as to whether it was man-made or natural. One important thing must be emphasized: enslavement operated, as a rule, only with the out-group. If the Greeks made other Greeks into slaves, they had to be from a different city-state. As Moses Finley has put it: 'despite the absence of the skin-colour stigma; despite the variety of peoples who made up the ancient slave population; and despite the frequency of manumission' the ancient world knew a non-biological, ethnocentric type of racism. The slave was in fact defined as a barbarian and an outsider (Finley 1980: 118).

In Ancient Greece we can see, then, the ethnocentric principle in operation, although the prejudice need not be based on biological assumptions. Racial prejudice is only one type of social prejudice: historically it has existed along with religious, national and other prejudices. What about the most common hallmarks of race, such as colour of the skin, hair or eyes? Objectively these features were there to be seen, and no doubt for centuries races were distinguished on the basis of these traits, but these distinctions did not necessarily have significant cultural or social consequences. Colour is certainly not the only somatic characteristic that can be used for racial classifications, although admittedly it is the most accessible, and we know of at least one African society in which body stature is what justifies social domination. It was not until the eighteenth century that the comparative anatomist Peter Camper discovered that different races exhibit different facial angles. As we shall see, with the general development of anthropology in the nineteenth century, certain techniques for the measurement of different parts of the body were developed. Particularly important were head measurements – craniometry – in so far as they allowed a classification of European populations into long-headed (dolichocephalic or Aryan) and round-headed (brachycephalic or Alpine) types. Towards the end of the century, craniometry became the foundation on which the brand new science of anthroposociology was erected.

The modern idea of race owes little to the Hellenic one. It is true that Plato, when comparing the Greeks with the Scythians and Phoenicians, introduced a racial element when he asserted that it was only among the Greeks that the intellectual element predominated. Certainly the racial conceptions of Ancient Greece were transmitted into the Middle Ages and were even visible in early modern Europe, but as Eric Voegelin has established, they had a very limited impact on our modern ideas. More important in Ancient Greece was the idea of the body. Voegelin maintained that the modern idea of race is a particular case of a general instance of body ideas. He defined a body idea as 'any symbol which integrates a group into a substantial whole through the assertion that its members are of common origin' (Voegelin 1940: 286). In the body symbolism of the Greek city-states, it is possible to observe the evolution from concrete family relations to a group in which descent is purely fictitious, but its symbolism is extremely powerful even after the four major types of descent groups were broken down and residential criteria were used instead for grouping.

It appears that in the Roman Empire there was neither racial nor ethnic discrimination. Unlike the Ancient Greeks, who had a restrictive criterion for belonging to the *polis,* the Romans aimed at integrating all conquered peoples by granting them Roman citizenship. In theory, then, all different nations were equal, and it is well known that even the highest echelons of the state were occasionally occupied by people from different parts of the Empire. As to the black population present in Rome, Frank Snowden (1970) seems to suggest that they were not disparaged, though there are plenty of examples in the literature that give one to believe the opposite – was it not Horace who said *Hic niger est; hunc tu Romane caveto*? Be that as it may, however, we do have enough literary evidence from Imperial Rome which points at the hostility felt against certain groups (as Tacitus made it clear in relation to Celts and Jews) and the profound contempt for Africans precisely because of their blackness (which as Juvenal showed was associated with a variety of negative feelings). It could be argued that the hostility towards the Jews was the result of the rebellious character of the latter (as exemplified in the various insurrections in Palestine) and of their peculiar religious practices (such as circumcision, the Sabbath, and rejection of the imperial cult).

It is proper to ask whether, as a religion, Judaism was not bound to elicit a certain amount of antagonism. After all, and as Leon Poliakov has recognized, Ancient Israel appeared to many as distant, aloof and hostile. As the 'chosen people', the Israelites seemed to be adopting a position of superiority towards gentiles in general. And yet, the Ancient Testament made explicit the unity of the human species in so far as all human beings were descended from Adam and Eve. What are we to make, however, of Noah's cursing of Canaan, son of Ham, whose descendants were condemned to be the slaves of the descendants of Shem and Japhet? The fact that Genesis 10 presents three genealogies grouping a variety of peoples in each, should not be interpreted as a racial classification. In fact, the affinity between the different peoples in each category is not racial but geographical and historical. But the traditional association of Shem with Middle Eastern populations, of Japhet with European ones and of Ham with African ones will be used in the modern period to justify black slavery.

More important, though, than the attitude of the Romans towards the Jews was the way in which early Christianity tackled Judaism. The recent discoveries of the Dead Sea Scrolls and of the Nag Hammadi papyri have shown an early Christian world deeply divided as to what constituted the true teachings of Jesus. It has been suggested that elements of Judaism and Gnosticism were present in early Christianity. In fact, however, this kind of statement only makes sense from the comfortable perspective of Christian orthodoxy, and this was not a reality until after AD 150. It is interesting that Christian anti-Judaism, as distinguished from anti-Semitism, was a religious reaction against the defenders of the Old Testament, and that it started with Saint Paul's doctrine being at the centre of the compiled New Testament. This is indeed the same Saint Paul who in his Galatians 3: 28 could state that in Christianity 'there are no more distinctions between Jew and Greek, slave and free, male and female, but all of you are one in Christ Jesus'. That until very recent times in Western culture the New Testament has provided a background for anti-Judaism is obvious from Marcion through Luther to Bultmann. But as John Gager has concluded: 'only in a highly restricted sense can Western anti-Semitism be said to originate in Pagan and Christian antiquity' (Gager 1983: 9).

Saint Paul is also relevant in another respect. He developed the idea of the mystical body of Christ. There is a Greek background to this theory and it has to do with the notion of like mindedness, which originally referred to the brotherly feelings that occurred within the boundaries of any symbolic group. By the time that Saint Paul was advancing his notion of the mystical body, a certain dualism was preserved: Adam was the common physical ancestor, Christ the spiritual one. In the idea of the mystical body a parallelism is established between Christ and human beings: they are both composed of body and spirit. For Voegelin the

> union between the human community is granted through the double nature of Christ as man and God. Every person who has been received into the membership of the community (*ecclesia*), participates in the spirit of Christ . . . Christ living in the members of the community constitutes the spiritual bond between them. (Voegelin 1940: 290)

Voegelin also insisted that, although the idea of mystical body was universalistic, with the process of secularization that took place by the Enlightenment 'the problem of community was reduced to finding a spiritual bond and new symbols may arise which do not cover all mankind but only particular groups' (Voegelin 1940: 293).

If the question of colour prejudice only touched the Middle Ages in a peripheral way – though the period certainly preserved the pagan belief that black was the colour of death, bad luck, sin and filthy excrements – it does not mean that medieval society did not exhibit procedures of exclusion and discrimination against certain ethnic categories. Certainly medieval Europe had very limited contact with the outside world, and hence the stories of the few travellers who ventured into the Orient – like Marco Polo – were often distorted by positing the existence of fabulous beings and monsters. It was a mythical world in which the most bizarre beliefs developed. The inhabitants of *finis terrae*, that is, of the peripheral regions in the medieval maps of the world were not only the North Africans (often called Moors at the time), but also an assortment of beings which were thought to be real (Amazons, Satyrs, Hermaphrodites, half human-half animal monsters . . .). This prodigious fauna was the way in which the medieval mind conceived of the savage. In fact, the Renaissance and the early voyagers did little to change the medieval mentality; in a sense, for a couple of centuries after the discoveries, travellers' reports seemed to confirm all the conceptions from the Middle Ages. Well into the seventeenth century the dividing line between Africans and apes was blurred to the extent that sexual intercourse was often assumed to take place between them. Even as late as 1781 Thomas Jefferson's *Notes on Virginia* (Question XIV), could present as factual the idea that orangutans had a sexual preference for black women.

The Middle Ages and the Jews

If the savage was to all practical purposes an imaginary being on which the medieval world projected all its fears, ignorance and prejudices, the Jew was real enough to elicit hatred, persecution, expulsions and organized massacres. But in the final resort these attitudes towards the Jews could only be justified if, as a group, they could be made to appear as aliens and dangerous to Christendom. To incarnate the quintessence of evil, their behaviour had to be seen as befitting the canons of medieval demonology. Three caveats should, however, be entered. First, I follow Poliakov's convention in distinguishing between anti-Judaism and anti-Semitism, and restricting the latter to attitudes that involve biological beliefs. Second, medieval anti-Judaism does not automatically follow from the fact that the New Testament and the statements of the early Christian Church contain hostile comments on Judaism. Third, anti-Judaism is a complex phenomenon in which religious, political and economic motivations are involved.

The medieval Christian Church, in its attempt to preserve its domination, fought successfully against three major challenges: internal heresies, Judaism (which was present amidst the Christian community) and Islam (an outside threat except in the Iberian peninsula). At the beginning of the Middle Ages, the existence of serious theological differences between Christians and Jews was no obstacle for the latter to be accepted as *bona fide* members of the community in a variety of capacities (agriculturists, officials, traders, and so forth). In the Iberian peninsula the coexistence of three faiths was an undeniable social fact, at least for the early period.

It was with the onslaught of the First Crusade that visible and repeated outbursts against the Jews started. They occurred in a climate of religious effervescence and intransigence. On their way to the Holy Land the crusaders left behind a trail of Jewish blood. Particularly vicious was the pogrom of the Rhine Valley in 1096. Accusations against the Jews were phrased not only in the traditional terms of the early Christian discourse – the Jews as recalcitrant non-believers in the Messiah, and Jews as the deicide people – but they were also progressively seen as perfidious and evil, that is, as diabolical creatures. A mythology about the Jews developed, most remarkably the belief that, at Easter, they were involved in the ritual killing of Christian children. The attitude towards the Jews became harder and the hostility increased.

By the mid-twelfth century this type of accusation was rife and the Jewish communities all over Europe (England, Germany, France) started to suffer the consequences: the Jews were either massacred or forced into exile. Encouraged by the Church, a variety of measures were taken by the authorities against the civil rights of the Jews. In many places the Jews were forced to carry a special piece of clothing (yellow lapel or hat) so that they could be easily identified. Towards the end of the Middle Ages the Jews were often attributed a specific genealogy (they were descended from the devil) and certain physical features (aquiline nose); furthermore, as we shall see, in the Iberian peninsula they were supposed to be the carriers of a biological stain that not even baptism could change. In general, we can say that the medieval hatred of the Jews has to be seen in the light of the Christian Church trying to preserve its unity and homogeneity whilst threatened by an external power (Islam) and by an internal one (heresies). In such a situation the Jews were chosen as the propitiatory victims (although, of course, there were other smaller groups, like the Cagots (Michel 1983), who were also discriminated against).

On the basis of the experience of medieval Europe, we can surmise that anti-Judaism was at root a religious attitude which progressively displayed other dimensions (political, economic and biological). Towards the end of the Middle Ages, and if we take the Iberian peninsula as a case-study, we can elaborate on Julio Caro-Baroja's scheme (Caro- Baroja 1961, I: 104) and try to explain the attitudes towards the Jews on the basis of the following reasons:

1 *Religious causes.* There is no need to belabour the doctrinal differences between Jews and Christians. As killers of God the Son the Jews suffered a collective stigma difficult to overcome and easy to manipulate.

2   *Economic causes*. The massive, often forced, presence of Jews in a variety of professions associated with the handling of money made illegitimately (such as money lending, usury, banking, trading) made them an easy target in times of economic crisis or when the interests of the Christian in rulers were paramount.

3   *Psychological causes*. With the appearance of Jewish ghettos, the Jews started to develop certain psychological features that were easy to identify and were culturally transmitted from generation to generation. In this way, Jews appeared as ethnically different from the rest of the community.

4   *Political causes*. The process of state formation required a certain degree of religious homogenization. The generalized expulsion of Jews and Moors in early modern Spain is to a certain extent a reflection of the needs of state building.

The case of the incipient Spanish state of the late fifteenth century exemplifies the transition from anti-Judaism to anti-Semitism. The presence of the notion of the purity of blood is the first sign that a religious and ethnic prejudice takes the form of a racial one. The key to this shift is not to be found in a reified conception of the Church or the state, but in the evolution of the Hispanic societies in the latter part of the Middle Ages. Whether in the process we privilege the economic or the ethnic element is a disputed matter. In 1965, with his *Inquisition in Spain*, Henry Kamen saw early modern Spain in terms of class struggles; in 1985 he seemed to be inclined to give more importance to ethnic struggles. The next chapter will deal with what could be called racial issues in sixteenth-century Spain.

Theorizing the 'Other': The Emergence of a Discourse on Race in Sixteenth-Century Spain

Introduction

The early modern Spanish state was a natural laboratory that produced the first modern experiment in ethnic-cum-racial subjection and homogenization. In the year of 1492, when their most Catholic majesties Queen Isabella of Castile and King Ferdinand of Aragon were reigning, three momentous events took place: the expulsion of the Jews, the conquest of Granada and the discovery of America. These occurrences represent the beginning of a new era; a period in which religious fanaticism pervaded Spanish society and determined the behaviour of the Spanish crown in relation to the outside world.

There seems to be little doubt that the Spanish monarchy upheld the idea that the kingdom – the result of a long process of unification and of Reconquest of Moorish-held peninsular lands – had been chosen by God as the true defender of the Christian faith. To be sure, Spanish society was class ridden, and behind ethnico-religious confrontations and differences economic interests often appeared, but the ubiquity and extremism of religious zealotry suggest the existence of a mental outlook that can only be explained as part of a long historical process (the so called Reconquest) in which ethnico-religious prejudice flourished.

For the Spanish economy the early modern period was not a period of primitive capitalist accumulation; the enormous riches in gold and silver extracted from America were dissipated in continuous military expeditions and in conspicuous consumption. The expulsion of the Jews (who specialized in banking, trade and crafts) and later of the *Moriscos* (who were skilful agriculturist in the Levant and in the South) had well-established deleterious economic effects, and, along with other factors, kept Spain out of capitalist development for centuries. The ethic of Spanish Catholicism, in its obsession with purity of blood, its disdain for work, and so forth, created the opposite of the spirit of capitalism (Benassar 1975).

If the *raison d'être* of the religious ideology of Spain was the establishment of a Catholic order by sword and fire against internal (Jews and *Moriscos*) and external (Islam and Protestantism) enemies in Europe, and idolatry in America, the instrument of such an objective was the Spanish state. The Augustinian opposition between the Divine City (*Civitas Dei*) and the Terrestrial City (*Civitas Terrena*) persisted throughout the whole period. But, how could the former be achieved without using the latter as means? The early Spanish state became an implacable machine to stamp out religious dissidents; if Catholic unity had to be achieved at all costs, then surely there was a need for a strong state, and because the religious and political objectives were the same, absolute power was justifiable. The Catholic Church might have banned Machiavelli's *The Prince,* but the Spanish princes unequivocally thought that the end (Catholic order) certainly justified the means (force) (Fernandez-Santamaria 1977)

For our purposes of tracing back the origins of racism to early modern Europe, the Spanish situation is particularly promising because, after all, to convince the majority of the population, the enemies of the Church had to be presented as dangerous and strangers, as aliens, often endowed with particularly hideous physical or characterological features. It was precisely this process of dehumanization of the other that made possible the appearance of racism at a later stage (Delacampagne 1983; Davis 1988). And this issue can be best examined by reference to the Spanish reactions to the discovery of America (Todorov 1984; Todorov 1995; Pagden 1993).

The Discovery of America and the Argument about the 'Indians'

Fifty years before America was discovered, the Portuguese had started to explore the African coast. It matters not whether the rationale for such explorations was to find a passage to the Indies, the spread of God's word, the pursuit of fabulous riches, or all at the same time. It is interesting to mention, however, that soon after the discovery of America, Spanish ideologists presented it as God's reward for the policies of Isabella and Ferdinand against the Jews.

America meant basically two things: precious metals and Indians. Gold and silver were necessary to the major glory of God; they were the means to finance the struggle against heretics and infidels of all sorts. The Indians were a problem. Were they human? If the answer be positive, how is it that they did not appear in the Bible? Influenced by medieval legends and by the primitiveness of Indian culture (particularly the Circum-Caribbean one), some denied the Indians their humanity. Of course, the existence of an urban civilization among the Aztec and Incas made it difficult to classify them as barbarians. But, if they were not humans, what were they: monsters, animals? It certainly suited Spanish colonists to see them as beasts of burden or as slaves. It is true that in his bull *Sublimis Deus*, Pope Paul III declared, as early as 1537, that Indians were fully-fledged human beings, eager to receive the true word of God. This papal bull had a limited impact, as subsequent theological discussions in Spain clearly show (not to speak of the practices of the Spanish settlers in America). Even those who agreed with the importance of teaching the Gospel to the Indians often suggested that American riches were a divine incentive to attract the Spaniards to America. The parable of the two sisters was often used to characterize the white and the Indian races. A father had two daughters whom he wanted to marry; one was beautiful and intelligent, the other was ugly and stupid. He had no difficulty in marrying the former, but the latter had to be handsomely endowed to attract any suitor. The gold and silver of America, the parable goes, were the dowry of the Indian nation, without which the continent would have remained unexplored and hence the Indians would have been left to their idolatry.

One of the most extraordinary developments of the first half of the sixteenth century was the attempt by the Spaniards to justify the enslavement of the American Indians by reference to Aristotle's theory of natural slavery. Eager for military glory, for religious conversion and for fast enrichment, the Spanish conquerors were reluctant to engage in any kind of physical labour – after all, they were all supposed to be hidalgos, noblemen. This meant that somebody else had to extract precious metals from the mines, till the soil and plant the crops. The obvious candidates were, of course, the natives themselves.

The Renaissance vogue of Aristotle was particularly strong in Spain, and his *Politics* was soon used as an authoritative argument for the subjugation of the Indian population. Now, Aristotle had distinguished between civil and natural slavery. The first conception assumed that the 'good' society required the presence of a category of people devoted to manual labour, so that a minority could have the leisure to indulge in a contemplative life. This conception was not only typical of ancient society but also of the medieval period. How did some people become civil slaves was purely a fortuitous matter (punishment, capture, and so forth). On the other hand, natural slavery referred to a special category of people who, given their intellectual or moral inferiority, were destined to servitude. Because of its psychological imperfections, the fate of the natural slave was to become a beast of burden. In Aristotle's mind the master-slave relationship was seen as beneficial not only to the master, but also to the slave. After all, a slave could not think on his own, but as a domesticated animal and in contact with the master, the natural slave was bound to improve his lot.

The first to use the Aristotelian argument in favour of labelling the American Indian as a natural slave was the Bishop of Darien, Juan Quevedo. The occasion was a disputation with Bartolomé de las Casas in the presence of the Emperor Charles V in 1519. There followed a series of bitter controversies that culminated in a great debate that took place in Valladolid in 1550–1, again in the presence of Charles V this time having as main contenders Juan Ginés de Sepúlveda and an old Las Casas. The long-lasting controversy was basically fought on the same lines, only the arguments had become more detailed and subtle. What was a stake was whether the Indians were irrational human beings who could not rule themselves and hence could be enslaved or rather whether they were similar to Europeans, but pagans, and hence with souls that could be redeemed. It could be said that these theologico-political discussions had limited effect on the actual practice of the Spanish conquerors . It is true that by the time the Spanish monarchs decided to intervene, millions of Indians had been enslaved and massacred, but by 1550 the Crown had promulgated a number of regulations destined to introduce principles of justice in dealing with the Indians.

The problem, of course, had started soon after the discovery of the new continent. By 1493, Pope Alexander VI in his bull *Inter caetera* gave to the Castilian crown the exclusive right to spread the word of God in the New World. Was it also the right to a territorial concession? The bull was ambiguous in this respect. Freely elaborating on the Papal disposition, the Royal Requirement of 1513 stated that the Indians had the duty to acknowledge the Spanish crown as their overlord and allow the preaching of the Catholic faith. In case of resistance, the Spaniards could use force to punish them, to take away their property and to enslave them.

While at the beginning the available information about the American Indians was rather patchy and unreliable, things started to change after 1520 with the publication of more factual texts. With the conquest of Mexico and Peru came information from societies that were very different, more culturally advanced than the rather primitive Caribbeans. It was on the strength of these texts that the different theological and juridical arguments were constructed. Except for Las Casas, who had first-hand experience of the Indies, the other participants in the disputations had to rely on the published sources.

The Theoretical Contribution of Francisco de Vitoria

Before considering the confrontation between Sepúlveda and Las Casas it may be worth looking into what the great theologian and jurist Francisco de Vitoria made of the American discovery (Vitoria 1991; Castillo-Urbano 1992)). In his *De Indis*, written in 1539, he set out to enquire whether the conquest of America was just and rightful. For Vitoria the problem was a theological one because the natives of America were subject to divine law. He admitted that there were a number of grounds on which the Indians could be subjected to the Spaniards. At the religious level, because they were either infidels (like the Turks) or sinners. Now, the first suggestion hardly applied to the Indians who had never heard of the Christian Gospels before the arrival of the Spaniards. As to the second reason, Vitoria maintained that it was not sufficient to justify the conquest according to natural law. More important were the arguments advanced at the intellectual level. Were the Indians simple-minded or irrational? If this was the case their enslavement would be justified, at least according to Aristotle. If these kind of natural beings existed, argued Vitoria, they were no different from animals and in consequence possessed no civil rights. But the evidence that had come from America could not justify such a conclusion because all their behaviour indicated their human condition. Finally, as to the question of Indian simple-mindedness, Vitoria concluded that this characteristic, as applied to human beings, was a freakish occurrence that could be predicated of a whole class of people. Accordingly, in their social affairs the Indians had a rational order peculiar to themselves. This conclusion was based on the fact that Indian communities exhibited a variety of social institutions (including religion, marriage, law, commerce, cities and crafts) which allowed them to be labelled polities.

With these arguments Vitoria dismissed the idea that the Indians could be considered Barbarians, in Aristotle's sense of the term. There were, however, a number of natural practices (such as cannibalism, and human sacrifices) among Indians that were difficult to explain unless one accepted that human beings were perfectible and could be improved through education. Vitoria's *De Indis* established the humanity of the Indians (they were not brutes belonging to a different species placed somewhere between human beings and monkeys, and hence created by God to serve the needs of humans), but it also suggested that they were not fully developed human beings. Because of this Vitoria felt that Indians required tutelage until they had come of age. In conclusion, if in his arguments Vitoria undermined the rationale behind the application of Aristotle's theory of natural slavery to the American Indians, his stance allowed that the Indians should be considered in a dependent position. As a whole, the theological School of Salamanca (which included Vitoria, de Soto, Cano and others), although hardly radical, attempted to look into the matter in the light of the principles of natural law. There is evidence that the Emperor was not always pleased with their position, that 'the king of Spain was tutor to the Indians and when they require no longer any tutor they ought to be left in liberty' (Pagden 1982: 107), and they certainly did not please the *encomenderos* either, who having originally been entrusted – from the introduction of this institution by Columbus in 1499 – with providing protection, Christian learning and a small salary for the Indians' labour, had practically used the Indians as slaves in the mines and the fields Pagden 1982: 34).

Compared with Las Casas, Vitoria's position was at best middle-of-the-road. He certainly abhorred the excesses of the Spaniards but nonetheless accepted that the kings of Spain had the right to colonize America. As the founder of international law (*ius gentium* or law of nations), his whole doctrine was based on the idea of natural law. The purpose of this law was to foster peace and order among nations (obviously for Vitoria applied only to the Christian commonwealth). In this context he was only following Aquinas's idea that humanity constituted a mystical body both spiritual and temporal, and that the destiny of the Christian world could not be separated from the destiny of humankind. The universal society had a law, *ius gentium*, based on natural reason and positive customs, which applied to all nations. Each nation had the right to existence, to juridical equality, to independence and to free communication and trade. Of course, when a nation was not capable of self-government, another, more civilized one, had the right to tutor her. A monarch could actually enforce these rights by a just war when another nation had transgressed them. For Vitoria was in agreement with the natural law that the kings of Spain should have the right not only to preach the gospel but also to travel to and to trade with the Indies. If the Indians were to resist such rights of access, then it was legitimate to use force to implement them (Méchoualan 1979: 885–7).

Las Casas and the Political Rights of Man

The name of Bartolomé de las Casas is well known (Hanke 1951; Various 1974; Las Casas 1992; Traboulay 1994; Mahn-Lot 2001). His *Very Brief Account of the Destruction of the Indies* (1542) depicted, in no rosy colours, the cruelties and ravages of the Spaniards in their first half a century in America – the pursuit of the three Gs: Gold, Glory and God. After its publication in Spanish the work was translated into most European languages, giving ample ammunition to the enemies of the Spanish Crown in Italy as in Germany, in France and Holland as in England; out of it developed the so-called Black Legend of the conquest. Las Casas was no theologian but rather a man deeply shocked by the horrors of the *encomienda* system. He witnessed at close range the way in which the Spaniards treated the Indians – no better than dogs. The Indians suffered the worst possible fate: their land was expropriated, their freedom coerced, their customs forbidden, their women raped, their children enslaved, their bodies tortured and their life taken away.

A man of good character, Las Casas went to the Caribbean for the first time in 1502 as a colonist, but it was not until 1514, when already a priest, that he concluded that everything that had been done to the Indians was, in his own words, 'unjust and tyrannical'. He decided on a radical change of life, and started to denounce the Spanish exploitation of the natives. After his conversion, he was involved in an attempt to change the system, but with little success in spite of his flurry of activity both in America and in Spain. His own utopian schemes for the creation of true communities of Spaniards and Indians failed miserably due to the uncontrollable greed of the Spaniards. Then, in 1523, and for a number of years following, he studied theology, law, and Indian history, and started to write *History of the Indies* (which he did not complete until the end of his life in 1564).

The bull *Sublimis Deus* (1537) reflected the ideas of Las Casas' religious order – the Dominicans – in that it professed the Indians to be rational beings and not talking beasts as many colonists called them. In his *Apologetic History* (1559) [*Obras Escogidas*, III: 165–6], Las Casas argued that the *sui generis* character of Indian culture was no reason to banish it from the realm of civil societies. He boldly stated that on the basis of the evidence from both ancient and modern times, it was clear that 'there were no races in the world, however rude, uncultivated, barbarous, gross or almost brutal they may be, who could not be persuaded and brought to a good order and way of life, and made domestic, mild and tractable . . . provided . . . the method that is proper and natural to men is used; that is, love and gentleness and kindness'. The reason for this truth was obvious to Las Casas: 'that all races of the world are men, and of all men and of each individual there is but one definition, and this is that the they are rational. All have understanding and will and free choice, as all are made in the image and likeness of God'.

Las Casas also strongly objected to the argument that before conversion the Indians had to be 'pacified' by arms. His *Method of Attracting All People to the True Faith* (1537) argued not only that the Indian wars were unjust, but also useless. Conversion could only take place by using rational arguments. His pleas had at least some temporary effects on Charles V, because for a while the Emperor forbade the *encomienda* system. Las Casas's uncompromising stand in favour of the Indians made him many enemies both in Spain and in America. By the late 1540s he was under attack from a variety of quarters, but his most redoubtable adversary was Juan Ginés de Sepúlveda, the Emperor's friend and chronicler.

Ginés de Sepúlveda and Natural Slavery

Ginés de Sepúlveda was an open and able supporter of the cause of the *encomenderos* and had brilliantly defended – in his *Democrates secundus* – not only the wars of conquest but also Aristotle's theory of natural slavery as applied to the Indians. In 1550 the Emperor ordered all the conquests in the New World to be stopped, waiting for the judgement to be passed by a commission of theologians and jurists that was to assemble in Valladolid. The Emperor's purpose was to elicit how 'conquests, discoveries and settlements be made to accord with justice and reason' (Hanke 1970: 41).

In the great debate in front of the judges, the main antagonists were Las Casas and Sepúlveda who, separately, defended their positions. No formal conclusion ever came out of these sessions, which lasted until 1551, but the legislation passed by the Spanish crown in the years to come revindicated, to a certain extent, Las Casas' standpoint, although the practice was probably more in accordance with Sepúlveda's views. It was, however, important that the Spanish crown decided 'not to stigmatise the American Indians as natural slaves' (Hanke 1970: 116).

Absent from this great debate was the black race. At a time when many of their people were being captured by the Portuguese in West Africa and shipped to the American plantations and mines, they did not find a protector of their humanity like the Indians had found in Las Casas. In fact, the latter had at some stage early in his life actually encouraged the substitution of Indians by black slaves – a suggestion that he later deeply regretted (Todorov 1984: 170). Slavery was, of course, not unknown in sixteenth century Spain itself. There were about 100,000 slaves (nearly 1.5 per cent of the population); many had been captured in Islamic lands, but increasingly they also came from West Africa. They were occupied mostly in menial capacities and in domestic positions, working for the Church, the aristocracy, and so forth (Benassar 1975; Dominguez-Ortiz 1970).

The most articulate and able defender of the theory of the natural slavery of the Indians was, as I have already indicated, Juan Ginés de Sepúlveda. May be he was not a great scholar, but he was certainly a brilliant and persuasive humanist. Around 1544 he had completed a dialogue entitled *Democrates secundus* in which he had tried to justify the war carried out against the Indians on the basis of Aristotle's theory of natural slavery. As his text was not in tune with the Victorian theologian establishment, it did not obtain a *nihil obstat*, and yet it was well received in other intellectual and religious quarters. The work, in the words of Pagden, was 'the most virulent and uncompromising argument for the inferiority of the American Indian ever written' (Pagden 1982: 106). In his *Apologia,* published in 1550, Ginés de Sepúlveda toned down his arguments and used other strategies to achieve the same end. According to Hanke the debate turned around the four basic propositions which, for Ginés de Sepúlveda, made it 'lawful and necessary to wage war against the natives' (Hanke 1970: 41). The propositions that justified war against the native Americans were the following:

1.- For the gravity of the sins which the Indians had committed, especially their idolatries and sins against nature.
2.- On account of the rudeness of their nature, which obliged them to serve persons having a more refined nature, such as the Spaniards.
3.- In order to spread the faith, which would be more easily accomplished by the prior subjugation of the natives.
4.- To protect the weak among the natives themselves (Hanke: 41).

Pagden suggests that Ginés de Sepúlveda restricted the argumental lines of *Democrates secundus* to three major enunciates: 'that the Indians are culturally inferior to the Spaniards and require "tuition"; that their "unnatural" crimes deprive them of their rights of *dominium*; and that the bulls of donation are a valid charter for the Spanish conquests' (Pagden 1982: 119).

What then was a 'just war' according to Ginés de Sepúlveda? If the Indians were inferior and with a limited capacity for reasoning, they were to be classified as natural slaves, and, not only did civilized people have dominion over them and hence the right to use them as beasts of burden, but they could also wage war against them according to the Aristotelian-Thomist doctrine. The main thrust of Sepúlveda's argument was in the construction and comparison of the ideal-typical characters of the Spaniards and the Indians. While the former exhibited courage, wisdom, nobility, prudence, religion, humanity, self-control and intelligence, the latter were barbarians, cannibals and subject to the lowest passions. The Indians were not proper human beings, they were at best 'little men' (homunculi), with no arts or letters, nor written laws or private property (Hanke 1970: 45–7). How could Ginés de Sepúlveda ignore the achievements of the Incas, Mayas, Aztecs and others can only be answered by Las Casas' dictum that 'God had deprived him of any knowledge of the New World' (Hanke 1970: 48). The expression *homunculus* as used by Ginés de Sepúlveda is particularly offensive in that it suggests, as Pagden notes, 'not only stunted growth but since *homunculi* were created by magic, also unnatural biological origins' (Pagden 1982: 117–18). Furthermore, the Indians are persistently associated with animals, hence completing their image as half-human beings only. After a just war it was perfectly legal that the defeated were either killed or enslaved and their property confiscated. As to the Indians who accepted Christianity and peacefully surrendered to the Spaniards, they could not be enslaved, but since they were otherwise inferior they could not enjoy the same rights as the Spaniards. In due course, when they had become humanised by being in contact with Spanish civilization, more freedoms and rights might be given to them, but they would never be able to become full members of a civilized nation.

Conclusion

The great debate of Valladolid in 1550–1 was an extraordinary intellectual and political event in that for the first time at the beginning of the early modern period the question of the inequality of races was discussed in great detail. The arguments used against and in favour (Burrus 1984) of the humanity of the Indians would reverberate in later centuries and up to the present. The discovery and colonisation of the Indies was no doubt a story of plunder and cruelty, but in the midst of the repressive, fanatical, racist, aggressive, messianic society that was sixteenth century Spain, a number of jurists and theologians raised for the first time in modernity the question of human equality and dignity and gave answers that had a long lasting if slow effect (see Defourneaux 1966; Benassar 1975; Méchoualan 1979; Kamen 1985; Traboulayu 1994).

That this should have happened in a society obsessed with purity and in which the fusion of politics and religion resulted in the cruellest and bloodiest of early modern persecutions, a society in which thousands after thousands of people, nominally, if not practically Christian but of Jewish and Moorish origin, were sent to the stake to be burnt by the Holy Inquisition, that this society should have allowed the discussions of Valladolid to take place is all the more miraculous. Sixteenth century Spain would remain the prototype of the totalitarian state of the future. The fact that it was organized on the basis of religion has no great significance, although the procedures of exclusion on the basis of religion were radical and had few restraints. It should be added, perhaps, that these totalitarian procedures were not a Catholic prerogative, as Barrington Moore (1958: 59–73) has clearly shown for the Geneva under Calvin.

–3–

Genealogies of Race

The Origins of Mankind: Early Speculations

We have mentioned before that the Spanish explorers, at least in the early period, saw the Indians through the ideological lenses of the Middle Ages. There were a number of themes that were regularly presented in the literature of the period. It all started with Columbus who actually believed that the terrestrial paradise must have been placed somewhere in the Indies. This was followed by the idea that America must have been the mythical reservoir of the monstrous races of man, along with all sort of other fabulous beings. The discovery of the New World gave a new lease of life to the many legends about mythological beings from ancient times. For quite a while it was actually believed that these fabulous beings had their *locus* in America – and beliefs die reluctantly (Hanke 1959; Malefijt 1968).

But the age of discoveries also provided increasingly reliable data on the racial varieties of mankind and their institutional, behavioural and intellectual characteristics. Understandably, one of the major mysteries about the American Indians was their origin. Because they were not mentioned in the Bible, was it still possible to maintain that they were descended from Adam? In his famous *Historia natural y moral de las Indias* (1590) – perhaps the finest of the earlier ethnographic texts and the first social anthropological treatise on the new continent – the Jesuit Joseph de Acosta along with many others favoured the idea that the American populations were of either European or Asiatic provenance, and that a passage must exist which links Asia with the Indies. Other authors favoured hypotheses that required no migratory movements – because for them the Indies appeared in the Bible under other names (such as the Ophir of Solomon) and the Indians were none other than the lost tribes of Israel. Finally, a complex providential argument was also used that suggested that God had decided to keep the Indians out of the Revelation so that their prompt and resounding conversion would be seen as a sign of the force of the word of Christ (Poliakov 1976: 55).

It is interesting to note that the sixteenth century also offered a 'primitivist' discourse on the American Indians. By primitivism is meant here the doctrine that 'whatever additions have been made to what is called the "natural condition of mankind" have been deleterious' (Boas 1973: 577). The American Indian provided a growing body of literature with the raw material to construct the model of the 'noble savage'. Most influential among the early texts was that of Michel de Montaigne's *Essais* (1580), and most particularly the section entitled *On the Cannibals*. The habits of the Caribbeans, which had contributed so much to the definition of the Amerindians as barbarous, became in Montaigne's pen just different ways of behaving, but in no way signalling cultural inferiority. These peoples may not have measured up to what the Europeans called civilization (literacy, law, trade, technology, and so forth), but this did not mean that they lacked morals or that their life was brutish.

In the long run, though, the question of the origins of the American Indians could not be properly solved within the framework of the model provided by the Bible. Interestingly, the first critics of the extensive use of the Bible appeared as early as the seventeenth century. Isaac La Peyrère was by far the most brilliant and colourful of them all. A Huguenot of Jewish origin who later converted to Catholicism, La Peyrère wrote in 1642–3 a treatise that he called *Pre-Adamitae*. In this book the raised the possibility that most of mankind (Jews excepted) could be studied outside the main Judeo-Christian tradition (Popkin 1974: 353). La Peyrère's basic thesis was that the Bible only described the history of the Israelites, and not the history of the world. All events referred to in the Bible were events localized in Palestine. The so-called Pre-Adamite hypothesis assumed that the state of nature existed before Adam and Eve, and that Jewish history exemplified the divine drama of salvation. La Peyrère's bold denial of the Adam-Noah origins of the peoples of the world opened up the way to the study of people's cultures independently of the Judeo-Christian context. In other words, it allowed the possibility of studying human behaviour from a variety of perspectives (geographical, climatic, economic, political, psychological, and so forth) (Popkin 1974: 354). Finally, implicit in La Peyrère's theory was the original diversity of the human races and the need to consider them in a naturalized and secularized framework. In retrospect, this was La Peyrère's most spectacular contribution, putting polygenism on the agenda of the modern world.

Following on the ideas of La Peyrère, the *Critical and Historical Dictionary* of Pierre Bayle – which was a source of inspiration for Hume, Rousseau and Voltaire – went a step further in moving from biblical to secular man. Human beings were not at the mercy of God's will but could rather be studied in terms of natural factors. If anything, the *Dictionary* demolished biblical stories presenting them as a history of human foibles, of crimes and misfortunes, in which the sexual motivations had the upper hand .

Before the seventeenth century came to a close, another type of development should be mentioned: the beginning of comparative anatomy. The Greeks, notably Aristotle and Galen, had certainly observed the structural similarities between human beings and apes. But it was not until Edward Tyson published his *Anatomy of a Pygmie Compared with that of a Monkey, an Ape and a Man* (1699) that we had a detailed description of a chimpanzee as compared to men and monkeys. Tyson felt that, on a number of accounts, the chimpanzee was close to man, while in other aspects it was more similar to a monkey. His conclusion was that, in fact, it belonged to a species between man and the apes. He was particularly struck by the similarity of the brain of the chimpanzee and that of human beings, and saw no anatomical reason why the former could not speak. Although brutes lacked souls, the rational-like qualities of the chimpanzee were a great source of amazement to Tyson. In the last part of his monograph there was an attempt to sort out the different references that he had found in ancient lore concerning man-like animals, and he concluded that many of them actually referred to the chimpanzee. Whether Tyson's study represents a landmark in the theory of evolution, as Ashley Montague remarked, may be disputed, but undoubtedly the text will stands out as an attempt to prove the existence of a scale of nature.

It is no coincidence that the names for higher apes in most Western European languages should refer to the disturbing morphological proximity between man and apes – chimpanzee is the native Angolan for 'mockman', orang-utan is the native Malay for 'man of the woods' and gorilla is the Greek word, of allegedly African origin, for hairy man. Finally, because Africa was the *locus* of the higher apes and of the black race, there was a tendency (and in Tyson it is quite obvious) to see blacks, if not as improved apes, at least as very retarded humans.

It is not surprising that, following the geographical discoveries the first racial classification should have appeared. François Bernier, in his letter to *Le Journal des Savants*, 24 April 1684, entitled 'Nouvelle division de la terre par les différentes espèces d'hommes qui l'habitent' divided the population of earth into five races (Europeans, Africans, Chinese, Japanese and Lapps). What is interesting is not the typology in itself, which was obviously incomplete, but the fact that Bernier separated very clearly Europeans from non-Europeans, attributing to the latter certain animal features. He was also one of the first to use the word 'race' to designate the coalescence of certain morphological features of the human body as well as, of course, pigmentation. But because his conception was ahead of his time, his classification was practically ignored. It is also important to notice how during the sixteenth and seventeenth centuries a crucial number of words relating to racial matters became common in most European languages. To start with the word race itself, but also terms like caste, black, *mestizo* (offspring of European and American Indian), and mulatto (offspring of European and black). Poliakov has noticed how the term mulatto (meaning young mule in Spanish and Portuguese) is a particularly derogatory term in that it assimilates the descendants of a white and a black person to the offspring of the horse and an ass. The emphasis is on the idea that whites and blacks belong to different species, and that their unions should be sterile (Poliakov 1976: 58).

The Dehumanization of Black Africans

One of the most striking things of the Enlightenment is a pervasive and vivid anti-black prejudice (Olender 1981; Banton 1983: Davis 1986). How this attitude developed in the previous two centuries is the objective of this section. I have already indicated that while the American Indians had found defenders of their humanity, black Africans were on the whole perceived – and treated – as racially inferior. This generalized anti-black mentality was the result of the continued interaction between certain stereotypes generated by the European contact with the African continent and the progressive identification of blackness with slavery. There is little doubt that the exploitation of blacks as slaves was justified with religious, scientific, aesthetic and other arguments. And yet it would be historically inaccurate to suggest that the ideological criteria used to perpetuate black slavery were all post facto. It was because in the slave societies of the Americas blacks were treated as beasts of burden and as cattle that they were perceived as non-human, as quasi-animals. And hence the early stereotypes were confirmed and crystallized into unmovable prejudices.

In *White over Black*, a most remarkable historical monograph on the early attitudes of North Americans towards blacks, Winthrop Jordan has depicted with dazzling and graphic detail, and in a style not exempt of passion, how the first impressions of the Africans on the English had long-lasting effects. What were, then, the distinctive marks pinned on Africans? First of all, Africans were perceived as blacks, that is, beings with black skin and black hair. The English, unlike the Mediterranean civilizations of the time, were unfamiliar with both dark-skinned and black peoples. The description of the English explorers clearly expressed a sense of shock and horror when referring to the colour and other features of the African peoples. Now, Jordan emphasizes that the contrast between white and black as colours was firmly established in English culture, and that why the former was clearly associated with purity, virginity, beauty and good, the latter was linked with dirtiness, sin, ugliness and evil (Jordan 1968: 7). The projection of some of the attributes of the word black into Africans is already visible in the English literature of the late sixteenth and early seventeen centuries. Colour prejudice was a well-known motif – of which perhaps Shakespeare's Othello is the most popular example.

Travellers, explorers, philosophers and commentators of all times were intrigued at how the black condition had originated. From the perspective of the Bible, if all human beings were supposed to be descended from Adam and Eve, at some stage within the limited and well-established biblical chronology of the world, human beings must have started to diverge in skin pigmentation as well as other body characteristics. The most probable cause advanced at the time was the effect of the sun, though this explanation was not without flaws (why were some American Indians, living in similar climates, not black?).

Although blackness was thought as an inborn and lasting condition (particularly after it was realized that blacks in Europe and in North American were not 'whitening', experimentally oriented minds often wondered how long it would take for black people to turn into white (and vice-versa). This idea stayed in the English and the European mind in general for a long time, to the extent that, even Buffon in the eighteenth century, could suggest that the only way of finding out how long it would take to change from black to white was to transfer a group of West Africans to Northern Europe, where people had the whitest skin and blue eyes, and have them intermarry for generations until the predicted changes occurred (Buffon 1971).

There was another explanation of the origins of blackness which was put forward in the sixteenth and seventeenth centuries and which had a long lasting and pernicious effect. It was based on a far-fetched exegesis of the Old Testament (probably borrowed from the Talmud and the Islamic traditions) which established not only that the descendants of Ham would become slaves, but that they would become black (Evans 1980).

Religion was another area that created a big gulf between English and African peoples. For a Christian the natives of Africa were defined as heathen, that is, an unenlightened people who lacked the moral principles common to all the major universalistic religions known at the time (Christianity, Judaism, Islam). On the whole no African ritual practices were seen as religious, at east in the early period of exploration. It is surprising, however, that the English, unlike the Iberians, were not engaged in any attempt to convert these heathen into the Christian faith. The chasm existing at the religious level contributed only to confirm the suspicion that black Africans were a completely different type of people.

Closely related to the issue of heathenism was the issue of savagery. The Africans were seen as unpolished, uncivilized people, due to the fact that all the different elements that constituted their culture were diametrically different from those seen as acceptable in the England of the time. Particularly shocking were, of course, the sexual mores of the African – but more of that later. The English, like other Europeans, had a morbid fascination for the minutine of the life of the savages. But as I have it hinted before, while there were attempts to dignify the figure of the American Indian as the 'noble savage', the African counterpart had hardly any apologists.

Jordan calls a 'tragic happenstance' that 'the Negro's homeland was the habitat of the animal which in appearance most resembles man' (Jordan 1968: 29). It is ironic that while blacks were likened to animals, the chimpanzees were likened to human beings. The line between apes and men became blurred, and black people started to be perceived as an intermediate grade. Copulation between apes and blacks was seen as occasional occurrence, and the existed of monstrous offspring possible, and even attested.

The final attribute of African was their lecherousness. This condition followed from their savagery and beastliness. Black Africans were perceived as beings with an uncontrollable sexual urge, if not completely engrossed in satisfying their lust. The fact that they were scantily clothed and were seen as promiscuous and incestuous, contributed to create this picture. This image of Africans as oversexed creatures was not completely new; in fact the explorer's reports from Africa only came to confirm the stereotypes that had existed in this respect from the later Middle Ages and that had filtered into the European folklore and literature from Islamic sources. Leo Africanus' *History and Description of Africa* (Italian original 1526; Latin tr. 1556; English tr. 1600).

Related to this vision of the African as a libidinous animal was the belief that the black male sexual organ was of an extraordinary size, while the female of the race was represented as being sexually overt and pushy. Furthermore, the images of bestiality, particularly of male apes copulating with black women, entered the eighteenth century and no doubt promoted the idea that there was a close connection between apes and Africans.

How far the coalescence of these five attributes mentioned by Jordan dehumanized black Africans to such an extent that in the mind of the settlers of the New World they became the sole candidates for slavery will always be open to contention. Why were Indians and white slaves little used may have to do, as Philip Curtin has remarked, not with the colour of the skin, but with the fact that the rates of black mortality were much lower than that of the other races. So there seems to be a sound economic explanation for black slavery in the Americas. In the context of the Mediterranean and of the Islamic world this rule does not apply because the environment was healthier, so whites and blacks were enslaved.

Another way of probing Jordan's claims is, of course, by inquiring to which extent Arab and European explorers (other than the English) shared the same stereotypes about Africa. There is a myth that presents the Islamic world as free from racial, anti-black prejudice. This is far from the truth. In fact, in the context of the Arab expansion there developed a perception of black people as inferior. The black poet Suhaym, born a slave, could lament his fate as early as the seventh century:

> Though I am slave my soul is nobly free,
> though I am black of colour my character is white.
> (Lewis 1971: 11)

During the medieval period the situation of blacks within Islam only deteriorated. By the fifteenth century, Ibn Khaldum, the most famous Arab philosopher of history of all times, could write in the Muqaddimah: 'The only people who accept slavery are the Negroes [Sudan], owing to their low degree of humanity' (Lewis 1971: 38).

It is also important to document the Dutch perception of Africa in the early period. If there is no doubt that there are strong parallels between the way in which the English and the Dutch perceived Africans, the Dutch discovered that black Africans were not completely savage. In fact, when compared with the Indians of the Guyanas, Africans were often materially more advanced, and their level of economic, social and political organization was more sophisticated. Although not so much obsessed with colour matters, the Dutch soon realized, however, that Africans were more appropriate for a plantation type of economy than the Indians.

It cannot be said that the early Portuguese and Italian African chronicles differed much in content or tone from the English ones. The descriptions that obtain are predictably ethnocentric, emphasizing those aspects of African cultures that were more likely to shock European audiences. African societies were depicted as bestial societies: without law, without religion, without sexual regulations. The latter feature was often highlighted as particularly offensive. It was said of Africans that 'are in carnal acts like beasts, the father has knowledge of his daughter, the son of his sister' (George 1958: 65).

By now it should be absolutely clear that the process of dehumanization of black people, which was characteristic of the early modern period, is not sufficient, in itself, to account for the appearance of generalized black slavery in the New World. An important point to remember is, of course, the persistence of slavery in the Middle Ages, particularly around the Mediterranean basin. In this area the existence of black slaves was of long standing. Portuguese explorers began capturing African slaves in the fifteenth century, and sold them in the Iberian markets. They found them particularly useful for the cultivation of a new crop – sugar – in the Canary Islands. With the discovery of America and the need for a cheap and resistant labour force to work in the mines and the plantations, the fate of the black African as a slave was sealed. No doubt the prejudices attached to the Africans that we have considered previously, meant that the African was the ideal candidate for slavery in the Americas. The rationale, however, was more economic than anything else, but by creating a cultural abyss between whites and blacks, the slave system was given a powerful justification.

Enlightenment and Prejudice

One way of looking at the Enlightenment is by condemning the *philosophes* for failing to conform to the moral expectations of the day. Leon Poliakov, *l'enfant terrible* of the history of racism, occasionally loves to challenge the cherished vision that we have of the Enlightenment: that of a century of universalism, cosmopolitanism and humanism. Whether it is Montequieu, Voltaire, Hume or Kant, it is always possible, and sometimes even easy (says Poliakov), to find in the writings of these authors passages that smack of racism.

In *l'Esprit des lois* (1748) Montesquieu sustained that slavery was against natural law, but he regarded blacks as little more than savages. Hume was even more outspoken in his sense of racial superiority: 'I am apt to suspect', wrote in his essay 'Of national Character', 'the negroes and in general all other species of men . . . to be naturally inferior to the whites' (Hume 1985: 208). The cosmopolitan European philosopher could not but feel pride for the civilizational attainments of the West, especially when compared with the backwardness of the peoples of America, Africa and Asia as depicted in the travellers' books. Voltaire, in the 'Introduction' to his *Essai sur les moeurs et l'esprit des nations* (1765), was tempted to account for this cultural retardation by positing, for example, that the black race was a different species from the white one, and that the intelligence of the former was vastly inferior to that of the latter. As to Kant, he was apparently anti-Semitic, as well as being in favour of preserving racial purity, although the ability of the different races to mate successfully convinced him of the unity of mankind.

It could be objected that none of these thinkers represent the scientific opinion of the time. It would make, however, little difference to bring to the fore the leading natural historians because, in the final resort, they share what with a presentist language we might refer to a racial prejudices. Linnaeus and Buffon are cases in point: both portrayed non-European peoples in no rosy colours. However, it is possible to say that while most *philosophes* espoused polygenist conceptions, naturalists believed that human beings originated in a common ancestor. An area that should also be considered is the issue of what constituted humanity for eighteenth century thinkers, and in which way it differed from animality. The *locus classicus* of this discussion is found in the Enlightenment's concern with the ape-man relationship.

Nobody has better expressed than John Greene the predicament of the Enlightenment with respect to human races: 'To the eighteenth century mind the basic issue concerning human races was whether they were to be regarded as separate species or as a variety of a single species' (1959: 221). A number of consequences followed:

1 Theologically, the problem was how to make compatible the Biblical belief in the unity of men as descendants from Adam if the polygenist hypothesis was accepted.
2 Politically, the issue was how to treat subjected peoples – and particularly if slavery could be justified.
3 Scientifically, if the monogenist hypothesis was accepted, how to explain human variation?

There is little doubt that by the eighteenth century racial prejudice was deeply ingrained in Western civilization, but more as a sub-case of Eurocentrism than anything else. It took the eighteenth century taxonomic drive to produce a hierarchical classification of *Homo sapiens*. The first natural historian to present a comprehensive picture of the place of man in the zoological world was Carl Linnaeus (1707–78). He was probably the most influential natural historian ever. He presented a system of classification of plants and animals that was the onset of the modern nomenclature. For the first time in human history humans were classified in a biological system. Linnaeus had the mind of an encyclopedist and managed to systematize a variety of information coming from different parts of the world. He was, however, a firm believer in the immutability of the species as originally created by the Supreme Being, though we was prepared to accept that time diversified species into varieties.

In Linnaeus's *Systema Naturae*, published originally in 1735 and ran into a number of new editions during his lifetime (the standard edition – the tenth – was published in 1758). The genus Homo, containing two species, was classified, in the 1758 edition, in the class of mammalia and in the order of primates, along with apes, lemurs and bats. It is interesting to note that in the first edition Linnaeus mentioned the existence of two dubious beings (*paradoxa*): the satyrs ('tailed, bearded, with a human body, much given to gesticulation and extremely lascivious') and the tailed men (much referred to by travellers) and which he classified in the genus ape, although he was not quite sure. As I have mentioned before, in the eighteenth century it was not easy to establish a clear-cut distinction between man and ape, because in the traveller's tales there was a humanization of apes, as well as the opposite (savages often presented as apes).

By the second edition (1740), Linnaeus classified *Homo sapiens* in four geographical varieties or races: white European, red American, dark Asian and black African. An interesting variation appeared in the sixth edition (1748): man was defined as 'know thyself' (Solon) and this saying was interpreted by Linnaeus in the light of the Graeco-Roman and Christian philosophy to mean the following:

Man is created with an immortal soul, after God's image. He alone is blessed with a rational soul for the glory of the Creator. Man is the lord of animals and the ultimate end of creation, for whose sake all other things have been made. Nature gives man kindred animals for use and food. Man is the most perfect and wonderful machine, and yet he is fragile like a bubble and exposed to a thousand calamities. To understand all these things is to be a man, that is, a genus very different from all others. (in Bendyshe 1863–4: 423–4)

The previous statement notwithstanding, the fact is that Linnaeus classified man as an animal, though admittedly on the top of the echelon, and as such as part of natural history. The definitive classification of the genus *Homo* occurred in the tenth edition (1758) Here Linnaeus distinguished and defined two basic types of *Homo*: *sapiens* and *troglodytes*. The first comprised the following subspecies:

1.- SAPIENS (*Homo diurnus*, varying according to culture and place)

    1.2. *Wild man* (four-footed, mute, hirsute).

    1.2. *American* (black hair, straight and dense; beardless; wide nose; speckled face; obstinate; jovial; paints himself with skilful red lines; Ruled by Custom).

    1.3. *European* (white; sanguine; muscular; hair galore; blue eyes; gentle; perspicacious; inventive; covered with tight clothes; Ruled by Law).

    1.4. *Asiatic* (yellow; melancholic; rigid; dark hair; dark eyes; severe; vain; avaricious; loose clothes; Ruled by Opinion).

    1.5. *African* (black; phlegmatic; relaxed; black hair; frizzled; silky skin; flat nose; thick lips; women's bosom a matter of modesty; breasts give abundant milk; sly; lazy; negligent; anointed with grease; Ruled by Caprice).

    1.6. *Monstrous* : a) by himself; b) by art

        1.6.1. *Alpine* (small; active; timid)

        1.6.2. *Patagonian* (large; lazy)

        1.6.3. *Hottentot*: single-testicle, hence less fertile

        1.6.4. *Chinese*: long-headed, conic head.

2.- TROGLODYTES

(Cave-dwelling man). Most nearly related to us. Sees distinctly by night. Lives within the borders of Ethiopia, Java, etc. No larger than a boy nine years old. White in colour, walks erect and has short, white, curly hair. Their eyes are orbicular: iris and pupils golden. A fold of skin hangs down the lower part of the abdomen, concealing the pudenda of women. Have a whistling language of their own, very difficult to learn. They affirm to be the former rulers of the world, but they were deposed by men; they hope to recover their empire at *Calendas Graecas*. In India they are used as servants.

It is easy to criticize Linnaeus for what appears to be his gullibility; in fact, he had to rely all too often on fantastic, outlandish and confusing descriptions by travellers and naturalists, having had himself limited access to either first hand knowledge or scientific accounts of the different types described (Broberg 1983). It is obvious that Linnaeus's second human type – *Homo troglodytes* – is a construct based on rather fanciful, vague and disperse information. And yet it fits nicely in his conception of the chain of being. That is, Troglodytes, could be envisaged as an intermediate being between humans and apes (Gould 1985: 264).

Finally, an important question arises from his classification of *Homo sapiens* in different varieties: is it a hierarchical typology? Jordan (1968: 221) is adamant that Linnaeus did not rank the different subspecies of man, though he admits that one of his students – Hoppiac – emphasized the gulf between Europeans and 'savages'. Now, it seems to me that from the descriptive table presented by Linnaeus it follows that the European subspecies is the one that fared better emotionally, intellectually and politically, whereas both Africans and Asians are presented in derogatory terms.

Louis LeClerc, Count of Buffon (1707–88), has the dubious honour of being the first naturalist to have introduced the term 'race' in the scientific vocabulary. His *Histoire naturelle* in 44 volumes (1749–1804) is perhaps the most ambitious and comprehensive history of nature ever produced. Buffon, who is noted for having said that 'the style is the man himself', left a very different imprint in the history of ideas from that of Linnaeus. His objective was to gather, arrange and summarize what was known about the natural world in his time. The world of nature might be orderly and subject to regularity, but unlike Linnaeus, Buffon never proposed a rigid system of classification. He was well aware of the artificiality of all classificatory systems. What mattered most to Buffon were forms, not systems.

One of Buffon's most cherished conceptions was that of the constancy of the species which, according to him, were real, natural entities defined as a group of individuals who were similar and inter-fertile. On the other hand, he questioned the fixity of the species and accepted that new species could arise. Most changes in nature, however, took place within the boundaries of a species and would solely constitute grounds for formation of new varieties.

The least that can be said about the *Histoire naturelle* (thereafter HN) is that it did not please the ecclesiastical establishment. Theological errors had been pointed out by religious zealots after the publication of the first three volumes of HN. Buffon insisted that he was a Christian believer, and even modified some of his most controversial propositions in line with the teachings of the Catholic Church. In private, however, he maintained his position unchanged. Catholic critics had good reasons to see his books as heretical; after all, Buffon had dispensed with the idea of God as the Great Clockmaker, and with it went out also the idea of final causes. The reasoning was simple: if God did not intervene in nature, natural phenomena had to be accounted for in terms of natural causes.

Another major challenge to the biblical story was his assertion that the geological time of the earth far exceeded the approximately 6,000 years specified by the Bible. In his manuscripts Buffon assumed that the earth could be a few millions years old. As a true man of the Enlightenment, Buffon was in favour of keeping religion and science as separate endeavours; this led inevitably to ideological skirmishes with the Faculty of Theology at the University of Paris.

The impact of Buffon's theory was widely felt in the Europe of his time. Witness to that are thinkers as varied as Goethe, Kant and Herder. Buffon's ideas were popularized by Diderot and d'Alembert in their *Encyclopédie*, and constituted a major component in the early development of anthropology. As to the theory of evolution, Darwin claimed Buffon as a transformist (although, as we have seen, Buffon tended to stress change in varieties rather than in species). Perhaps, as it has been remarked, Buffon's work both fostered and hindered the propagation of evolutionary ideas in biology (Lovejoy 1968: 111). In any case, he was one of the first to put forward the hypothesis of organic evolution. Not only did he believe that humans and apes had a common origin, but generally speaking he thought that plants and animals had a common ancestor.

The unity and diversity of man was a topic that Buffon considered in many places, but most specially in the first three volumes of his HN. Man is indeed an animal, but an animal endowed with reason, thought Buffon. The intellectual and moral superiority of man notwithstanding, he cannot hide the fact that his faculties originated in the animal kingdom. The science of natural history, however, functions with a single methodology: no distinctions are made between humans and animals and the same laws apply to both of them.

In *The Image of Africa*, Philip Curtin (1964) has suggested that in the eyes of many eighteenth century writers the contrasts between whites and blacks were so noticeable that they could hardly believe that Europeans and Africans belonged to the same species. However, for somebody like Buffon the reproductive compatibility between the different races or varieties of man was a decisive reason to assert the unity of the human species. None the less, it cannot be said that for him races were the same in terms of perfectibility or aesthetics. He was quite emphatic that not only was white the primitive colour of mankind, but that it was also in the white-inhabited temperate zones where the most beautiful specimens of humans were found.

In so far as other races had deviated from the white one, they had become more ugly and less-proportionate. As Roger has remarked: 'the physical and moral picture of all these [non-European] peoples is rather sombre' (1989: 239). Following Maupertuis, many commentators believed that the human forms that had originated from the natural type of man were to be envisaged as degeneration caused by environmental factors. Buffon agreed wholeheartedly with this kind of explanation. Temperature was an important factor in shaping different peoples; both extremes of cold and heat were conducive to human degeneration. In northern regions, Buffon found that people like the Eskimo and the Lapps were small, ugly and unintelligent. As to those who lived in the tropics, they were also seen as savages, nearing the animal stage. Both mind and body had degenerated due to the unfriendly environment.

The beauty of Buffon's environmentalism is that it rejected racial essentialism and hence it allowed for a process of reversion to come into operation. Peoples who had degenerated could see their characteristics return to their original form, if only they were transported back into a moderate climate. In fact, Buffon believed that in ten generations or thereabouts a black population would turn back into its original white condition. In addition to climate, Buffon thought that human variation was also the result of dietary practices. This argument he used to account for colour differences among neighbouring populations. Finally, energy expenditure affected also body shape and general appearance: civilized peoples were on the whole more aesthetically pleasant than savage ones, simply because they exerted themselves less (Eddy 1984: 37).

This was Buffon's theory of racial degeneration as presented in his early writing of 1749. If anything changed in later years was the growing predominance of the organic over the environmental. He became convinced that the most important changes that account for human variation were produced by the food ingested. This led Buffon to place the onus of racial degeneration, which by then included mental weakness, on the level of civilizational development. Because savage peoples were unable to control their environment and the type of food they consumed, some of them were so degraded as to resemble apes. He even thought it conceivable that black women had viable offspring after having copulated with apes. However, he later rejected this idea because he became convinced of the spiritual unity of the human species. None the less, the physical and mental inferiority of Africans and American Indians, when compared with Europeans, hardly offered any doubt to Buffon (Eddy 1984: 34).

In his attitude towards non-European people there is little doubt that Buffon was a child of his age. His judgements about the ugliness, the laziness, the stupidity, and so forth, of the so-called savages have been amply documented. And yet to affirm the unity of the human species not for theological but for scientific reasons, was an intellectual event of major proportions. In any case, it is fitting to close this brief examination of Buffon's theories by bringing a text which denounces the inhumanity of Europeans who enslaved and generally mistreated Africans:

> Why black people may lack in esprit, they are full of sentiment . . . Their present state is miserable due to slavery . . . In addition, they are often mistreated and punished as if they were animals. Humanity revolts against this ignominious treatment which is justified by the thirst of money . . . How can human beings with an element of humanity consent to such harshness? (Buffon 1971: 283)

To close this section on natural historians I would like to refer briefly to Georges Cuvier. Although he is perhaps a post-Enlightment man – he lived between 1769 and 1832 – he is an influential figure in the history of the theory of evolution and man's role in it. To the question of whether man was the highest of animals, Cuvier's response was to assert its qualitative difference, although earlier in his career he was tempted to consider man as the most perfect animal, the summit of the evolutionary scale. He openly admitted the structural similarity between man and ape, the main difference being the different size of the brain.

Cuvier went along with the threefold classification of mankind – Caucasian, Mongolian, Ethiopian. Some peoples, like the American Indians, were outside this classificatory system. He strongly maintained the idea that the human species was one – the reason being that the different groups were interfertile. According to Cuvier, colour was not the main feature that distinguished the races; more important were physical traits such as the shape of the head, the form of the nose or lips, the configuration of the lower jaw, and so forth.

It would be fair to say that Cuvier did not often delve into the issue of race and civilization, that is, whether there were differences of intelligence among the races. None the less, it is obvious from his writings that he shared with most of his contemporaries a sense of European, that is, Caucasian superiority. He was convinced that no other race had contributed so much to the development of the sciences, arts, literature, religion, and so forth. Like so many of his naturalist peers, he was of the conviction that Africans were close to animality. In a course of public lectures delivered in 1805–6, Cuvier could say:

> It is not for nothing that the Caucasian race has gained dominion over the world and made the most rapid progress in the sciences, while the Negroes are still sunken in slavery and the pleasure of the senses and the Chinese are lost in the obscurities of a monosyllabic and hieroglyphic language. The shape of their heads relates them somewhat more than us to the animals. (Coleman 1964: 166)

Coleman (1964), however, rightly rejects the accusation that Cuvier could be construed as a sort of white supremacist *avant la lettre*. His attitude towards the 'inferior races' is best described as paternalist. He certainly acknowledged that they were all human beings endowed with reason and sentiments. The cultural 'inferiority' of Africans did not justify their mistreatment; an institution like slavery said more about the inhumanity of Europeans than the animality of Africans.

-4-

The French Revolution and the Early Critics of Modernity: The Legacy of Maistre

This chapter deals with a rather long historical period, from the mid-sixteenth century to the nineteenth century. The French races form a topic that it is particularly prominent up to the French revolution, although it is far from disappearing from the nineteenth century discussions. As a reaction against the French Revolution by the extreme right-wingers we have, particularly in the figure of Joseph de Maistre, the appearance of a totalitarian doctrine. In the words of Isaiah Berlin, this author is essentially the proto-fascist thinker *par excellence*.

Two French Races

In her detailed study of the idea of race in France between 1550 and 1616 Arlette Jouanna insists that approximately 100 texts were published on the topic. According to the author, the idea of race is well established in the social order, separating quite radically the noblemen and the ordinary people. The people of the noble race are exemplary models that can be imitated by the inferior race; any sexual mixture can proof to be disastrous because keeping the purity of the blood is essential for society. It is interesting to note that while the ordinary people accepted the racial division, the growing bourgeoisie and the professionals expressed a sense of superiority vis-à-vis the general population. It is plain that in this time the hierarchical principle becomes stronger and more visible. An interesting assumption is the appearance of what could be called 'hereditary determinism', which is essentially connected with the sociological importance of birth (Michel 1847).

During the period under consideration the Wars of Religion were dominant. It is obvious that the aristocracy believed that it was racially superior and that the socially inferior people had practically no 'race' and no lineage. In the *Etats Généraux* of 1614 it is plain that there was a confrontation between the views of officialdom and that of the aristocracy, which expressed a pride in the conquering role of their ancestors and their natural superiority. This will become crucial and will affect the key thinkers of the eighteenth century, authors like Boulainvailliers and Montesquieu. In this context, what was being defended was the idea that the noblemen were descendant from the victorious Franks and that the peasants were descendant from the vanquished Gallics. This viewpoint of the War of the Two Races was a novelty after a long period in which the idea of a conflict between the conquering Franks and the conquered Gallo-Romans had disappeared. A final point worth remembering is that the sixteenth- and early seventeenth-century expression of 'race' had a variety of meanings like category, species, lineage, descent, and nation.

In Michel Foucault's *Il faut défendre la société*, which was the College de France course of 1975–6 but which was not published until 1997, it is noticeable that the starting point is Clausewitz's modified statement: politics is the continuation of war by other means. What Foucault is trying to say is that while French society was governed by the war of two races from the sixteenth to the eighteenth century, what happened in the nineteenth century was the appearance of state racism. However, the early modern discourse of the decadent aristocracy finds a peculiar continuity with the nineteenth century bourgeois ideology, which visualizes society as being threatened by criminals, workers, barbarians, and so forth. Not surprisingly, Foucault's book tries to account for the genesis of racism, indicating as well that it is the principle of the twentieth century totalitarianism (for example, fascism, nazism, communism).

In a nutshell, what constitutes the centrality of modern history is the idea of race war, based on an early stage in invasion and usurpation of power of, for example, Germanics over Gallo-Romans and Normands over Saxons. In other words, what is important, insists Foucault, is not envisaging history in terms of sovereignty, obedience, limits on power, contractualism, law, and so forth, but emphasizing and remembering conquests, invasions, expropriations, servitude, and exile. The class that was behind this type of discourse was originally the decadent aristocracy, followed by the bourgeoisie. One can say in advance that the nineteenth-century bourgeoisie conceived the idea of war as an event that happened within their own society. In other words, social order was subverted by a variety of internal enemies: the criminals, the workers, the degenerates, the colonized and the Jews. In a borrowing of Darwinian concepts, war was conceived in terms of the survival of the fittest, the strongest, the mentally healthier and the Aryan.

As we have noted at the beginning of this chapter, the idea of race appeared in France in the sixteenth century. As Barzun (1932: 251) noted in a pre-Foucauldian text published in 1932:

> The very roots of French history since the sixteenth century have been buried deep under and around the issue of race; that in determining whether the France of their day was chiefly German, or Roman, or Gallic, the historians of each century, as well the obscure pamphleteers of each party, have touched on every important national issue.

An important French historian who wrote on these issues was Marc Bloch. In a paper written at a time of an imminent Franco-German war (mid-1939), he emphasized that one should begin the issue by approaching the century in which there was an 'intense political fermentation, that of the Wars of Religion' (1940–5: 58). This century was, of course, the sixteenth century. In fact, it can be said that between Gregory of Tours and the end of the Middle Ages there was no negative reference against the Frankish invaders, and no opposition between the descendants of the Gallo-Romans and those of Germanic origins.

To start at the beginning, the first names to mention in the mid-sixteenth century are those of E. Pasquier and F. Hotman. They rejected the belief that France was a product of

> Trojan descent and suggested that the Gauls did not suffer the Germanic conquest, but were the French-Romans those who became dominated. In this respect, the Franks were presented as the liberators of the Gauls, who were oppressed by the Romans. It was a fact, they insisted, that the French nobility was descended from the Franks and the Gauls, and hence the noblemen were entitled to own the land. From the title of Hotman's work published in 1543 – *Franco-Gallia* – it is obvious that the crucial issue defended was that the Gauls had never accepted Roman domination. In fact, the assumption was that the Franks were descended from people who were originally Gauls and had crossed the Rhine towards the east. It is important to remember that the Franks were in favour of democratic ideas. The thesis that the Franks were descendants from the Gauls was maintained over a century by people like Pasquier, Bodin, Bellefort and Audigier (Amselle 1997: 792).

This state of things changed radically by the eighteenth century. In fact, by the end of the seventeenth century the Count of Boulanvilliers maintained that in France the 'Nordic' nobility was the only legitimate power. This was the result of a conquest that involved the use of force. To put it in a more direct way: the dominant class were the Franks and the subordinate one were the Gauls. His two major propositions were that there emerged a principle of racial hatred after the Frankish invasion, but that there was a Golden Age period, which happened under Charlemagne. It is interesting to notice that Boulanvilliers asserted that the history of the Frankish nobility showed a loss of prerogatives and status which were deviated, first to the Church, and later to the bourgeoisie. He insisted that only the aristocracy should have the right to attend the Parliaments (estates-general). In his classical text, entitled *Histoire de l'Ancien Gouvernement de la France,* Boulainvilliers defended the idea that in the French monarchy the right of the aristocracy is fundamental. According to Foucault it is obvious that Boulainvilliers' scheme imagined the medieval period in terms of two orders, nations or races and that each group is characterized by certain features, usages, mores and laws. It is important to emphasize that what is at stake is a scheme of domination, of subjection, from the right of conquest.

The reaction against Boulainvilliers was predictable and instantaneous. In the work of Dubos, for example, we can observe a reversing of the discourse of Boulanvilliers: there was no Frankish invasion and hence there could not have been subjection of the Gauls; he insisted that the power of the monarch derived from the Romans. With Dubos triumphed the Latin thesis in so far as he maintained that the conquest of Gallia by the Franks was a myth. According to the author there are a number of important points:

1 The settlement of the Franks was not oppressive but peaceful.
2 The Frankish rule was only a justified continuation of the Roman rule.
3 There was a mixture of the two races (Gallo-Romans and Franks) at once, and there was no major differentiation.
4 The state was characterized by an absence of slavery and the presence of freedom. (Barzun 1932: 169–70)

The reaction against Dubos was also predictable. It was up to the moderate and prestigious Montesquieu to make an extreme criticism of Dubos. In a rather expressive statement he maintained that 'nothing pushes back the progress of knowledge like a bad work by a famous author, because before instructing, one must begin by correcting the mistakes' (Montesquieu 1989: 639). Montesquieu insisted that the Franks were not friends of the Romans and actually had conquered the Gallia. Although he agreed with Boulainvilliers on the importance of the royal absolutism, he rejected his idea that the Franks enslaved the formerly free Gallo-Romans. His idea was that only the Gauls were enslaved and that his image of the Franks was like that of raiders, that is, a conquering tribe that most of the time left the Gallo-Romans free from interferences. This is compatible with the fact that the Franks required the payment of a ransom and dispossessed the natives of some of their lands (Barzun 1932: 202–3). It would be fair to say, as Bloch has remarked, that Montesquieu did not believe that racial antagonism between Franks and Gallo-Romans lasted forever. In fact, he insisted that the modern French nation was forgetting the distinctions of origins and the presence of castes. It is interesting to note that these ideas had an important influence on German thinkers, particularly in Herder.

Much could be said about further discussions during the eighteenth century. In brief terms, one can refer to Mably, who was the spokesman for the Third Estate, and insisted that the Frankish invasions had challenged Roman absolutism and had represented a breath of freedom. Voltaire, on the contrary, saw the Franks as no better than hungry savages. The contribution of E. Sieyès in *Qu'est ce que le Tiers Etat?* (1789) emphasized that this institution was the embodiment of the nation. For him, the nation was composed of by the descendants from Gauls and Romans; as to the Frankish they were aristocrats that had to be defeated. As is well known,

Sieyès suggested sending the Franks back to the German forests where they came from. The strange reality is that after the Revolution the aristocrats seemed to follow his advice and many migrated to Koblenz.

The French Revolution seemed to quieten the racial issue. Many regarded modern France as a fusion of Gallic, Roman and Frankish elements. For example, the leading historians of the early nineteenth century, people like Michelet, Thierry and Guizot, presented a picture of France as the result of the happy blending of races, which gave a well-balanced culture and modern outlook to France. To use a well-known statement by Thierry, one can say that the French had inherited the free and valorous character of the Frankish, the impetuosity and mysticism of the Gauls and the practicality and organizing genius of the Romans (Barzun 1932: 256). Generally speaking, it is correct to assert that the admiration of the French writers for the Nordic genius survived until 1870. People like Madame Stael, Guinet, Cousin, Guizot, Nerval, Berlioz, Renan, Gobineau and many others were influenced by German writings. It is not surprising to observe that after the French military defeat and the loss of territory, there was a return to Gallic preferences. Quinet, for example, had by 1857 rejected the idea that the French institutions had Germanic origins and Renan started a Celtic revival.

A final point is worth mentioning concerning the work of Fustel de Coulanges. His *Histoire des institutions politiques de l'ancienne France* (1875–92) favoured the Gallo-Roman thesis. It would be fair to say that his perspective is closer to that of Dubos rather than that of Boulainvilliers and Montesquieu. According to Bloch's perspective Fuster de Coulange's theses are the following:

1   The idea of a Germanic invasion is doubtful because the phenomena is rather complex and took place over a long period of time. It is more correct to refer to what could be called a slow infiltration.

2   Another wrong point of view is to suggest that the invasion can be presented as a struggle and victory of the Germanics over the Romans. The Germanics, however, were not a unity but a rather disperse group. As Fustel de Coulanges put it: 'The struggle between the Roman Empire and the regime of the war band was like the struggle between the sedentary state and the stable state' (Fustel de Coulanges 1875–92, Vol. IV: 326).

3   The natural conclusion is that because the invaders were unstable and without a past, they accepted the institutions of the solid political civilization of the invaded.

4   The Germanic invaders accepted the social inheritance of the Gallo-Roman society. The idea of a national, ethnic, or racial confrontation only makes sense in modern times; it was non-existent in the medieval period.

The French Revolution and its Critics

The French Revolution was the most momentous event of modernity. The echoes of its revolutionary ideals – *Liberté, Egalité, Fraternité* – reverberated not only all over Europe, but also in distant places such as Port-au-Prince, Buenos Aires, Cairo and Moscow. The hopes raised by the French Revolution were boundless: it promised to do away with human ignorance and drudgery and it heralded the coming of the Age of Happiness. But with the Revolution came Terror; the dreams of Reason produced monsters. The French Revolution not only did a *tabula rasa* with the ancient regime but devoured its own children. After 1792 the French Revolution became chaotic, self-destructive and despotic.

The first important issue is to find out, at the very beginning, how did the Enlightenment prepare the way for the French Revolution. There are four major points worth mentioning:

1   It weakened the traditional religion that had been allied to the monarchy for time immemorial. In this way they encouraged the poor and unprivileged to think more about the earth than about heaven.

2   It taught a code of ethics which was fundamentally secular and that rejected religious beliefs and dogmas. The main doctrine was essentially humanistic.

3   It developed the critical spirit of analysis and taught to ordinary men that traditions should not be accepted.

4   It created an historical sense that encouraged belief in progress and freedom.

It would be fair to say that in the beliefs of the Enlightenment the millennium was at hand. What was expected was a radical change of life, with the high standards on freedom, security, happiness, virtuosity and wisdom. The basic assumption was that human beings were rational and sociable. It was up to the educational system to provide the rules of conduct; these were the result of an accessible human understanding. In practice, there are laws that govern the natural and the social worlds. The respect of the laws of society creates stability and happiness. Another point emphasized is that, for educated people, the government should be kept to a minimum and the freedom of the individual enshrined. In the final resort, it is possible to assert that all good and appealing things are perfectly compatible.

These ideas were disseminated in a powerful way through a variety of procedures and in a variety of places. One should mention the salons, the clubs (particularly those against slavery and in favour of the French Revolution), the theatres, and the educational system. As to the techniques of diffusion one can refer to the following: books and tracts, periodicals, the *Cahiers de Doleance* and the revolutionary pamphlets (the last two issues crucial in 1788–89).

Following these developments, which implied putting into practice the objectives of the Enlightenment during the French Revolution, a number of voices,
particularly those of Burke, Maistre and Bonald appeared who maintained that no
matter how imperfect society might be, revolutions cannot be justified because they
make things worse. Only a return to royal authority and divine legitimation would
save society from the revolutionary disasters provoked by rationalism, individualism, liberalism and secularism. Bonald and Maistre represent the beginning
of modern reactionary thought. While Burke set the foundations of modern conservatism and it is quite appropriate to see Bonald as a reactionary, only Maistre
qualifies as the heralder of modern totalitarianism. As we shall see, Maistre's
thought is often violent and sinister, with a touch of religion (Catholic fundament-
alism). However, when freed from its religious shell it appears close to modern
fascist ideology.

Before discussing these classical counter-revolutionary thinkers, there is an
interesting issue considered by a variety of authors concerning the political status of
J. J. Rousseau. These authors have suggested that Rousseau exhibits an extremist
conception. In this sense, Rousseau's ideas would assert that totalitarian society is
one that contends that it can cater for all the basic needs of human beings; to achieve
that end it requires that all individuals should be totally subordinated to the collectivity.

It has been suggested, among others by J. L. Talmon (1952) and L. G. Crocker
(1968), that Rousseau endorsed totalitarianism, although he would hardly have
approved the means used by fascists and communists. According to Lebrun (1972:
895):

four basic characteristics of totalitarian societies are present in Rousseau's utopia:

a) A charismatic guide or leader.

b) An organic ideal of community in which all owe unlimited loyalty and obedience to
the community.

c) The precept and goal of unanimity.

d) The numerous technique used to mobilise and control the minds, wills, and emotions
of people.

The conclusion of Lebrun's analysis is that there was a longing in Rousseau for
a perfect society in which the selfish and social tendencies of the individuals would
be reconciled. The alternative to pure democracy was not imperfect democracy but
rather theocratic despotism. It is an interesting question, as Lebrun's formulates it,
whether Rousseau comes ideologically close to the author Maistre – an author who
will be considered in the next section. Suffice it to say at this stage that Talmon and

Crocker suggest that they are both totalitarian thinkers. They would emphasize the fact, however, that Rousseau's language of democracy is misleading because he in fact favoured a 'system of cultural engineering that would reduce freedom to an index of illusion' (Crocker 1968: 167). The kind of socialization postulated by Rousseau and Maistre meant a total 'identification of the individual with the collectivity' (Crocker 1968: 169). Undoubtedly, Rousseau does not refer to divinity or suggesting that the democratic polity will be founded on the mystical unity of the general will.

One of the effects of the French Revolution was the revival of organicism among counter-revolutionary thinkers. The idea that society was a natural organism and should not be tampered with was very much at the centre of the vigorous criticisms used by the enemies of the French Revolution. For these thinkers the Enlightenment had only succeeded in creating an atomistic society in which the individual had lost its place in the social order. Edmund Burke believed in the idea that social life was basically organic, that individuals were held together by emotional, non-rational bonds. He contrasted this holistic vision of society with the atomistic, contractual and utilitarian perspective typical of the Enlightenment. The idea that society was a natural outgrowth and that it was not up to human beings to impose an artificial order, was also central to Burke's political philosophy. Both Bonald and Maistre idealized the medieval society of *Stände* (estates), as a consensual and happy one, and stigmatized the egalitarianism of the *philosophes* which had only led to the conflict, struggle and terror of the France of the turn of the nineteenth century (Frank 1956).

It is a well-known fact that some of the early critics of modernity, and I am referring specially to Louis de Bonald, had a profound impact in the French sociological tradition of the nineteenth century (Saint-Simon, Comte, Tocqueville and Durkheim). Bonald was essentially a positivist and an organicist, and maintained that both historically and morally society preceded the individual. He emphasized the limitations of reason; he insisted that its use lead to major mistakes in socio-political affairs. Bonald relied heavily in a 'God-centred, community-anchored theory of language and knowledge' (Ready 1995: 51). This is no doubt the bedrock of his anti-individualism. Although he was a conservative and an ultra-royalist, he was definitely not a proto-fascist like Maistre. He was only disenchanted with the values and institutions of modernity and a critic of Western individualism.

According to R. Nisbet (1952), there emerged an attitude towards the French revolution that could only be called conservatism. There are ten commandments highlighted by Nisbet:

1 Society is an organic entity with internal laws of development, and not an aggregate of individuals. Society cannot be created by individual reason, but can be weakened by it. The roots of society are in the past; it is a partnership of the dead, the living and the unborn.

2   Society has also primacy over the individual (historically, logically and ethic-
ally). Social institutions have preceded man and his ideas; these institutions are
God given. It is important to emphasize that society constitutes the individual, and
not vice-versa.

3   Society cannot be broken down into individuals. The individual is a pure
fantasy and the atom of society must be a social relationship.

4   Social phenomena are interdependent. This follows from the organic character
of society. Consequently, any attempt at reforming a part of society will clash with
the complex lines of relationship.

5   There is the principle of needs. These are the primary needs of the humans. A
deep knowledge of human nature is required to find out what they are. This shall
not be confused with fictitious natural rights.

6   There is also the principle of function. According to it, every person institution
or custom serves some basic need in human life and contributes a service to other
institutions.

7   Against individualism what is stressed are small social groups (such as religious
and occupational groups, family and neighbourhood). These are the intermediate
associations that the French Revolution wiped out. The Revolution equalled
disorganization and social disorder.

8   There is a value of the sacred, non-rational and non-utilitarian elements of
human existence.

9   The principle of hierarchy and status is essential and it is against equality,
which creates unsuitability.

10   Finally, the legitimacy of authority occurs when it is traditional and it proceeds from the customs of a people.

Early French Totalitarianism (Maistre)

It is a well-known fact, that the confusion, chaos, destruction and terror that went
along the French Revolution convinced Maistre that political order was the paramount objective to be achieved. It was human folly and intellectual pride that had
led humans to undermine tradition (Ravera; 1986: Lebrun 1988: Alibert 1990:
Fisichella 1993: Darcel 2000). No matter how imperfect society might be, revolution

cannot be justified because it will make things worse. The kind of conflict-free society that Maistre dreamt of could only be achieved if human beings humbled themselves before two key institutions: Church and monarchy. It was possible, he alleged, to uncover the social design of the divinity; only by following this 'providential order' could society aspire to peace, happiness and contentment. Maistre's main criticism of the Enlightenment and the French Revolution is that they rejected the traditional authority based on an alliance of throne and altar. However, he 'recognised and approved of Rousseaus's reliance on a legislator and on religion as an instrument of social control' (Lebrun 1972: 897).

Lebrun is an author who, incidentally, points out that Maistre was more 'honest' than Rousseau in so far as Maistre never raised any hopes about the idea that society could be freer (Lebrun 1972: 898). In some respects Rousseau and Maistre are 'totalitarian thinkers', the main difference being that Rousseau's language of democracy is misleading because he in fact favoured a 'system of cultural engineering that would reduce freedom to an index of illusion' (Crocker 1968: 167–9). The kind of socialization postulated by both Rousseau and Maistre meant a total identification of the individual with the collectivity. A final point worth quoting is what Maistre thought of this author: 'Rousseau, one of the most dangerous sophists of our century, and yet the one who was the most deprived of true knowledge, wisdom and especially of profundity, with only an apparent depth that was all a matter of words' (Maistre 1993: 34).

Maistre made no bones about the need to submit to traditional authorities; in so far as religion was placed above the state, there was a chance that the individual would have a resort against the all-encroaching state. Of course, for Maistre the final argument was that the divine providence created and legitimated the authority of popes, kings and aristocrats. It is obvious that Maistre appeared as an author who rebelled in a radical form against the key ideas of the Enlightenment. In his long article 'Joseph de Maistre and the Origins of Fascism', Isaiah Berlin (1991) offers what could be called the basic beliefs of Maistre, and which can be envisaged as the total opposite of the Enlightenment:

1   No a *prioris* of human nature, but the facts of history, zoology and common observation.

2   No ideals of progress, liberty and human perfectibility, but salvation by faith and tradition.

3   No goodness of human nature, but incurably bad and corrupt nature of man, hence the need for authority, hierarchy, obedience and subjection.

4   No science, but primacy of instinct, Christian wisdom, prejudice (fruit of the experience of generations) and blind faith.

5   No optimism, but pessimism.

6   No eternal peace and harmony, but divine necessity of suffering and conflict, sin and retribution, bloodshed and war.

7   No ideals of peace and social equality based on the common interest of men and on man's goodness, but inherent inequality and violent conflict of aims and interests as being the normal condition of fallen men and nations.

A shrewd commentator, Isaiah Berlin pointed out as early as 1953 that Maistre was the first modern representative of totalitarian thought. What motivated the onslaught of Maistre was the conviction that the French Revolution, which dethroned both God and King from the French soil, could only be understood as a Satanic rebellion. But behind the French Revolution was the Enlightenment, which particularly in the figures of Voltaire and Rousseau provoked in him an accentuated moral outrage. The Enlightenment undermined both Christianity and monarchy, and hence was the immediate cause of social dislocation that culminated in the events of 1789. The French Revolution represented an unfurlement of boundless evil; when left to themselves, without the guidance of Christianity, men lusted for power in a disordinate way. This leads to error, decay and destruction, with the inevitable result: punishment for having sinned against the Creator. The divine order can only be broken at a costly price: terror and bloodshed.

It is in the seventh of the dialogues that Maistre (1993) tried to show how the rule of violent death is written everywhere in the animal world. When it comes to killing other human beings, war is the law of the world, and it this sense man undertakes war with great enthusiasm.

Returning to the issue of Maistre's opinion on the French Revolution it is difficult to know whether he had detested it from its very inception or not. What is a fact is that by the early 1790s he could be already considered an ideological adversary of it. His conservatism, however, was of a long standing; the idea that law, customs and institutions inherited from the past could be overthrown at will was totally alien to Maistre's way of thinking. When Burke published his *Reflections on the Revolution in France* (1790), Maistre found in them a corroboration of his anti-democratic sentiments. By 1795 his convictions had hardened to the point that he felt the ideological basis of the French Revolution had to be thoroughly challenged. For Maistre the French Revolution is not a hazardous event, but the unfurling of a supernatural plan. However, because it is the irruption of evil into history, it has a satanic character. The defence of monarchy and religion passed through the undermining of the ideological roots of the French Revolution, and this meant a concerted attack on Rousseau's seductive and pernicious political philosophy. The result of this feverish undertaking was the writing of *De l'état de nature*, an unpublished tract aimed at undermining the ideological foundations of the Enlightenment and at restoring a truly anti-democratic society.

Maistre's objective in *De l'état de nature* is straightforward: to justify philosophically and historically the contradictory nature of man; a being who is, on the one hand, sociable, reasonable and perfectible, but, on the other hand, morally bankrupt, politically inept and psychologically unsatisfied. From this state of things Maistre concludes that what humans need is a rigid social order, the outstanding feature of which is strict obedience to God and throne (Darcel 1976: 24). His task can be envisaged as a refutation of Rousseau's *L'origine de l'inégalité parmi les hommes*. For Maistre, Rousseau is not only wrong, he is also evil; his doctrines have contributed in no minor way to a revolution that has been ruthless and bloody. Maistre often deforms Rousseau's thought to suit his polemical bent.

One of the consequences of Maistre's attack on Rousseau is that the myth of the Good Savage took a sinister turn. For Maistre savages were originally civilized men who had degenerated. For him, the sight of these quasi-animals was repugnant because of their multiple vices and bloody practices. In his *Saint Petersburg Dialogues* he wrote an extremely disparaging picture of primitive people:

> One cannot glance at the savage without reading the curse that is written not only on his soul but even on the exterior from the body. This is a deformed child, robust and ferocious, on whom the light of intelligence casts no more than a pale and flickering beam. A formidable hand weighing on these benighted races effaces in them the two distinctive features of our greatness, foresight and perfectibility . . . The natural vices of humanity are even more vicious in the savage . . . He has an appetite for crime and no remorse. The son kills his father to spare him the inconvenience of old age, his woman destroys in her womb the fruit of their brutal lust to escape the fatigue of nursing it. He rips off the bleeding scalp of his living enemy, he tears him into pieces, roasts him, and devours him while singing . . . He is visibly perverted; he has been stricken in the deepest layers of his moral being. (Maistre 1993: 46)

In the same text, there is a culmination of what could be an affinity with the modern fascist mentality. Although we will see it in more detail, it is relevant to offer a picture of the world which is conceived in terms of blood and death:

> The universal law of violent destruction of living beings is incessantly fulfilled. The entire earth, perpetually steeped in blood, is nothing but an immense altar on which every living thing must be immolated without end, without restraint, without respite, until the extinction of evil, until the death of death. (Maistre 1993: 217)

In a rather peculiar way we can see how Maistre takes always the most extreme of the ideological positions. For example, in 1815 he defended the Spanish Inquisition in the most radical way. In the pursuit of controversy against free thinkers he denied the statement that this was an intolerant institution. In fact, in his words it 'was one of the mildest and wisest civil tribunals within the range of civilization' (Maistre 1977: 172). If the Inquisition attacked the Jews and Muslims of Spain it was because they threatened the very survival of the incipient nation. The kings of Spain behaved hence in a highly patriotic manner. Since the Catholic Church possessed the monopoly of religious truths, concluded Maistre, it would have been better for the spiritual health of Europe had the Inquisition remained in its place during the Enlightenment.

The text on the Spanish Inquisition is presented as a letter to a Russian gentleman but it is, in fact, a rather harsh text that preaches violence against those who are against the state. Maistre sees it as an essential political axiom that violence has to be answered with violence. The best means are those that succeed, independently of their severity. The reason for the establishment of the Inquisition in Spain was the formidable power of wealth of the Jews, to the point of endangering the Spanish nation. The Muslims, though weakened, represented also a threat to the survival of the Spanish nation. These groups represented superstition, barbarism and despotism, and were the negation of humanity. The heresies of Judaism and Islam were dangerous because they were both forbidden races (*races proscrites*) who had important connections with the people in power.

The Inquisition, insists Maistre, is the state, and not a religious institution, although it has the religious imprimatur. Those condemned to death were so by the state. The Inquisition judged only real crimes, that is, acts that broke the existing laws of the country. Maistre insists that any repressive measure, including torture and death, is acceptable provided that it is within the law of the land. Major crimes against the state (religion included) have to be punished severely. For him, a heretic is the worst of criminals because it undermines the basis of society.

An important point is that Maistre subordinates the individual entirely to the state, hence he can be pinpointed, as we shall see, the herald of the totalitarian state. According to the Maistre the people have no rights; they are at the total mercy of the state (the sovereign, to be more precise); as he put it, the people are always children, always lunatic and always absentee. In consequence, the people will always accept their masters and never chooses them; and power must be seized without the knowledge of the masses. It is not surprising, then, that Maistre has been presented as an extreme defender of absolutism, theocracy and monarchy. For him, society can only function under the iron dictatorship of God, king and executioner.

We are coming to the issue of the topicality of Maistre. Before presenting the detailed and fascinating picture presented by Isaiah Berlin, it is perhaps worth bringing the ideas of E. M. Cioran. For him, the irony about the 'actuality' of Maistre is that it has been the inhumanity of the twentieth century that has made him a contemporary; in other words, his monstrous and odious doctrines ensure that he is remembered today. The reason is obvious: war and cruelty are essential and inevitable parts of recent human history. As we have seen, for Maistre the French Revolution is totally bad. Cioran insists that *Les soirées de Saint-Pétersbourg* is about the role of providence in human government. Evil is everywhere as it exceeds well in 'indestructibility and plenitude' (Cioran 1991: 35), to the extent that in God co-exist good and evil.

Cioran insists that Maistre was an enraged and fanatical thinker, ready to taken us down his abyss. Maistre's main obsession was to slay the spirit of the eighteenth century. According to him, being free produces an intolerable vertigo that can only lead to tyranny. In this respect, one could say that Maistre expressed in theological terms what totalitarian thinkers of the twentieth century would express in secular terms. When Maistre said that human beings are bonded to God by a supple chain which makes them 'freely enslaved', is not that a prelude to the twentieth century Molochs's state that created such existence of incongruity as the idea of the 'freedom of necessity'?

For Cioran there are a few more crucial ideas worth mentioning. War fascinated Maistre. He had said 'war is therefore divine in itself, since it is a law of the world' (Maistre 1993: 218). In consequence, he was reconciled to the idea that wars were necessary. On the other hand, he was fascinated by the pomp of the throne, and the vindictiveness and fearsome of the God of the Old Testament. Finally, for Maistre, maintains Cioran, man is too corrupt to deserve freedom, hence the need for ruthless theocracy.

According to Berlin (1994), Maistre spoke the language of the monarchical *ancien régime*, but his importance for the twentieth century is that his writings encapsulate the essence of totalitarian thought. As we have already mentioned, he was originally a Man of the Enlightenment, but the French Revolution – and particularly the period of Terror – led him to become 'an implacable enemy of everything that is liberal, democratic, high-minded; everything connected with intellectuals, critics, scientists, everything which was to do with the kind of forces which created the French Revolution' (Berlin: 1994: xiii). Maistre ended up by abhorring one of the key assumptions of the Enlightenment: that man could be improved by force of reason and that freedom and happiness were attainable. He saw as his objective to demolish these illusions.

The idealistic conception of man as a free and perfectible being was to be substituted by an empirical approach to society and history which suggested that man was evil and needed subjection; he worshipped tradition and the past as repositories of virtue. He gave primacy to what was instinctive, even if it that meant superstition and prejudice. War and conflict were part of human society; indeed, they were a divine necessity, a punishment for the exit of man. In a word, he was the unrelenting prophet of irrationalism and his avowed aim was the destruction of the whole Enlightenment, with all its virtues and vices. Apparently, an ultramontane Catholic, his doctrines go far beyond the philosophy of the Church.

Maistre insisted in his empirical approach: he accused the eighteenth century philosophers of idealizing nature. He believed, however, as we have quoted, that nature was brutal and bloody, red in tooth and claw. Berlin interprets this line of thinking as an affinity with the paranoid mentality of the twentieth-century fascists. Of course, for Maistre the final outcome is the victory of God; in any case, the individual has to expiate his original sin through 'blood, pain and punishment' (Berlin 1991: 115). In this context, Maistre praises the role of the executioner in history as that of the person who, in the final instance, brings order in society:

> Remove this mysterious agent from the world, and in an instance order yields to chaos: thrones fall, society disappears. God, who has, created sovereignty, has also made punishment. (Maistre in Berlin 1991: 117)

It is not that Maistre was a sadist, but he believed that human beings could only be saved if they were subjected to a terrorist authority. Life has to be constantly subjected to suffering and humiliation. The debunking of reason was Maistre's main objective. For him, society is not the result of a national project, but of tradition, of the weight of the past; society is more like a spontaneous organism that has to be left alone, not interfered with. As a fervent follower of the Christian idea of original sin, Maistre states that 'man is by nature vicious, wicked, cowardly and bad' (Berlin 1994: xxi). The only way of controlling this perverse nature is by subjecting human beings to a rigid discipline. As we have seen, it is obvious, then, that the contractualist doctrines of the eighteenth century (and particularly that of Rousseau) are anathema for Maistre. In any case, for him society has been in existence for a long time and in the work of God, not of man.

Generally speaking, Maistre criticizes the idea that social institutions are a conscious outcome of rational decisions taken by human beings. Maistre is also against the idea that there is something called MAN as the subject of natural rights. In an often-cited passage he says:

> In the course of my life I have seen Frenchmen, Italians, Russians . . . I know, too, thanks to Montesquieu, that one can be a Persian. But as for a man, I have never met him in my life; if he exists, he is unknown to me. (Maistre in Berlin 1994: xxiii)

In Maistre's mind the pillars of social order are religion and subordination. In his advice to the Russian emperor he explicitly said that if the Christian Church and serfdom were undermined, monarchical authority would come to an end. In this respect it is important to underline that in Maistre's approach two principles are essential:

1 The idea that the causes of society are arcane and mysterious.
2 The idea that long lasting social institutions (language, marriage, monarchy, etc.) are irrational.

Maistre believed that there was a conspiracy against social order from the part of the intelligentsia; as a matter of fact, he blamed Protestants, Jews, and American revolutionaries, as well as, liberals, intellectuals, scientists and artists. Because knowledge is dangerous for societal order, the scientists were the main object of hatred. On the hand, he perceived that fatal revolutions, both in America and in Europe, represented a sort of satanic order, full with violence and fanaticism.

The description that we have offered of Maistre's ideas it is hopefully indicative of the rich presentation elaborated in Berlin's essays. In a final summary, the author insists in one of his basic ideas: that Maistre was a forerunner of fascism. Why?

1 Because he was a chilly, harsh and sardonic thinker, who favoured shackles and obscurity.
2 Because he had a low measure of human capability and virtuousness.
3 Because he believed that the essential part of life was discomfort, immolation and submission.
4 Because he was against people's sovereignty.
5 Because he believed that the source of power was the divinity.
6 Because he stressed tradition, the past, the unconscious and dark forces.

–5–

Racial Theories of History: The Legacy of Gobineau

Prelude

In his inaugural lecture to the College de France, Claude Lévi-Strauss intriguingly referred to Gobineau as an irremediably lost ancestor of anthropology (Lévi-Strauss 1967: 9). On the other hand, in his popular textbook *Sociology*, Anthony Giddens has called Gobineau 'the father of modern racism' and has stated that his ideas, particularly that of the superiority of the white race, became 'influential in many circles'. Furthermore, these ideas 'were propounded as supposedly scientific theories' and they influenced Hitler (Giddens 1989: 255). Is this characterization correct? We shall see. Michael Biddiss (1970b), the sole British specialist on Gobineau, wrote a book entitled *Gobineau, Father of Racist Ideology*, and has often associated Gobineau's name with the founding of Aryan racism. How can Gobineau, the recognized father of racism, be an anthropological ancestor? Are we to disbelieve historians of anthropology when they unanimously claim that their discipline was, from its very inception, in the forefront of the battle against racism? Or shall we conclude that the statement by Lévi-Strauss is a *faux pas* resulting from that common form of Gallic chauvinism, that consists in praising all things French?

In my research on the history of the idea of race in general and the work of Gobineau in particular, two things have struck me. First, that many historians of anthropology have suppressed or minimized the fact that in the eighteenth and nineteenth centuries most thinkers took the view that some races were not only different but also inferior in intelligence to others. In other words, that the racial interpretation of history was considered a perfectly acceptable scientific hypothesis. Second, that although one can hardly deny that the author of the *Essai sur l'inegalité des races humaines* (1853–5) put forward a theory of history in which the decline of civilisation as was explained in terms of racial miscegenation between a superior race (the Aryans) and the other races, an exploration of Gobineau's writings on the Orient (particularly Persia) showed him a convinced cultural relativist and and anti-colonialist, as well as a fine observer and bright analyst. Have we finally unravelled the mysterious Lévistraussian coded reference to Gobineau? Perhaps. In any case this chapter is not only a descent into the anthropological inferno to save a lost soul from eternal oblivion.

What was Gobineau's background? As a first approximation, one can say that he lived from 1816 to 1882, and in that he was a contemporary of Marx. He was a Frenchman who identified with the aristocratic values of the *ancien régime* and was extremely critical of the French Revolution. He was authoritarian, anti-liberal and anti-democratic. Although diplomat by profession, he was a self-styled man of letters by choice.

Gobineau's life from the early years to the *Essai*

Ernest Sellière, who in 1903 was the first Frenchman to dedicate a full-length book to the study of what he called the 'historical Aryanism' of Gobineau, observed how crucial the family background of Gobineau was to a full understanding of his racial philosophy of history. More recently, the work of Jean Gaulmier (1965) and Jean Boissel (1967, 1973, 1981, 1993, 1981), to name only the leading specialists on Gobineau, has not only reinforced this psychologistic point of view, but has actually replaced the tarnished image of Gobineau the scientist with that of Gobineau the poetic visionary.

It would appear as if Gobineau's multifarious intellectual endeavour, and particularly his life-long racial pessimism could be partially explained in the light of an early fixation with the infamy of his Creole mother and the weakness of his traditionalist father. There seems to be a consensus at present that the Aryan paradise that Gobineau created for himself in his fiction and in his (pseudo) scientific writings was no more than a romantic refuge for a man trying to escape from a degenerate family, a decaying country and a declining civilisation. Some people would go as far as to suggest that Gobineau's love for the Orient was a futile attempt to recover a spiritual dimension long lost in Europe. Be that as it may, the danger in assuming that Gobineau's discourse was a pure reflection of his inner fatalistic world is that we are condemned to ignore his historical and sociological insights.

In 1855, when Gobineau had published his *Essai* and left for the Orient , he was, at 37, an unsuccessful literary man and an incipient diplomat. He was born in 1816, near Paris. His father's family belonged to the Gascon bourgeoisie with mild aristocratic pretensions: Gobineau's father was a staunch Catholic, who served the cause of the Bourbon dynasty as a man of arms. His mother, a Creole of Martinique, was said to be the illegitimate granddaughter of Louis XV. The marriage of Gobineau's parents was an absolute failure.

As an adolescent, Gobineau acquired an inclination for the Orient. This was not just intellectual curiosity but an important aspect of Gobineau's personality. He developed a sort of passion for things Oriental; and it was not a passing fad, but rather a lifelong affair. When he went to Paris in 1835 he pursued his Orientalist interests in a scholarly way, but with no school certificate of any sort, he could only be an external student at the College de France. The absence of independent means meant that Gobineau had to abandon his illusions of a scientific career as an Orientalist. If Gobineau was always somewhat amateurish in scientific matters, it can no doubt be attributed to his failure to obtain proper university training.

Between 1835 and 1849 Gobineau lived in Paris. What happened in these fifteen years is crucial to understanding the development of his literary and scientific interests, his political standpoints and his attitude towards life in general. Gobineau went to Paris a romantic young man with literary ambitions and Oriental leanings, a faithful royalist (legitimist) and an ardent desire to marry his sweetheart. His dreams were soon to be shattered by the cruelty of destiny: his loved one made a marriage of convenience, literary success was constantly evading him, the internal squabbles and intrigues of the royalist circles drove him into despair, and financial stability through a remunerated position never became a permanent reality. Gobineau made a number of friends in aristocratic and literary circles, but the event that changed his existence was his encounter with Alexis de Tocqueville in 1843. Over the years a somewhat lopsided friendship developed between the two men, which lasted until Tocqueville's death in 1859. Gobineau owed him not only a certain sense of intellectual confidence but more importantly the beginnings of his diplomatic career. That Tocqueville disapproved of a number of Gobineau's stands on politics, religion, race, and so on, did not stop the friendly relationship.

In 1849 Gobineau went to Berne, and a completely new horizon opened for him. It was the beginning of his career as a diplomat – a profession that took him to Germany, Persia, Greece, Brazil and Sweden among other places. It was doubtful that he saw his occupation with a sense of calling, but as a belated Renaissance man he drew many pleasures and inspiration from living in alien lands; this is particularly true of his first sojourn in Persia from 1855 to 1858. He served Empire and Republic alike, maybe not wholeheartedly – 'I am a Barbarian at the service of the Empire', he once said – 'but in an efficient and faithful way like a modern *condottiere*'. For Gobineau, diplomacy did not, could not become an end in itself; rather it was a more or less appropriate means of earning a living. Come what may, nothing could change the sacred commitment that the young Gobineau had made to become a man of letters. His contemporaries may have failed to appreciate his literary, scientific and artistic qualities; this did not deter Gobineau from a self-appointed mission, though it no doubt contributed to his increased paranoia, as well as his pessimism about his fellow human beings, his country and the civilization to which he belonged.

It was during his stay in Switzerland that Gobineau started and completed the four volumes of the *Essai sur l'inegalité des races humaines* (Gobineau 1983). There is little factual evidence as to what prompted him to embark on the project of writing a book on the inequality of races. Boissel (1981: 126) has ventured the hypothesis that, in the final instance, the *Essai* is an attempt to explain the decadence of the French nation. But in his writings of the 1840s race was not the all-explanatory concept that Gobineau used at a later stage to account for the unfolding of history. Worth mentioning as well, is the point that Gobineau, who until then had cultivated literature (poetry, short story, novel and political journalism) started a new genre: the writing of historical and ethnological essays. We have no satisfactory answer to the question of why Gobineau decided to focus on the racial factor, but we know how he wrote the book through the correspondence of the period. It was more the result of personal intuition, combined with a powerful impulse, as Buenzod (1967: 326) has remarked, rather than the painful, dedicated achievement of an inductive process of carefully collecting data about past societies. Certainly, once the idea that race could explain the rise and fall of civilizations had seized Gobineau's imagination he then undertook frantic research to illustrate and confirm this initial, revolutionary discovery.

The actual preparation and writing of the *Essai* was done in a relatively short period of time for such a long book (about 1,000 pages). His correspondence shows him in an exhilarated state of mind. He was obviously hoping to impress the intellectual class of his time and to renew radically the historical disciplines. One of the first people to react to the publication of the first two volumes of the *Essai* in 1853 was Gobineau's friend and protector Alexis de Tocqueville, and his comments were echoed by many after him. For Tocqueville, a racial theory of history was not only wrong, but could also be positively dangerous and pernicious. He argued that perhaps Gobineau was just trying to prove the validity of some of his most instinctive and deep-seated ideas, but others would surely find applications for the *Essai* that Gobineau neither approved of nor foresaw.

Like Marx, Gobineau was accused of being a materialist and of denying human beings free will. For a man who considered himself a Catholic – no matter how *sui generis* – this accusation must have been extremely painful. In fact, the *Essai* satisfied nobody: philologists were scared of the biological overtones; naturalists were frightened by its historical sections; French readers did not like lack of patriotism; and both right and left found strong reasons for disagreeing with Gobineau. It would be fair to say that the *Essai* received very little scholarly or public attention during Gobineau's lifetime. It was only reprinted, with a new preface, in 1884, two years after Gobineau's death. Towards the end of his life Gobineau saw the *Essai*, along with the *Histoire des Perses* and *Histoire d'Ottar Jarl*, as what might be called an ethnic trilogy with personal overtones: an attempt to explore his own racial instincts. The classical know thyself became in Gobineau's version: know your own lineage and your own race. He even maintained that his ethnic quest had been the prime motivation of his life.

Gobineau's *Essai*: Main Theoretical Points

What are the sources of Gobineau's *Essai*? Without wanting to enter into the details of it, we can safely suggest the following:

1   The two nation/class/race theory (Frankish versus Gallo-Romans) which developed in France between the sixteenth and eighteenth centuries (as discussed in the previous chapter). Particularly important were the discussions in eighteenth century in which Boulanvilliers, Dubos, Montesquieu and Sièyes participated.

2   A personal interest for the Orient (discovery of the 'Aryan language and of the 'Aryan' race).

3   The development of the sciences of man. Here the key texts to take into account is James Cowles Prichard's *Researches into the Physical History of Mankind* (1836–47) and Victor Courtet de l'Isle's *La science politique fondé sur la science de l'homme* (1837). According to Boissel (1972), the author of *La science politique* was the first racial theoretician who sustained the superiority of the white race in its Germanic variety. The reasons for this superiority were varied: anatomical, historical and civilizational.

4   The romantic vogue, with the association of race, language and nation.

It is fair to say that in the eighteenth and nineteenth centuries many social scientists took the view that some races were not only different but also inferior in intelligence to others. In other words, the racial interpretation of history was considered by many as a perfectly acceptable scientific hypothesis.

In his *Essai sur l'inégalité des races humaines* (1853–5), Gobineau put forward a theory of history in which the decline of civilizations was explained in terms of racial miscegenation between a superior race (the Aryans) and the other races; surprisingly, such conception went along, in Gobineau's mind, with a cultural relativistic and an anti-colonialist stand. Gobineau wrote about race. There is no doubt that he was convinced that in the principle of racial hierarchy he had discovered the key to the rise and fall of civilizations. But his discourse about races referred to a long gone past. As to the future, he was very pessimistic and saw no chance of stopping the decline of human civilizations.

In his *Essai* Gobineau applied the scientific method as it was known to him at the time. The hypotheses he used, although extremist, were not eccentric or outlandish, but perfectly in tune with the anthropological and historical developments of the period. It is a futile, and facile exercise – if undertaken from the vantage point of view of today's biology – to dismiss his work as pseudo-science or, even worse, as mythology or superstition. He might have been wrong, but then the history of the sciences is full of theories that have been refuted. In the second half of the nineteenth century the concept of race seized the imagination of the scientific community. The working hypothesis was that with race scientists had discovered a solid principle of human classification. The fact that one could group human beings according to the size of their skull, the colour of their skin, the shape of their nose, the texture of their hair, had in itself a limited interest, particularly for social scientists. However, if a correlation could be established between race, on the one hand, and intelligence and character on the other, an extremely important principle would have been discovered, which would undoubtedly throw light on problems that had puzzled historians for generations:

1 Why are some peoples civilized and others not?
2 Are some races unable to attain civilization?
3 How can the emergence and collapse of civilizations be explained?

It can be said that the main objective of the *Essai* is to explain the rise and fall of civilizations. Gobineau's starting point was to criticize and reject the following traditional explanations of social decay:

1   Fanaticism. Some societies, like the Aztecs, were extremely ferocious against their own people, and yet they did not collapse for that reason.

2   Luxury. It certainly occurred in many societies long before they started to decay; this is the case of Greece, Persia, Rome and many modern societies.

3   Corruption. It is not a sufficient cause. It was very common in ancient times (for example, in Sparta, Phoenicia and Rome). Furthermore, morality changes all the time.

4   Irreligion. There are plenty of societies with strong religious beliefs that none the less collapsed: this was the case with Persia, Judea, and Central and South American civilizations.

5   Government. It is precisely at the beginning of the development of a nation (organism) when the administration, the legal framework, and so forth, are at their weakest, and none the less they survive.

6   Institutions. Who creates institutions, asks Gobineau, but peoples (races)? Hence they should be envisaged as effects rather than causes; furthermore, they preserve the genius of the nation. Here Gobineau insists that the idea of national character is incompatible with racial equality.

7   Environment. Neither climate nor soil nor geography are determining factors. The world has seen plenty of barbarism and civilization everywhere. It is the people who give to the land its moral, economic and political value.

8   Christianity. The explanation why Christianity is not a civilizing power lies in the fact that non-European peoples who have embraced this religion have not become civilised even after many centuries.

Gobineau' s conclusion is that none of the previous factors can be considered a general cause for the decline of civilizations; his argument is to provide historical examples of civilizations that have survived or even prospered under these conditions. He agrees that the cause of the destruction of a nation has to be found in the social organism itself, and this cause can be none other than degeneration. Nations die when they are composed of elements that have degenerated, not in the sense that they have lost the virtues of their ancestors (such as morality and government), but because they have lost their vigour.

Degeneration is a key concept in Gobineau's vocabulary. It is conceived as a condition that affects a people that no longer has the same intrinsic value that it had in the past. How has that occurred? Simply, as a result of continual adulterations in the quality of the blood by miscegenation with inferior peoples. Here is where the concept of race becomes crucial. Now, Gobineau is under no illusion that races have been kept pure since time immemorial. The history of mankind shows a great variety of racial formations, from the Adamite man through to secondary, tertiary and quaternary formations. In modern times the three great races are the black, yellow and white ones. Gobineau conceives of race as blood and as biology, but also as national character and national culture.

As I have said above, Gobineau's main concern is to account for the rise and collapse of civilizations. By civilization he meant a state of relative stability in which individuals try to satisfy their wants in a peaceful and refined way. Two points are worth making in this context. First, history shows that left to their own means most societies do no raise themselves above a rudimentary type of organization. According to Gobineau, this includes the majority of pure yellow and black races. Second, only a small, gifted number of societies have managed to attain civilizational status – and they are mostly white.

It is now perhaps the time to see how Gobineau characterizes each of the three races. Starting at the lowest end of the hierarchy, the black race is described as showing an animal character, both anatomically (shape of the pelvis) and intellectually (limited mental capacity). It is, however, a race endowed with a powerful energetic drive; it exhibits also a strong intensity of desire and of will. On the whole, it is more sensual than the other races, but it is also unstable, capricious and violent (killer instinct). The yellow race is the opposite type of the black one. It has little physical energy and it is inclined towards apathy. It is not a race of excesses or of constant desires, though they can be obstinate. It is inclined towards utility, comfort and order, but cannot understand the sublime or deep thoughts. They are clearly superior to blacks and constitute what Gobineau calls a good middle-class civilization, though by themselves they could not generate it. Finally, the white race comes at the top of the hierarchy. Gobineau believes that it is endowed with a reflective energy. Although it can be utilitarian, the white race is more idealistic than the yellow one. One important feature is the love of liberty, although it also values order. Unknown to other races, the idea of honour figures prominently among whites. Cruelty, a conscious kind of cruelty, is also a feature of this race, which in the area of the senses is vastly inferior to the others.

It should be by now clear that for Gobineau a society is an assemblage of individuals who basically share the same instincts and ideas. They should exhibit a high degree of social unity, though Gobineau did not require that their political unity was that perfect. It is important to keep in mind that the political is hence more transitory than the social, unless there is racial mixture. In other words, a stronger state might defeat a weak one, but a civilization (that is, a social organism) will never die if it remains eternally composed of the same national elements (for example, blood).

Gobineau listed ten world civilizations: Indian, Egyptian, Assyrian, Greek, Chinese, Roman, Germanic (Western), Alleghanian, Mexican and Peruvian. He had little to say about the American civilizations. As to the others he insisted that they all had some more or less important white influence. In particular he emphasized the presence of Aryan blood in India, Egypt, China; it was Aryan blood that created these civilizations, though in Egyptian case it was mixed with black blood and in China with yellow. Assyrian civilization originated with white invasions, and it included a variety of Middle Eastern peoples: Jews, Phoenicians, Iranians, and so forth. The Aryan presence was also important in Greece, although mixed with Semitic elements; as to Rome, it was produced by an amalgam of Aryans, Celts, Iberians and Semites. Finally, Germanic civilization was made with a solid Aryan stock, though mixed with other western European peoples. There is nothing terribly novel in such a list of civilizations. What is important are the conclusions that Gobineau extracted from the comparison. Three major points are worth highlighting; they encapsulate the essence of Gobineau's theory about the rise and fall of human civilizations:

1 No spontaneous civilization is found among the yellow and black races; only when their blood is mixed with white blood does a civilisation arise.
2 Among the white-based civilizations the Aryan branch is predominant.
3 When the Aryan blood is exhausted a civilization stagnates.

Gobineau's *Essai*: Main Methodological Points

In this section it is my purpose to provide a summary and a running commentary of the introductory section to the *Essai*. It appears at the offset of Book I under the misleading title of 'Dedication'. The immediate concern of Gobineau, after insisting that his book is the result of 'long meditations', is how to account for the revolutionary changes that have taken place in Europe between 1789 and 1848 (the age of revolutions). Two approaches are possible: the first (the commonsensical or vulgar) focuses on the short term and on extraordinary but surface events; it is basically subjective and propelled by narrow personal interests. The second approach, which is the scientific one, tries to uncover the 'hidden causes' of these events. To explain these phenomena one must be familiar with human nature and with the annals of the past. What Gobineau proposes is essentially a science of history.

Gobineau was well aware that his self-imposed task was a common endeavour among thinkers of the eighteenth and nineteenth centuries. However, his concern took him not only to study the immediate but also the distant past and in the end the whole past. Trying to make sense of the fragmented past in a huge fresco was no easy undertaking, but once the pieces of the puzzle fell on their place, Gobineau felt compelled to project his conclusions unto the future. The key methodological tool that he used to achieve such an objective was the analogy – a well-known procedure employed both by natural historians and philosophers alike.

As we have seen, the idea that a society can be equated to an organism was central to Gobineau. The social body has an organic cycle: birth, growth and death. Disease is a key feature of the social organism past and present, and presumably future. Social disease is, then, a worthwhile objective to unravel.

Gobineau believed that his own time was privileged in that it made easier the task of explaining the origins of the social malaise of nations. While revolutionary change seems to force upon us a sort of historical chemistry, scientific developments in the historical disciplines uncovered the origins of other than our own Western civilizations. The metaphor he used is the atmospheric one: what was clouded, foggy and dark, becomes clear and shiny; science dissolves the obscurities of the past and makes reality transparent to the enlightenment man.

Greece and Rome, but also the Germanic peoples, appear in a new light; the latter, we know it from Gobineau's early writings, are at the origin of the political institutions of Western civilization and, with Christianity, they constitute the two angular stones of this civilization. Also important are Egypt, Assyria, Iran and India, that is, the ensemble of Oriental civilizations. For Gobineau, these discoveries allow us to see in a new light, that is, to better understand the classical texts of Homer and Herodotus; even Genesis – and here it is important to emphasize Gobineau's formal respect for the Bible – if approached with an enlightened mind will continue to be a source of wisdom, richness and rectitude.

What kind of data are the best suited to Gobineau's hypotheses? Not chrono-logical tables, lists of dynasties, or a sequence of events. What mattered for Gobineau was the information concerning the manners and customs, usages and arts of the foregone nations. By knowing the physical and moral life of a nation, as well as its private and public life, it is possible to reconstruct what Gobineau called the personality of a race and what determines its value. The idea of a racial personality refers basically to cultural features, like those mentioned above.

The existence of 'positive facts' makes obsolete certain type of discourse that Gobineau calls abstract and hypothetical, typical of a sceptical philosophy. Social relations are extremely complex and the causes of the rise and fall of civilizations too intricate for these past discourses. Facts are there to be interrogated; they are everywhere and must be respected. It is no longer acceptable, insisted Gobineau, to create, like the revolutionaries do, imaginary beings that are easy to manipulate in the political arena. We have finally come across the real human beings in the flesh and all fantasies must be discarded. Our problems are too pressing to allow any more games, which are often impious and always nefarious. It is only the severe court of history that can properly judge the character of humanity.

For Gobineau the heroic ages of the past hardly compare with the situation of the present. Not that the former is without stain. But where can one find religious faith, political honour and moral duty? Modern man is only capable of developing the knowledge established in the past, laughs at the virtue of our ancestors, has transferred energy from human beings to steam, no longer creates poetry and does not believe in prophets. We have reached a stage in which the only things that matter are material interests.

The key question for Gobineau was: can the races of modern times regain their lost youthfulness? History taught him that renewal occurred quite regularly in the past. But his reading of the present and of the future was rather gloomy. However, he tried to explore the past more thoroughly in search of proofs that could offset such negative predictions. The method used for that purpose was historical induc-tion. As he puts it: 'Passing from one induction to another, I came to the conclusion that the ethnic question overshadows all other problems of history, and the in-equality of races from whose fusion a nation is formed, is sufficient to explain the whole course of the destiny of peoples' (Gobineau 1983: 138).

This obvious truth had been perceived before by many people in one form or another. How could one ignore that the irruption of certain human groupings in a country suddenly transformed the pre-existing way of life? It follows that there are strong and weak races, and Gobineau's book analyses their qualities and their historical meandering. What Gobineau thought to have discovered by using the method of tracing back the genealogy of the strong races was that 'all that there is of great, noble, and fruitful on earth, that is, human creations such as science, art, and civilisation derives from one single race' (Gobineau 1963: 139).

Finally, Gobineau insists that his book is not intended as a form of contemporary polemics, but that he places it in the realm of scientific discussion. The book deals with long historical periods and in this sense it can be catalogued as a sort of moral geology. The books is neither about man in general (or even less about the citizen) nor about fortuitous nationalities or states. In fact, it deals with the different ethnic groupings, races, societies and civilizations, and in that sense is an historical book.

Gobineau and his Contemporaries

In his *Principles of Political Economy*, published in 1848, John Stuart Mill said, referring to the supposed differences of race, that 'of all vulgar modes of escaping from the consideration of the effect of social and moral influences on the human mind, the most vulgar is that of attributing the diversities of conduct and character to inherent natural differences' (Mill 1987: 253). Now this is a rather unusual, though not totally unique kind of statement for the nineteenth century; the historian Henry Thomas Buckle, in his *History of Civilization in England*, warmly subscribed to these remarks. However, racial explanations of history were the official currency of the second half of the nineteenth century and Gobineau was the father of such an ideology.

In this section I intend to compare Gobineau's ideas to those of some of his contemporaries. I have chosen rather well-known figures and I have tried to indicate convergences, as well as divergences. I think it is perhaps appropriate to start this exercise by looking at Tocqueville and Gobineau.

Alexis de Tocqueville (1805–59) is considered by R. Aron (1989, II: 237) as one of the founders of sociology; he was essentially a political sociologist who wrote two major books: *De la démocracie en Amérique* (1835–40) and *L'ancient régime et la Revolution Française* (1856). In his works he compared systematically and fairly two distinct types of societies (aristocratic and democratic), emphasizing the advantages and disadvantages of each type. An aristocrat, he accepted the coming of democracy but he hoped that it would be balanced by religion, law and custom. Although an aristocrat like Gobineau, his attitude towards the French Revolution was very different. He shared its liberal aspirations, while rejecting the excesses of the period of Terror (including the extreme egalitarianism). He emphasized the fact that continued revolutionary violence endangered freedom.

Tocqueville's trip to the United States in 1831 brought him into close contact with the racial realities of that society. He was shocked by the treatment endured both by American Indians and black people. Tocqueville strongly believed that in the eyes of God all human beings were created equal, and that it was society that forced them into inequalities. Particularly striking for him was the fact that even where black people were free, racialism was still rampant. Tocqueville emphasized that the memories of slavery dishonoured the black race and perpetuated among whites the bad habits of the past. As to differences in intelligence between blacks and whites, Tocqueville denied its existence. The only solution to racial problems were mixed marriages; in the long run, this would create a new civilisation free from the prejudices of the past. Biological determinism was then to be excluded. Blood does not make some people free and others subjected. A lot of things affect the temperament of a nation, including climate, religion and race. To give primacy to racial explanations is a sign of intellectual poverty.

Tocqueville and Gobineau were friends of sorts; Gobineau became Tocqueville's political secretary and his protégé. The Tocqueville-Gobineau correspondence of the 1850s suggests that Tocqueville found Gobineau's racial theory both unscientific and immoral. For him Gobineau's book was poorly researched; furthermore, his theories were scientifically false and socially dangerous. The letters exchanged *à propos* of the *Essay* show that Tocqueville grew impatient with Gobineau. He insisted that the differences between nations are not eternal and unchangeable, and that they do not depend on race – which is a theory that cannot be proven. Gobineau's fatalism disturbed Tocqueville, who doubted the good sense of telling people that their society is inexorably decadent. For Tocqueville, man's destiny, both at the individual and at the national level, is not the result of fate but of will.

Although a comparison between Gobineau and Marx may appear at first sight as outrageous, in fact there a number of parallels worth mentioning. Barzun (1941) and Biddiss (1970) had coincided in stressing the 'materialism' of both Gobineau and Marx. In any case, let us look at what can be fathomed from a comparison between these two nineteenth century prophets:

1   They were virtual contemporaries: Gobineau lived from 1816 to 1882 and Marx from 1818 to 1883.

2   Both use racial, ethnic and national stereotypes, although Marx read and annotated the *Essay* with mostly hostile comments.

3   Gobineau is essentially a social pessimist: the decline of civilization is unstoppable. Marx is essentially a social optimist: future communism will mean the end of exploitation and a period of human progress.

4   Both put forward comprehensive interpretations of history that have been identified as giving primacy to economic (Marx) or racial (Gobineau) factors. In fact, they both explain historical development as a result of class struggle, except that Marx understands class in socio-economic terms, while Gobineau in racial ones.

5   They both use the same type of 'evidence': a) universal histories and b) national and racial characterization.

6   Both Marx and Gobineau have been used and abused by twentieth-century totalitarian regimes (Marx by communism, Gobineau by Nazism).

Perhaps more interesting and relevant is an attempt to place Gobineau's ideas on race in the wider intellectual tapestry of the second half of the nineteenth century. In this period race appeared as a more-or-less important explanatory factor in the philosophies of history of the major French intellectuals (who happened to be positivists of sorts). I will consider the contributions of Comte, Littré, Renan and Taine.

The author to start with is Auguste Comte, the founder of positivism. His ideas on race are expressed in his *Course* (1830–42), but more especially in his *Système de politique positive* (1854–6). In Comte the concept of race is closely related to that of milieu. He distinguished between social and biological milieux; the biological milieu counts race among its factors. However, between race and milieu there is interplay, though in the short run races exhibit a constant character. In any case, Comte asserted that human beings were dominated by their ancestors (*'les vivants sont sans cesse dirigés par les morts'*). Although Comte does not emphasize racial hierarchy and insists in the complementarity of races, he still suggests that blacks are more emotional, yellows more active and whites more speculative.

According to him three factors determine social facts: climate, race and political/social action. However, neither race nor climate can be classified as being always dominant; that is, they do not have always a true positive character. Civilization often annuls the influence of climate and race, but the latter is more important than the former. It is also the case that race was more important in the past (in primitive societies) than in the present day.

Another important positivist was the famous author of the *Dictionnaire de la langue française*, Emile Littré; he was more interested than Comte in the issue of race, though fought energetically against Gobineau. He saw history as partly determined by race, though the rise and decline of civilizations had to be accounted in terms of a variety of factors. In his *Études sur les barbares et le Moyen Age* (1869) he maintained that the barbarians, that is, the people of Germanic stock were inferior, civilizationally speaking, to the peoples of Latin stock. For Littré the Romans were the true creators of Western civilization.

Ernest Renan was perhaps, along with Hypolitte Taine, the most influential cultural philosopher of the second half of the nineteenth century – and not only in France. Gobineau accused both Renan and Taine of having plagiarized his ideas on race. In a positivist mode, Renan held that race and climate were the mainsprings of history, although ideas (Comte) also played an important role. While not as extreme as Gobineau, Renan is another founder of the racial philosophy of history. He actually stated that the idea of race remained the major explanatory factor of history (*'l'ideé de race reste la grande explication du passé'*). It is in this sense, that an early twentieth-century commentator, Ernest Sellière, could talk about strong parallels between Gobineau and Renan.

He is not altogether clear about the relations between race and language. Although, on the one hand, he stated that there is on single criterion to recognise Semites, and that is language, he insisted, on the other hand, that languages tell us nothing about the blood of those who speak them. Renan emphasized the existence of linguistic and racial differences between Semites and Aryans, suggesting that the latter had contributed to civilization much more than the former. The main contributions of the former are in the religious sphere, whereas the latter have made important philosophical and political contributions (like the idea of freedom). In the long run, Semites cannot adapt to Western civilization and become the enemies of Aryans; the result of this clash will be the elimination of the Semites.

At a more general level, Renan distinguished three types of races: inferior (non perfectible), civilized (China, east Asia, and so forth) and noble (Semites and especially Aryans). In the encounter between superior and inferior races only two outcomes are possible: the annihilation or the subordination of the latter. The primordial influence of race is balanced by the effects of the milieu. As to racial mixtures and the decline of peoples, Renan did not accept Gobineau's correlation, because when a race was atrophied nature has others on reserve.

We come finally to Taine. He was the mentor of the turn-of-the-century generation. Race, along with the milieu (environment) and the moment (epoch), are for him the key factors of history. He identified race with 'innate and hereditary dispositions', and for him there was such a strong connection between race and nation that it is not always possible to separate one from the other. Milieu and moment, however, modify the influence of race. Taine used, then, the concept of race to encompass the consistent characteristics and mental habits that a people exhibit across their history. As a Lamarckian, he believed that heredity transmitted national traits and modes of historical behaviour. He also used the word race to refer to nation and national character. He believed that literary works reveal more about the national character than historical or political documents.

Some Provisional Conclusions

What do we know about Joseph Arthur de Gobineau beyond the bare fact that between 1853 and 1856 he published the infamous *Essai*? That he was the father of racist ideology (Biddiss 1970b; Castradori 1991)? That he was the forebear of Hitler? There are some people whom we love to hate; they are the scapegoats for the stalags and gulags that have marked the lowest ebb of human existence in our most civilized twentieth century. Psychologically it is always reassuring to know that blame can be apportioned to a few select evil doers. But the twentieth century should not be allowed to escape with an individualized collective responsibility. It is appropriate that we should feel guilty; after all our hands are dirty: we have all contributed to the struggle of race against race, of state against state, or man against woman, of human being against human being. Our spirit is polluted by the constant, unceasing degradation of the human species. What is man, if not another expandable animal? And what is civilization, if not a superficial layer of hypocrisy painted on our primeval passions and feelings? Self-deception is the everyday religion of man. We hope to exorcise the crime of our times – genocide – by invoking the spirit of a nineteenth century prophet of race to whom we can easily transfer our feelings of guilt.

Gobineau wrote about race. There is no doubt that he was convinced that he had discovered, in the principle of racial hierarchy, the key to rise and fall of civilizations. But his discourse about races referred to a long gone past. As to the future, he was pessimistic and saw no chance of stopping the decline of human civilizations. The work of Gobineau is little known, although his name is notorious enough and is often conjured up to signify the quintessence of white racism and aristocratic elitism.

The classical discourse of Gobineau was distorted, in the first instance for ideological and political purposes, and later on, in the Nazi period, to justify the discrimination against and the extermination of certain racial groups (Jews, Gypsies) (Lemonov 1972). Although I abhor the a-historical procedure of attributing present events to past ideas, this is an all too common way of writing history, particularly by those who are intellectually lazy, sociologically naive or profoundly dogmatic. Plato, Jesus, Luther, Marx, Nietzsche and many others have often been blamed for what others have done in their names. Unfortunately, this extremely idealistic vision of history is shared by conservative and radicals alike. It ignores the fact that historical events are the result of a variety factors that operate at different levels (economic, political, military).

Let there be, however, no misunderstandings. My point is not to whitewash classical racial theory but rather to place it historically. It is important to disentangle the doctrines of Gobineau from the tissue of misrepresentations in which they have been mixed up from the late nineteenth century to the present. What surprises me most is not that the ideologists of National Socialism manipulated and twisted Gobineau's ideas to fit their specific ideological and political demands, but that historians of the social sciences, by propagating such inanities, have also contributed to the creation of Gobineau's myth.

We have come full circle. By distorting the past, by locating the evil spirits of racialism in one figure of the nineteenth century, we hope to appease our bad conscience for what the twentieth century has allowed to happen to certain racial and ethnic groups. All in vain. What makes genocide possible is the cowardly nature of our everyday existence, our submission to the powers that be and our boundless egotism. Let it be known that when you hear the bells of despair they do not toll for Hitler but for thee.

–6–

Darwinism and Social Darwinism: The Legacy of Galton

Background on Darwin

Charles Darwin is today a fashionable author. Many scholarly and popular books and articles have been published on his work (Desmond and Moore 1991). The impact of Darwin is well established in a variety of disciplines – modern genetics and palaeontology among others (Futuyama 1995; Richards 2000). It can now be maintained what a portentous revolutionary event was the publication of *The Origin of Species* in 1859. At the dawn of a new century many intellectual idols of the twentieth century have shown they have feet of clay (and I am thinking particularly of Marx and Freud). But this is certainly not the case with Darwin who emerges as a towering figure, comparable only to Copernicus, Galileo and Newton. What is the interest of Darwin for this book? It is not because he was an exemplary scientist, but because the supposed application of his theories to human affairs gave rise to pernicious social doctrines referred to under the general rubric of Social Darwinism.

One of the purposes of this chapter is to praise Darwin, not to bury him. That indeed he was a child of his time nobody can deny. Shakespeare warned us that 'the evil that men do lives after them; the good is often interred with their bones'. Interspersed in Darwin's writings one may find statements that reflect the prejudices of his class, race, gender and nationality. But is there anything more inane and futile that to project our morality, which is the product of our own era and hence transitory, to the Victorian past? To do what may give us a sense of moral superiority, but is unavoidably anachronistic, out of place. What is important to emphasize in the case of Darwin is that, beyond the vagaries of his own environment, his theory of evolution has not only withstood the test of time, but it has come out reinforced.

As Gould (1980) has remarked, Darwin was not the first thinker to be an evolutionist, but his forerunners had presented rather speculative theories that could not be tested and which were not based on empirical evidence. He not only provided ample evidence for his theory, but also suggestions for further research. What made for evolution were the small changes that occurred in nature. By insisting on what can be observed and measured, Darwin was able to examine the process of evolution. He made evolution a workable science.

It would be fair to say that his concern was not 'progress'; in fact, he was against the idea of inherent progress. Natural selection is just a theory of local adaptation to changing local environments. Furthermore, for Darwin variations occur by chance, randomly. Again, Darwin's theory did not suggest that evolution was working for a purpose, say the good of the species. The only thing that exists is the struggle for individuals to succeed; in modern terminology, to pass their genes into other individuals.

Finally, it is essential to say that in Darwin's theory there is no room, or rather role, for a god, or a spirit, or a vital force. This has nothing to do with whether Darwin was an atheist or not. It is just that his theory did not require a god watching over nature.

At this stage it might be of some relevance to offer what I believe are Darwin's assumptions about human nature:

1 Human nature is an extension of animal nature.
2 Humans and animals share a number of features.
3 Different features between humans and animals are explained away by continuity. On the other hand, no qualitative difference between man and beast can be predicated.
4 Against anthropocentric assumptions, one must say that humans are not the centre of nature.
5 Human characteristics are selected for specific environments: the intellect is appropriate for certain conditions, the physical strength for others.
6 The standard idea is to assume the intellectual superiority of the white race.

Generally speaking one can say that the impact of *The Origins of Species* on Western civilization was tremendous. Perhaps the single most important effect was to destroy the quasi-theological frame of mind in the sciences, so those biologists no longer concerned themselves with the Biblical story of the creation of the species or geologists with the story of the Flood. Darwin's proof that species change in a gradual orderly way under the influence of natural causes, used the same uniformitarian principle (that is, ancient changes in earth's surface are caused by the same physical principles acting today) made Lyell the founder of scientific geology. The adaptations of plants and animals to their environment, were accounted by Darwin without any reference to divine purposes. In other words, Darwin explained the living world in naturalistic terms.

The importance of Darwinism on the conception of man was central; many of the social and human disciplines were radically affected by Darwin's revolution. From his early work on *The Origin of Species* (1859), it was clear that human beings were not descendants of an historical Adam created by God in 4004 BC, but from remote pre-human ancestors. Thomas H. Huxley presented some of the implications of Darwin's work in the area of bodily traits in his *Man's Place in Nature* (1863).

The Darwinian theory found stiff opposition among theologians, but also there was a popular reaction against it. On the other hand, the upper class felt that it threatened their privileges. They associated the doctrine of evolution with the atheistic material that had been part of the French Revolution. Those who believed that human beings could improve their lot overthrew the ancient regime by their own efforts; Darwinism was believed by many to belong to this family of radical ideas. Many Victorian conservatives felt that the doctrine of evolution by natural selection was a threat to Church and State, though Darwin had declined that Marx's offer to dedicate his *Capital I* to him. The success of the Darwinian scheme of explanation was felt in a number of methodological points influenced subsequent science:

1 Darwin showed that explanation could be historical without losing its scientific character. In biology one is often to explain phenomena by showing how they originated and developed. To understand the tree of life one has to understand how it grew.
2 By getting rid of idealist elements in his treatment of natural selection. Darwin established evolutionary science on a scientific basis. He then introduced 'statistical' or population conceptions to permit generalizations to be made about the changes that selection produces in individuals.
3 *The Origin of Species* explained what happened in evolution as an outcome of both orderly and accidental events. Natural selection is an order generating process. The occurrence of variations, the survival and reproductive success of organisms, and so forth are matters of accident or chance. It thus became clear that a discipline does not need to establish what must necessarily happen according to universal laws in order to be a science.
4 The Darwinian explanation showed that, although adaptations are not the result of design, they are nevertheless purposive. They serve certain ends and must be so studied. Thus a scientific concept of teleology can be admitted, but at the same time theological and metaphysical teleology are rejected.

Social Darwinism

Social Darwinism is the theory that individuals, societies and races are subject to the same laws that Darwin had perceived in plants and animals in nature. To the question, was Darwin a social Darwinist? The answer is in the negative, but it is always possible to find some passages in the *The Origin of Species* and especially in *The Descent of Man* that are ambiguous enough to justify such a reading.

Some authors, like J. C. Greene (1981), tend to see Darwin as a social Darwinist, that is, somebody who believes that competitive struggle between individuals, tribes, nations and races has been the chief engine in social evolution. Greene maintained that, in his early writings, Darwin suggested that he was concerned with how population pressures shaped the early development of mankind, struggle for existence, migrations, encroachment and extinction of races and tribes, suscept- ibility to disease, and so forth. In other words, these are the same mechanisms that affect the general theory of evolution. Darwin was also concerned with the issue of race formation, both in terms of body form and intelligence. Central to his conception of human evolution is the idea of the struggle of races, believing that those races with the highest intellect would gain the day. Another point emphasized by Greene is that Darwin considered the idea that natural selection acts on man's 'moral faculties', as well as on his physical and intellectual capacities. The progress of intellectual and moral faculties is the result of natural selection on individuals, tribes, nations and races. Natural selection means that the better and higher specimens of the human race will increase and spread, the lower and more brutal will die out. However, Darwin accepted the idea that the mental level of the lower races can be improved.

As I have said, looking at Darwin's texts, some passages seem to suggest that progress is the outcome of the struggle for existence of individuals, tribes and nations. However, other references to the role of education, of religion, of human- itarianism suggest the opposite. Michael Ruse (1980), for example, sees Spencer, and not Darwin, as the main culprit in the spread of social Darwinism. In any case, as we shall see later in detail, Ruse maintained that Darwin was, in a certain way, a social Darwinist. At this stage it is perhaps relevant to mention the importance of Darwin's nephew, Francis Galton, who, as we shall see, contributed to the issue of heritability of the mental and moral capacities.

Why did the expression social Darwinism came into existence? It appeared only after Darwin's death and it banked on the fame of Darwin to prop up a theory that was otherwise weak. If the rider 'Darwinism' was tagged along a given social theory, it was rightly believed that it would make it more appealing, giving it a scientific authority which would otherwise not have. One can say that the basic assumptions of social Darwinism are the following:

1 There are weak individuals (and societies, and races) and there are strong individuals (and societies and races).
2 The life of individuals (and societies, and races) is characterized by the 'struggle for existence' and it is ruled by the principle of the 'survival of the fittest'.
3 The state should not intervene in society to protect the weak, otherwise the process of natural selection would not operate and hence society would cease improving.

4 Social stratification should not be tampered with because it was the natural outcome of some people being industrious and frugal and others being lazy and spendthrift.
5 At the international level, social Darwinism was in favour of imperialism and racism.

According to Michael Ruse (1980), social Darwinism is a many-sided expression. It means different things to different people. Generally speaking, it refers to the 'theories of human social development and maintenance which are in some way inspired by biological evolutionary theory' (Ruse 1980: 23). He sustains that the two main sources of inspiration can be found in relation to Social Darwinism: Charles Darwin and Herbert Spencer. Both owe their original ideas to Robert Malthus.

The last edition of Malthus's *An Essay on the Principle of Population* (1826) was the one actually read by Darwin and Spencer. Against the optimism of the eighteenth-century progressivists (particularly Condorcet and Godwin), Malthus put forward a pessimistic theory about the potential of human society for real material progress. He maintained that the human populations of the world would increase in a geometrical progression, were it not that a large fraction of the progeny in each generation failed to survive and to reproduce.

Malthus's argument ran as follows: since population increases at a geometrical rate while food supplies only grow at an arithmetic rate, there will inevitably be a struggle for existence to grab the scarce goods and hence the weak will loose to the strong. There follows an infernal picture of 'struggle, want, disease, hunger, war and death' (Ruse 1980: 24). Welfare can only postpone the fate of the wretched of the earth. The only way of checking the struggle for existence is to control the population growth by means of the restraint from marriage.

In one sense, then, the *Essay* can be seen as a precursor of social Darwinism, in so far as Malthus generalizes by means of analogy from the plant an animal world to the human world; but in another sense, he is at variance with it in that he did not accept an evolutionary perspective, and hence he did not accept the possibility of change in either the plant/animal world or the human world.

It was in the 1850s, that Spencer developed certain evolutionary and social Darwinist themes. A key idea of Spencer is his Law of Progress from the simple to the complex, from the homogeneous to the heterogeneous. He applied this law to the whole cosmos: from the inorganic to the organic and to the human. For Spencer, everything social was subjected to this law, whether it was commerce or literature, government or language. Evolution or change is central for Spencer.

Spencer had a deterministic and teleological (end-directed) conception of human progress. In his *Essays* (1890) he said that progress is not an accident, not a thing within human control, but a beneficent necessity. He emphasized that the hierarchy of animals and of human societies at all levels (physiological, intellectual and so forth); not surprisingly, the English are seen as the pinnacle of this evolution.

For Spencer the evolution from simple to complex could be accounted for in terms of the Lamarckian doctrine, that is, the inheritance of acquired characteristics. In reality, certain stresses occur; these sets up needs in the organism, or family, or society. The response is the new characteristics of some kind (such as diversification, increased complexity, more heterogeneity) and these characteristics can and will be passed on to future generations. He applied the Lamarckian doctrine to all realms, especially the social (social Lamarckism).

Spencer reversed the Malthusian argument and suggested that the cause of evolutionary change is population pressure. The struggle for existence, which is the result of the increase in population and the scarcity of resources, triggers off all the tensions and needs for the working of the Lamarckian mechanism. The main difference with Malthus is that Spencer assumes a deistic beneficence that challenges the inevitability of Malthus's pessimistic conclusions. If the struggle for existence can be checked it is because the beings that are higher up in the evolutionary scale are less fertile. A peculiar assumption was that the more brain the less sperm, because they are made of the same stuff. That is why he believed that the Irish were more fertile than the English.

We can now consider Darwin's position. His main publication on the human species did not come until *The Descent of Man* (1871). By that time Spencer had already been publishing on the topic for at least twenty years (Freeman 1974). However, Darwin's idea of treating the human species on a par of other animals dates from 1836. Darwin started with the Malthusian premises and applied them back to the organic world. Ruse tells us that like Spencer, Darwin also turned Malthus on his head. Using artificial selection as an analogy he hypothesized the existence of a natural selection; after all, in the struggle for existence some organisms are more successful than others. This is due to the fact that these organisms exhibit characteristics that are better adapted to the environment and that's why they are selected. In a number of generations this leads to evolution.

There is no doubt that Darwin wanted to transfer his biological theory to the physical and psychical dimensions of human beings. The better intellectually endowed is a human being the more likely it is that his descendants will be greater in number. Man's animality requires two minor caveats. First, in reply to Wallace's spiritualism Darwin relied on the secondary evolutionary mechanism of sexual selection (males compete for females and females choose the male that they find most attractive). Second, when dealing with human moral sense Darwin was not clear as to how natural selection operated (he could not explain how an altruistic morality could help the individual; the bravest man was likely to leave no descendants).

However, Darwin offered two hints as to how morality can help the individual. These are the two mechanisms formulated by the sociobiologists today: kin selection (the altruistic death of a individual may improve the reproductive changes of close relatives: thus a capacity for morality could be passed on) and reciprocal altruism (the only way of getting help is by helping others). Darwin saw humans as a product of natural selection brought about by the struggle for existence. Ruse maintains that, in a way, Darwin agreed with the imperialist ideas of his day, even if he disagreed with the *motto* might is right. Finally, he was also worried that the progress of medicine would put an end to the beneficent effects of natural selection in suppressing the chances of the unfit people to reproduce themselves.

It is plain that for Ruse both Darwin and Spencer deserve the label social Darwinists, but for very different reasons. What brings them together is their debt to Malthus and the idea of total evolution. There were, however, important differences. Spencer was Lamarckian, progressionist and believed that the struggle for existence would come to an end because of reduced fertility. For his part, Darwin was a selectionist and saw struggle for existence as a pervasive and enduring phenomenon; he was non-progressionist in so far as he believed that the human race could degenerate (medicine).

What then is social Darwinism? Two elements emerge from the previous discussion. First, the existence of evolutionary progress as man and culture push teleologically towards some better state (Spencer). Second, the existence of a bloody struggle for existence ('nature red in tooth and claw') as the weakest individuals and societies are eliminated (Darwin). As we have seen, authors like Greene suggest that Darwin and Spencer are not that different, and in any case the 'merit' for creating social Darwinism should be bestowed upon Spencer. Ruse, however, although conceding the following three points still disagrees:

1   It is true that both Darwin and Spencer draw from Malthus, Lyell and von Baer. These three authors opposed evolution, although Von Baer (in embryology) showed the change from simple to complex and this is obvious in Spencer's law of progression from the simple to the complex and in Darwin's belief that ontogenies and philogenies go from the simple to the complex. But both Darwin and Spencer differ from Malthus and with each other (Spencer thought that Malthus'ideas would become intellectually bankrupt; Darwin believed that they would hold forever). Again, in relation to Von Baer's theory, Spencer took it to be a metaphysical absolute whereas Darwin took it as an empirical point to be tested.

2   It is suggested that both Darwin and Spencer adhered to Victorian values. This is true in so far as it affects the classification of human groups (inferiority of non-Europeans; inferiority of women, and so forth). This overlap shows that they were a product of their cultural environment.

3   Although Spencer supported progressive Lamarckism and Darwin was in favour of less progressive natural selection, both partly accepted each other's mechanism. Spencer came to accept the idea of survival of the fittest and Darwin the Lamarckian principle of inheritance of acquired characteristics.

It would possible to suggest, still following Ruse, that this overlap does not imply identity. Spencer preserved both selection and the inheritance of acquired characteristics until the end of his life. His *laissez faire* policy in no way contradicts his standpoint. He did not condone the oppression of the weakest; the struggle led people to greater effort and to Lamarckian progress upwards. The whole point for Spencer was that, working as individuals, people do more for their fellows than they would were the state in complete control. For his part, Darwin preserved natural selection and sexual selection (for humans) as the key mechanisms. Even if after 1860 Darwin paid more attention to Lamarckism (due to his difficulties with heredity), the primary cause of evolution was selection (he acknowledged the role of inherited effects in the transition from pre-hominids to hominids). As to progress, Darwin opposed the idea of its inevitability and even contemplated the possibility of involution (degeneration). Perhaps one could say that, in relation to 1970s anthropology, neo-Spencerians (Service and Sahlins) and neo-Darwinians (the sociobiologist Wilson) were poles apart. At present, although sociobiology is scientifically accepted, it is still rejected by social anthropologists.

More recently, Futuyma (1995: 209) has maintained that 'Social Darwinism, the doctrine that human progress is the outcome of competition and struggle among individuals, races, and nations, had its origins before Darwin. It chief proponent was Herbert Spencer, who attempted to synthesise all of physics, biology and human history into a grand evolutionary world view before Darwin published the *Origin of Species*'.

For an individualist like Spencer, the key to the understanding of human society was competition. The famous phrase 'the survival of the fittest' was Spencerian in origin, although Darwin used afterwards. For Spencer 'social progress could only occur if the fittest were allowed free rein' (Fukuyma 1995: 209)). State intervention in social life (in welfare, education, business and so forth) was counter-productive; it encouraged the survival of the unfittest, it broke the laws of nature at the price of creating a decaying, degenerate society. Darwin did not agree with such a reading of his theory.

It is interesting for our purposes, that Futuyma maintained that in addition to laissez-faire capitalism, eugenics was another offshoot of social Darwinism. The initial assumption of eugenics was that it was possible to improve a population, to create a 'healthier' stock (or race). Superior (that is, richer, more intelligent and healthier) people were encouraged to have more children, while inferior (that is, poorer, less intelligent and less healthy) ones were supposed to be prevented or discouraged from reproducing. When applied to races this led to imperialism abroad (Anglo-Saxon races seen as superior, hold sway over lower colonized races) and Nazism in Europe.

In conclusion, it is fair to say that people of very different political persuasions used *The Origin of Species*. While it is true that laissez-faire capitalism and fascism plundered the Darwinian reservoir in search of justifications for their political philosophies, on the left socialists like Marx and anarchists like Kropotkin also jumped into the Darwinian bandwagon. Marx stated that Darwin's book was very important and served him as a basis in natural science for the class struggle in history. Marx was willing to use natural selection as an example of class struggle, but not for individualistic, capitalist competition. For his part, Kropotkin, in his book *Mutual Aid* (1904), took a rather different standpoint. What he saw in Darwin's book was that co-operation among the members of a species could often be advantageous in their struggle for existence (Walicki 1979: 282–5). To Kropotkin, the existence of co-operative social behaviour in a number of animal species (such as wolves and monkeys) showed that nature teaches us to eliminate competition by co-operation (Futuyma 1995).

Francis Galton

It is a well-known fact that Francis Galton was Darwin's nephew and that *The Origin of Species* had an inspirational impact on him. He became an enthusiast of studying human nature – an objective that affected all his life (Fancher 1983a, 1983b; Keynes 1993; Gillham 2001). Perhaps the most obvious feature in mind is his universal scientific authority. Areas as varied as human genetics and the science of statistics were invented by Galton; more relevant to this book is the fact he was the founder of eugenics (Kevles 1985). It is, of course, arguable how committed he was to these invented disciplines. For the believers in the Nazi horrors of eugenics it is convenient to label Galton as the person that created an approach that was 'racist, sexist and class-biased' (Lewontin 1986: 317).

The term eugenics was coined by Galton in 1883 in the work *Human Faculty,* although he had already written on the topic nearly twenty years before. In fact, in 1865 he made a contribution to *Macmillan's Magazine* on the topic of race improvement that can be equated to eugenics. At the beginning of the twentieth century Galton was well aware that the ideas of hereditary talent and character were not accepted. The term eugenics, maintained Galton, is originally Greek and means 'good in stock, hereditarily endowed with noble qualities' (Galton 1904: 46). The assumption was that some people were energetic and better gifted than others. Galton had also observed that scientists were superior to others. As he put it as well, in any scheme of eugenics, energy can be easily transmitted by descent.

It was not, however, until the beginning of the twentieth century that Galton returned to the topic. In his 'Preface' to the *Essays in Eugenics* (1909) he was well aware that the topic of eugenics had to be dealt with discretion and safety, otherwise an unpleasant reaction would take place. For him eugenics is 'the science which deals with all the influences that improve the inborn qualities of a race. The improvement of the inborn qualities, or stock, of some human populations, will alone be discussed here' (Galton 1909: 35). It is obvious that his definition has to represent the best individuals of each group in term of their health, friendliness, energy and ability.

On the other hand, Galton was well aware that the qualities just mentioned could be improved or impaired depending on the social environment. The radical differentiation between a group of human beings who were intellectually able and hard working and another group who were morally and intellectually mediocre was a matter of fact. It is worth emphasizing that the latter are not very effective human beings and, on the whole, they tend to block progress. A consequence of his conception recommended that eminently advanced individuals should increase their fertility and vice-versa. Generally speaking, the author maintained that it would be appropriate to suggest that physically and mentally ill people should not be allowed to marry and reproduce; whether this referred to either specific races and classes or, in general, is not always clear.

In his *Memoirs of my Life*, published in 1908, he dedicated chapter 21 to race improvement and eugenics. The author was in favour that 'stern compulsion ought to be exerted to prevent the free propagation of the stock of those who are seriously afflicted by lunacy, feeble-mindedness, habitual criminality and pauperism' (Galton 1908: 311). He hoped that the democratic societies would, in the near future, forbid the marriage of ill-omened people, in other words, the undesirable classes should not be allowed to propagate their children. Marriages should become, as he would put it, eugenic, and they should take into account the social position, the adequate fortune and the similarity of creed of those involved.

It is clear for Galton that there are three classes of married people in terms of their offspring: 'a small class of desirables, a large class of passable and a small class of undesirables' (Galton 1908: 322). It is important that the country of reference should support the desirables socially, morally and materially, and not the undesirables. It is also important to expect that eugenics 'ought to become one of the dominant motives in a civilised nation' (Galton 1908: 322).

It is plain that for Francis Galton the aim of eugenics is twofold. On the one hand, the objective is to 'check the birth of rate of the unfits instead of allowing them to come into being, though doomed in large numbers to perish prematurely'. The second object is 'the improvement of the race by furthering the productivity of the fit by early marriages and healthful rearing of their children' (Galton 1908: 323). Finally, one can say that it is actually possible that 'natural selection rests upon excessive production and wholesale destruction; [and] eugenics on bringing no more individuals into the world than can be properly cared for, and those only of the best stock' (Galton 1908: 323).

To conclude this section on Galton, it is perhaps useful to look at his interesting list of subjects for eugenic enquiry that he published in 1905 under the title 'Studies in National Eugenics'; it is, as he insisted, a programme that he considered sketchy and that had to be consulted. He provided the following list (Galton 1909):

1   In the first issue one has to consider the context of the estimation of the average quality of the offspring of married couples from their personal and ancestral data. Talking about families one must distinguish between the gifted ones, the capable but not gifted ones and of those that are below the average in terms of health, mind and aspect. An interesting thing would be to look at how each social class is related to the type of families just mentioned.

2   An important issue is to consider the effects of actions by the state and public institutions. The first group to be examined is the habitual criminals. They should be segregated for a long time. The objective is that they are restricted in their opportunities to be violent and in the production of inferior children. The second group is formed by what Galton called the 'feeble minded'; the inquiries should be addressed against those institutions that promote their marriage and the production of offspring. A third category refers to the intellectually unable young people who are given grants for higher education. He is against this policy for two reasons: the intellectually unable will not profit from the education and not all of those who are intelligent will have access to money to study.

3   There are other influences that further or restrain particular classes of marriage. A selection should be developed on a judicious basis in which marriage should be regulated. At present, religion, law and custom have a dominant power on marriage.

4   Concerning heredity, Galton suggested that an investigation should be developed concerning the merits of the different races and the production of mixed races.

5   The final point refers to the idea that individuals should be offered eugenic certificates with reference to their physical and mental capacity.

In conclusion, one could suggest that for Galton eugenics was an important discipline (Mazumdar 1992). As such it is founded upon the idea of evolution and has as its major objective to direct the course of evolution. In that sense, Galton believed to be a faithful follower of his brilliant uncle Charles Darwin; whether his ideas were shared by Darwin is doubtful in some cases, and definitely not in others. Eugenics, as we shall see in connection with Vacher de Lapouge, was a discipline that became popular among intellectuals and scientists in Great Britain and the United States in at least the first quarter of the twentieth century (Paul 1984). When eugenics became not only a theory but also a radical and ruthless practice in Nazi Germany, it was inevitably going to the subjected to criticism and rejection for quite a long time.

Crowd Theories: The Legacy of Le Bon

Introduction

Crowd studies appeared at the turn of the twentieth century. The inspiring spirit behind all these studies was the multi-volume contribution of Hyppolite Taine, entitled *Les origines de la France contemporaine* (1875–93), in which the excesses of the mob during the French Revolution were highlighted. Taine's texts incorporate a critique of the rosy conception of human nature as presented by J. J. Rousseau and the Enlightenment thinkers in general. Furthermore, Taine emphasized the 'primitive' character of the 'people' who actively participated in the French Revolution (the third estate and the *lumpenproletariat*); they are depicted as having no education, with a poor mind, gullible, and so forth. However, as Le Bon will note, Taine may have perfectly observed the facts but failed to see the 'potential violence of human nature that leads the mass movements' (Thiec 1981: 414).

Taine's key theses on the French Revolution, according to Ginneken (1992: 39–40), are as follows:

1 The year 1789 meant essentially the collapse of law and order.
2 The defining aspect of the period was 'anarchy and mob rule'.
3 Responsible citizens were progressively excluded giving way to 'demagogues'.
4 Authoritarian rule prevailed after Jacobins seized power.
5 The new regime became more despotic than the ancient regime.

The key original contributions to the study of the crowd were published in the early 1890s, and they were all indebted to Taine. There are complex, unsolved issues concerning primacy and plagiarism. The facts are that the first publication was by the Italian Scipio Sighele's *La folla delinquente* (1891), followed by Henry Fournial's *Essai sur la psychologie des foules* (1892); Gabriel Tarde published two articles on the topic in 1893–3 (included in his book *Essais et mélanges sociologiques*, 1895), as well as two more papers in 1898-9 (incorporated in his book *L'opinion et la foule*, 1901).

However, the book that had the widest impact was Gustave Le Bon's *Psychologie des foules* (*The Crowd*) (1895). Sighele accused both Fournial and Le Bon of plagiarism. History has credited Le Bon with being the father of crowd psychology, and in some respect this is right in so far as Le Bon was the author who most influenced early twentieth-century thinkers writing on crowds and masses. Both Sigmund Freud's *Massenpsychologie und Ich-Analyse* (1921) and William McDougall's *The Group Mind* (1920) take Le Bon's *The Crowd* as the starting point of their intellectual endeavours.

According to Le Bon:

1 Crowds are typical of our liberal-democratic times.
2 In a crowd the unconscious element prevails over the conscious activities of the individual.
3 A crowd is more than the sum of the individuals that compose it.
4 Crowds tend to be destructive.
5 Leaders conduct crowds.
6 The features of a crowd are the result of two psychological mechanisms: contagion and suggestibility.

A passage from McDougall's *The Group Mind* (1920: 45) provides an excellent description of what Le Bon meant by a crowd:

> A group which is excessively emotional, impulsive, violent, fickle, inconsistent, irresolute and extreme in action, displaying only the coarser emotions and the less refined sentiments, extremely suggestible, careless in deliberation, hasty in judgement, incapable of any but the simpler and imperfect forms of reasoning; easily swayed and led, lacking in self-consciousness, devoid of self-respect and of sense of responsibility, and apt to be carried away by the consciousness of its own force, so that it tends to produce all the manifestations that we have learned to expect of any irresponsible and absolute power. Hence its behaviour is like that of an unruly child or an untutored passionate savage in a strange situation, rather than like that of its average member; and in the worst cases it is like that of a wild beast rather than like that of human beings.

Freud pointed out that Le Bon's crowd was basically a transient group, while there exist both primeval groups (determined by what Trotter called the herd instinct or the instinct of gregariousness – of which the horde is an example) and stable associations. The latter, according to McDougall, are highly structured groups with a higher collective mental life that the crowds. Their key features are:

1 They exhibit a degree of continuity.
2 Members of the group are aware of the structure and aims of the group.
3 They interact with similar groups.
4 They possess an array of traditions, ritual and rules.
5 Members of the group are allocated specific tasks and functions.

Le Bon's ideas were prescient ones and his statement that the age that was entering at the end of the nineteenth century was the 'era of crowds' was prophetic. His interest on mass society was followed by many authors: Vilfredo Pareto, Gaetano Mosca, Joseph Schumpeter, José Ortega y Gasset, Franz Neumann, Hannah Arendt, Erich Fromm and many others. Another prophecy was the growing importance of popular culture among the crowd people. The importance of mass movements, so central to the American sociologists like Robert Park and Ernest Burgess, came obviously from Le Bon.

It is widely believed that French thought was the original source of modern totalitarian thinking. If Isaiah Berlin proposed Joseph de Maistre as the key thinker of the early nineteenth century, Zeev Sternhell suggested Gustave Le Bon as the protagonist at the turn of the next century; that is to say, as a clear theoretical precursor of fascism. On the other hand, Gaap van Ginneken (1992) has insisted that is not easy to label Le Bon either ideologically or politically. What cannot certainly be said, however, is that he was a liberal-democrat. He has been labelled male chauvinist and racist, militarist and reactionary. However, his followers can be communist or fascist, but also democratic and Zionist. Lenin, as well as Hitler and Mussolini, Roosevelt, de Gaulle and Herzl admired part of Le Bon's ideas. According to Rouvrier (1986: 255), the politician who was closer to Le Bon was Charles de Gaulle – a leader who used Le Bon's ideas on the psychology of the masses 'measurably and democratically'. As we have pointed out, it is arguable how original was the *Psychologie des foules,* but Le Bon's book was a brilliant and influential synthesis of the idea of his time and it changed the political horizon of the twentieth century.

A final point worth mentioning concerns the relationship between Le Bon and Durkheim. First, there is no doubt that it was a difficult one. The reason is simply that Le Bon did not belong to the university circles; partly as a result of that he was either ignored or rejected by these circles – the Durkheimian School included. Furthermore, Le Bon represented social psychology and Durkheim sociology – two approaches highly incompatible then and even today. That is why Le Bon has always been welcome by the social psychologists (as one of the theoretical founders of the discipline) and rejected by the social scientists. However, as we shall see in the conclusion, Le Bon's impact on Durkheim is not to be discarded.

The Early Writings: An Anthropologist in the Making?

For a period of nearly fifteen years, as detailed by Marpeau (2000), Le Bon had an anthropological interest; before 1880 he was essentially a specialist and writer on medical topics, after 1894 he became a specialist in mass psychology for a number of years. Soon as well he became a critic of socialism, wrote on education and politics and was involved in discussing philosophy and physics. The writings published between 1881 and 1893 showed that Le Bon's interest was truly varied and remarkable.

The publication of *L'Homme et les Sociétés. Leur origine et leur histoire* took place in 1881. This text is presented as a scientifically oriented book in which concepts like observation and experience are considered as the alternative to dogmatism. According to Le Bon, there is a general scientific approach which is applied to physics and biology, but the main aim is to show that the origins and evolution of human beings is regulated by the same mechanisms that operate with the objects of the other disciplines. The book was no doubt an accurate picture of the anthropological discipline

There is an early and obvious concern in this period with what could be called physical anthropology. More specifically, Le Bon was concerned with establishing a relationship between the intelligence and the size of the skull. He was convinced that modern science showed that human beings exhibited important physical and intellectual differences at birth. He insisted in stating that, in any given civilization, males were distinguished from females at the intelligence level. It is obvious that, for him, the biological and the social were equated. On the other hand, the differences in civilization and class differences were also emphasized. In any social hierarchy intelligence determines the position of different groups, which are classified from large to small skulls. At the level of mankind the divisive element is the race. There are superior (large-skull) and inferior (small-skull) races; these racial differences emphasize social differences. Their position has to be justified scientifically, by reference to the skull measurement. To prove this hypothesis, Le Bon studied societies historically and comparatively. In fact, in his 1881 book he tries to show that it is essential to know the history of peoples, with the objective of finding out the reasons for their transformation.

In 1884 Le Bon published *La Civilisation des Arabes*, this was meant to be the first study of the great large civilizations, with an emphasis on his main scientific concern: 'To describe the successive forms of the physical and intellectual evolution of man' (in Marpeau 2000: 62). His next publication was *Les Civilisations de L'Inde* (1887) in which he used India as a society that exhibited different races and civilizations; in fact, India displays the whole history of mankind, from primitivism to modern civilization. However, when comparing the Indians with the Europeans it is possible to conclude, suggested Le Bon, that only a very small minority (perhaps 0.5%) of the latter is intellectually superior to the former. A few years later, in 1889, Le Bon published *Les Premières Civilisations*. In it the author highlights the importance of the progress of science, emphasizing the progress of mankind towards civilization in spite of the fights and struggles that affect nations.

Darwin is very important in Le Bon's period work, although the influence of Lamarck and Malthus is also visible, hence producing a different image of Darwin.

Le Bon would prefer to insist on the idea of a continuous progress of humanity. In this respect, Le Bon was original in the interpretation of authors like those mentioned. For Le Bon 'the evolution of the character of a race was slow, by accumulating progress transmitted through inheritance' (Marpeau 2000: 69). An author who is given a pre-eminent place in *L'Homme et les Sociétés* (1881) is Herbert Spencer. The reason is simple: he was involved in the project of 'constructing a synthetic thought which combined life sciences and human sciences' (Marpeau 2000: 70). In some respect one can say that Le Bon's project represented a shift from medicine to a historical and sociological work. In addition, his connection to Théodule Ribot, the editor of the *Revue Philosophique*, showed Le Bon's clear preference for scientific philosophy.

Between 1878 and 1882 he was involved with the *Société d'Anthropologie de Paris*, publishing number of articles in the *Bulletins et mémoires de la société d'anthropologie de Paris* and in the *Revue d'anthropologie*. His theses on racial issues were often criticized by his contemporaries. The important scientist Clement Royer, for example, rejects Le Bon's thesis on the psychological inferiority of women. A more general point, that which assumes that the larger the skull the more intelligent the brain, was rejected by Paul Broca (the founder of the *Société d'Anthropologie de Paris*), who insisted that some races, like the Mongols, were less intelligent than the Europeans, in spite of the fact the size of their brain was bigger. As for European women, if they were inferior to men, this was the result of their different education. These disagreements with him from two important members of the anthropological society may explain why Le Bon moved towards the geographical society from 1880 to 1892.

In the 1880s, perhaps the most obvious colonialist ideology of Le Bon emerged quite clearly from his various writings. He saw no possibility of a deep contact between colonizers and colonized due to the cultural distance that existed between them. For him, colonies were nothing else than arenas to be economically exploited. Many colonialists, who aimed at civilizing the colonial world, did not approve this cynicism. Writing in the *Revue Scientifique* of 24 August 1889, Le Bon asserted that education was unnecessary and dangerous for the natives. In the same year, and in a public discussion on the colonial question, Le Bon's position was widely criticized.

While Ginneken (1992) has categorized the Le Bon between 1881 and 1894 as a 'colonial anthropologist', Pierre-André Taguieff, has labelled him as perhaps the best able vulgarizer of 'evolutionary racialism'. Le Bon's main theoretical emphasis was on racial studies and physical anthropology. It would be fair to indicate that, according to Ginneken, Le Bon's theoretical position was that of an anthropologist who had a sophisticated knowledge of the period, reflecting a 'Spencerian and Darwinian (or rather Lamarckian) style' (1992: 136). It could be said, however, those in the 1880s major thinkers like Renan and Taine moved progressively from race to nation. The latter is understood as a spiritual or mental principle. On the other hand, Fouillée's position that ideas shaped social reality was also influential on Le Bon and Sorel who developed the concept of political myth.

It is important to emphasize that there were a number of political events that affected the position of Le Bon at the end of this period; the most important ones were the following:

1 The so-called Boulanger episode (1886–89). It refers to a period in which there were proto-fascist policies of mass mobilisation of both right and left.
2 An increased working-class movement (1889–95).
3 The Panama scandal (1893). It meant, among other things, a crisis on the reliance on parliamentary democracy for international businesses.
4 An anarchist campaign based on violence (1892–4).

These developments were characterized by mass movements that endangered 'elite liberalism'. Van Ginneken (1992) has insisted that the writings of Le Bon between 1894 and 1902 present a right-wing, nationalist and elitist alternative to the socialist threat. But this is another issue, not the main concern of this chapter.

'The Psychology of Peoples'

In 1894 Le Bon published *Les lois psychologiques de l'évolution des peuples* (published in English in 1898 under the title *The Psychology of Peoples*). This book is a brilliant, though somewhat unconnected, summary of the conclusions that Le Bon had reached in his previous anthropological books. It is a short and dazzling book, with the aim of being appealing and successful (20,000 copies were sold in his time). It was an attractive book that represented a major change in Le Bon's writing style: from the comprehensive and bulky text to the short, sharp and direct one. In this section it is crucial to present a summary of this unknown text (focusing on the 'Introduction' and the 'Conclusions').

Le Bon starts the book by emphasizing the key role played by a few leading ideas in the civilization of a people. From these key ideas derive the institutions, the literature, and the arts of a nation. He emphasizes that these ideas appertain to what we would call today the 'long run'. These ideas take a long time to be formed and they are very slow to disappear; in this sense one can say that ideas exhibit a slow tempo. Furthermore, Le Bon suggests that even when the intellectual elite has shown certain ideas to be erroneous, they persist in the depth of the nation. To impose new ideas is no less difficult than to discredit old ones. In a word, humanity loves to worship dead ideas and dead gods.

From the very beginning of the book Le Bon is clearly a critic of egalitarianism. The idea of the equality of the individuals and of the races is, according to him, a product of the eighteenth century; it was suggested by philosophers who had ignored three basic things:

1 The primitive history of mankind.
2 The variations of the mental constitution of human beings.
3 The law of heredity.

For Le Bon (1894: 2) it is an obvious social fact than some ideas are more appealing than others; the idea of equality was seized by the masses and 'ended up by firmly implanting itself in their mind and speedily bore fruit'. The effects of this idea were shattering: it shook up the foundations of the *ancien régime*, gave birth to the French Revolution and created a series of violent and lasting convulsions in the Western world. The fact that there were some obvious inequalities was attributed to differences in education (institutions). This was the panacea propounded by modern democracies. The principle that all human beings are born equally intelligent and good had triumphed.

Le Bon insisted that the progress of science (anthropological science presumably) had shown that 'the mental gulf created by the past between individuals and races can only be filled up by the slowly accumulating action of heredity' (Le Bon 1894: 2). According to him, modern psychology and experience showed that what, from an educational point of view, may be appropriate to a given individual or race, is harmful to others. Philosophers cannot change ideas once they are in circulation; this is what happens with the idea of equality. The author also insists in the nefarious effects of egalitarianism on society and the family. As to socialism and feminism, Le Bon depicted them in a rather critical way, insisting that mental and physical differences between races and sexes cannot be ignored.

At another, extremely relevant area, Le Bon insists that, concerning ideas, what is important is not whether they area true or false, but the social influence that they have on people's minds. It is when ideas become sentiments fixed in the masses that all their effects are felt. He stated that the objective of his work was 'to describe the psychological characteristics which constitute the soul of races, and to show how the history of a people and its civilisation are determined by these characteristics' (Le Bon 1894: 4). Le Bon's interest was not in races per se, but in the 'formation and mental constitution of the historical races, that is, of the races artificially formed in historical times by the hazard of conquest, immigration and political changes; our objective will be to demonstrate that their history is determined by their mental constitution' (Le Bon 1894: 4).

Le Bon was also interested in a number of other issues:

1 The degree of permanence or variability of the characteristics of the races.
2 Finding out whether there is a tendency towards equality or differentiation among individuals and peoples.

3 Examining whether the elements composing a civilization (arts, institutions, beliefs) are the different manifestations of the soul of the races, and hence whether they should be passed from one people to another.
4 Determining why civilizations decay and die out.

In principle, although many factors may determine the history of peoples (including accidents) there are great permanent laws that govern the general course of each civilization; of these permanent and general laws, the most primordial are those that derive from mental constitution of the races. For Le Bon (1894: 6) there was an invisible soul. On the other hand, the life of a people, with its institutions, its beliefs and its arts is all about the visible expression of this soul. An important issue to take into account is that reformers have not succeeded in changing the 'secular characters of the soul of the races'. As to the illusionary world of the socialists, this absurd dream of equality ignores the basic teachings of science: the irreducible character of the differences between human beings. For Le Bon it is plain that old age, death and inequality are unavoidable features of nature.

I would like to turn now to the general conclusions that Le Bon reaches at the end of this fascinating and extremely rich text. In my view the most important points are the following:

1 Races exhibit certain psychological features that are as permanent as physical characteristics. Changes only take place over a long period of time.

2 While the mental features of a race are in principle permanent, the environmental ones are modified constantly.

3 The ancestors of a race are the fundamental elements that constitute the mental elements of a living people; both morality and unconscious motivations depends on them.

4 What beyond the average separates races are anatomical and psychological differences. In practice there are superior and inferior races, that is, people with more developed and less developed brains.

5 While inferior races exhibit basically similar individuals, the more one enters into the superior races, that is, people who climb up in the civilizational scale, the more individually different they become. Civilization is correlated with increasing inequality, both mentally and socio-economically.

6 What determines the life of a people is its invisible type of soul or mind, while the external circumstances, particularly political institutions, do not play a key role in history.

7 The mental constitution of a people, that is, the expression of certain ways of thinking and feeling, cannot be culturally transmitted; only the external signs of a civilization can be transmitted.

8 Different peoples, with different minds, they tend to think, feel and act in different ways. Many types of war are the result of these disagreements between the different races.

9 A race is often the result of an aggregation of individuals of different origins over a long period of time. In practice, a race is a collective soul, living in a given milieu and in which the people have developed a common framework of beliefs, interests and sentiments. In the present historical conditions of civilized peoples, the only races that exist are artificial ones, created by historical conditions.

10 Mixed races are seriously affected by the changes of the milieu, whereas old ones are more resistant unless they are forced to disappear in the unstoppable decadence.

11 Societies are destined to age and to disappear. It is an historical lesson to learn that while they can take a long time to be formed, that is, to develop a mental constitution, they can disappear very quickly.

12 Finally, ideas, particularly of the religious type, are important in the development of a civilization. It is crucial to insist in the fact that ideas are only important after a long time of existence, when they have been transformed into feelings and they are part of the national character. Each civilization is based on a small number of fundamental ideas that are accepted universally. As to religious ideas, they are most important in all civilizations. Historical changes tend to be the result of religious changes; historical gods are more important than historical monarchs. Gods are the children of our dreams and, consequently, they are extremely powerful.

I have tried to present Le Bon's ideas without entering into criticism or defence. His concept of race will be seen as extremely revolting. For Taguieff (1998) it is important to note that Le Bon's book expresses the standards of the contemporary racialism. The most important elements are: primacy of suggestionism, racial determinism, cultural relativism, biological-and-racial pluralism, anti-universalism, polygenism and social life affected by unconscious factors ('soul of the race' and 'soul of the people'). However, I would like to close this section by presenting a long passage on Le Bon's idea of race from one of the leading twentieth-century American sociologists, that is, Robert K. Merton:

Le Bon shared with many others of his time what he called the fundamental notion of race as one of the mysterious master-causes that rule our destiny. Yet, as it turns out, this is anything but the kind of racism that a mid-century Gobineau made basic to the permanent ethnocentrism that furbishes the rationale for exploiting inferior races. Race, for Le Bon, was an ill-conceived idea corresponding loosely to what has since been described as 'national character structure'. We see this, for example, when Le Bon refers to the hereditary instincts of the Spanish race or when he casually remarks on the feminine characteristics of crowds everywhere, but finds Latin crowds to be the most feminine of all. Race is a loosely defined tag that hung on nations and peoples, reflecting Le Bon's anthropological ignorance rather than his ethnocentric malevolence. (1977: xxxviii)

'La Psychologie des Foules' – Crowds, Masses or Fools?

What are we to think today of Le Bon's *The Crowd*? If we look at practically all introductions to the social sciences there is no reference to Le Bon's work. If we consider, for example, the long and successful introductory textbook *Sociology* by Anthony Giddens, Le Bon is not considered an author worth mentioning; on the other hand, Gobineau is referred to, although of course he is presented as the father of modern racism (Giddens 1997: 218). The famous *International Encyclopaedia of the Social Sciences* (1968) dedicated a rather uninteresting short piece to Le Bon, which was signed by the social psychologist Jean Stoetzel.

It is appropriate to indicate that in the past fifty years Le Bon, like so many other social scientists of the turn of the nineteenth to the twentieth century, have been repressed and forgotten. It would be fair to say that the only remnant of the French landscape of the past is Emile Durkheim, and even his picture is often presented in a distorted way. It should be pointed out that social psychologists have never ceased to admire Le Bon's contributions to the discipline. In the way that in 1954 Gordon W. Allport saluted *The Crowd* as 'perhaps the most influential book ever written in social psychology', in recent years Serge Moscovici (1985) has dedicated much attention to Le Bon's work.

If we have to point out a social scientist who was been sympathetic to Le Bon and who has actually produced a remarkable introduction to *The Crowd*, this person was the leading American sociologist Robert K. Merton. The passage from his work that we have just cited is extremely favourable to Le Bon. His 'Preface' to Le Bon's book was prepared for the Penguin Books Edition of 1960. The importance of *The Crowd* is based, according to Merton, on the fact that Le Bon's contribution was in the area of mass behaviour and that he was able to tackle along a list of crucial problems. According to Merton (1960: viii), these are the following ones:

1 Social conformity and over-conformity.
2 Levelling of the taste.
3 Revolt of the masses.
4 Popular culture.
5 The other directed self.
6 Mass movements.
7 The self-alienation of man.
8 The process of bureaucratization.
9 The escape from freedom into the arms of a leader.
10 The role of the unconscious in social behaviour.

Merton insisted that Le Bon's main contribution was not problem solving but rather problem-finding. However, at a time when scientific opinion about human beings was rather optimistic, Le Bon's vision of humans as irrational and selfish, impulsive and capricious, violent and fraudulent, represented a radical change. There is no doubt that Le Bon reflects in a comprehensive and articulated way, the 'cultural atmosphere' (Merton 1960: xviii) of his time. His way of perceiving the political reality of his days was extremely accurate and was vastly appreciated, as the success of Le Bon's book suggests.

As we have pointed out in the previous section, Le Bon, having observed the political adventures of Georges Boulanger in the late 1880s, concluded that 'in the genesis of prestige nothing succeeds like success . . . [while] in the precipitous decline of prestige nothing fails like failure' (Merton 1960: xxiv). What can be deduced from such an event and other similar ones that occurred at the time (the collapse of Ferdinand de Lesseps and the Dreyfus Affair) is that crowds were unstable, suggestible and credulous. However, it would be fair to observe that the social psychology of crowd behaviour that he analysed was essentially drawn from instances of the French Revolution and the Napoleonic Era. His social scientific method, concludes Merton, might be faulty, but a good number of his ideas were sound.

The most important concept presented in the *Psychologie des foules* was the idea that crowds eliminated the autonomy of the individual. There is obviously a clear difference between an individual psychology and a crowd psychology. In certain circumstances a crowd psychology is formed; the reasons for this event are varied, being behind a material or an emotional background. What is crucially important is the existence of a process of alienation in which individuals loose their autonomy and individuality and form part of a collective identity. It is important to remember that Le Bon stated very clearly that individuality was abolished. For Marpeau (2000: 98), Le Bon's thesis postulates that 'human beings in a crowd are assimilated to being hypnotised'.

A second, important point is Le Bon's idea that the behaviour of the crowds does not follow a rational motivation. In other words, the individuals lose a critical consciousness, they are essentially dominated by an unconscious type of personality. The only dominant idea in a crowd is intellectually inferior to the isolated individual. An important feature of the crowd is its versatility. The crowd has different points of view that will dominate it separately. Crowd behaviour, then, is extremely variable, and it is obvious, according to Le Bon, that the crowd cannot reason; in other words, sentiments dominate more than reasoning.

Le Bon emphasized the importance of knowing the crowds well so that they could be governed in a positive way. That this knowledge also allows the leaders to govern the masses in a totalitarian way is an historical fact. In this sense, appealing political leaders left, centre and right, acquire the basic rules of crowd psychology. No doubt they hope to appeal to the people often through the art of deception. A fascinating mixture of Le Bon's is presented by Barrows:

> To seduce the masses the leader must penetrate the irrational minds of the crowd, feign sympathy for the plight of the oppressed, flatter them, make exaggerated promises he has no intention of honouring, and a perfect rhetoric of seductive images. (1981: 174)

As to the individuals in the crowds, one can only refer to Le Bon's own emotive language:

> By the mere fact that he becomes part of an organised crowd, a man descends several ranks on the ladder of civilisation. Isolated, he is perhaps a cultivated individual; in a crowd he is a barbarian, that is, a creature of instinct. He has the spontaneity, the ferocity and even the enthusiasm and heroism of primitive beings. (1895: 14)

It is interesting to remark that, according to Barrows, although the attitude of Le Bon towards Napoleon, a man perhaps to be admired, was positive it was doubtful that Lenin and Hitler would fit the same picture.

In some respect, Le Bon generalizes his ideas from the crowd to the political institutions. The democratic system is compared to the crowd; the people who vote are not critical or reasonable; they tend to be irritable, credulous and simplistic. Elections tend to be dismissed by Le Bon because they are presented as extravagant. As to the parliamentary assemblies, the defects are obvious in so far as they are not very intelligent and critical. It is possible to assert that these features were already typical of the French Revolution. An important point about the political assemblies is the fact that leaders, who use appealing though rather mediocre speeches, manipulate them. Robespierre was a good case in point of somebody who was very attractive and impulsive, but his speeches were in reality extremely incoherent (Marpeau 2000).

Le Bon referred frequently to psychiatry as a framework to account for crowd behaviour. What seems to happen is that human behaviour has to be explained by reference to the subliminal and the unconscious. For Le Bon, individuals who form part of a crowd became hypnotized as a result of the influence of a leader who uses his abilities to achieve such an objective. It is unclear how convincing this explanation is. A point worth making is that the hypnotized person is no longer in contact with the physical world; what happens is that the individual is controlled by images that the person produces automatically. There is a clear connection between false imagination and unconscious automatism. Furthermore, the person who suffers from hypnotism is bound to behave under the order of the hypnotizer.

Le Bon emphasized that there was a clear connection between words, images and acts. What are the consequences of this assumption? In the first place, anybody who is a member of a crowd will be affected by the images referred to by a leader who uses hypnosis; as a result of the procedure, the reality cannot be empirically or rationally challenged. The second point, mentioned to a certain extent in the previous citation from Le Bon, is that the crowd people are no longer rational; they belong to an earlier human stage in the scale of evolution. In other words, they are dominated by an automatic, instinctive and unconscious pattern of thinking and behaving. In this respect, modern crowd behaviour exhibits features typical of contemporary children and primitive tribes (Metraux 1982).

A point that I have already partially referred to is that according to Le Bon all the individuals of a group have the same images and patterns of behaviour and goals because they reflect the features of the leader. This is why one can refer to the homogeneity and singularity of the crowds. As a consequence, they can be easily manipulated. Le Bon emphasized the fact that crowds exhibit features of irrational behaviour if the leader is perverted and aggressive; however, if the leader is adequate they may behave heroically. This latter point opens an avenue to military behaviour, which can be done rationally and with clear objectives. It is obvious that a contradiction exists between these two conceptions, although Le Bon assumed that both realities were possible.

It was an extremely obvious point for Le Bon, in this respect like for Durkheim, that the individual was subjected to an external pressure or coercion. However, for Le Bon the biological reference was essential; the crowd dominated the individual. The existence of a collective unconscious was also essential, and it was conceived as a hereditary and was associated with the notion of race We have already seen in Le Bon's previous book his concept of race, which is reproduced in *Psychologie des foules*. There is no doubt that for him human racial variety is an important feature of human beings; it is a distinction that, as we have seen, is not only physical but also psychological. For Le Bon important social changes only take place in the long run, whereas historical changes are superficial. The former framework implies a challenge to both the historical races and the psychological species. He insisted that historical peoples like the English and the Italians are characterized by few permanent features and many others that are changeable; only the former are to be considered as the crucial elements of each history. For example, certain peoples (French included) show a clear need to be governed in an authoritarian way which is manifested by different historical events (absolute monarchy, Jacobinism and Bonapartism).

The decisive, explanatory element in the theory of races is the existence of a long past. What is being suggested is that during centuries certain characteristics developed and were transmitted; they became rather permanent and determined the type of each people. The race was seen by Le Bon as the key factor of the historical evolution; he considered race as a permanent factor. The behaviour of human beings depend on the characteristics inherited from the ancestors. As Le Bon put it:

> To understand the true meaning of the term race, it must be projected simultaneously towards the past and future. Much more numerous than the living, the dead are also much more powerful than them . . . It is by their dead, much more than their living, that a people is conducted. (1894: 12–13)

What this sentence suggests is that a people's history is subjected to a rigorous determinism. This is the reason why any racial mixture destroys the soul of the races; both at the level of ideas and feelings. Le Bon insisted that only racially approximated groups could be fertile in producing a new entity; on the other hand, the mixture of whites and blacks, for example, is pernicious and produces a decadent population.

A race, according to Le Bon, is often the result of the living together of dissimilar units that in the long run mix producing a set of common characters and feelings. This may lead to the appearance of a civilization. However, this result is not everlasting, but tends to fade away. As he put it: 'To evolve from barbarism to civilisation following a dream; later, its decline and death comes when this dream has lost its force; so it is the life cycle of a people' (Le Bon 1895: 125)

There is an important conclusion that Le Bon reaches in his *Psychologie des foules and* that we have already mentioned: a man who belongs to a crowd exhibits a civilizational level that is much lower that the present one. According to the author, modern civilizations imply fixed rules, discipline, rationalism, high culture and a perception of the future. Two major features characterize civilization: self-control and the capacity to reason. In addition to that, there is a sense of foreseeing the future. There is no doubt that Le Bon considers civilizations as institutions that are extremely positive. Races have an essential role for societies. Le Bon distinguished four types: primitive, inferior, medium and superior. Only the Europeans have produced great artistic, scientific and industrial inventions, although others (medium races) have created high civilizations. The evolution of the idea of race is related to evolution from irrational to rational human beings. What is at stake in the system of classifying races is the principle of hierarchy. This phenomenon explains the separation between inferior and superior groups.

Not surprisingly, an historian like Zeev Sternhell (1989) considers that this material makes Le Bon a pre-fascist, but, of course, Merton thought differently. Here the main point to emphasize is that Le Bon described procedures that became popular among fascists, but also communists and other politicians. However, there is obviously no direct connection and it only shows his tremendous ability to capture a modern tendency. One of the most impressive ideas of Le Bon is that of the images of Jesus and Mohammed, amazingly ignorant characters at the beginning, and who came to dominate an extensive part of the world for hundreds of years. What an appealing statement to people like Lenin and Hitler, who were desperate to dominate the masses in the twentieth century! No doubt, Le Bon was well aware of the ambiguity of the relationship between the leaders and the masses, in the sense that reason is perhaps typical of philosophers alone. However, the features of the many virtues required to maintain a civilization, from religious faith to love of one's country, are typical of political leaders.

A final point that I have already mentioned in passing has to do with the absence of Le Bon from the French university system and the fact that he was despised, detested and boycotted by the Durkheimian School explains the fact that Le Bon was extremely resentful and critical of the university system. However, it must be pointed out that Le Bon was in contact with, and had impressed, a large number of scientists, intellectuals and politicians. It must be emphasized that by studying non-rational factors in human behaviour, Le Bon, like Sorel, added a new dimension to our understanding of the way human beings act, and that was the world of emotions. To an extent, while Durkheim presented a theory of social cohesion which aimed at protecting the Third Republic of France, Le Bon believed that the masses would not behave rationally (Nye 1973)

The idea that irrationality presided over history was the result, as we have mentioned, of basic factors such as race and milieu. At the end of the day, Le Bon accounts for revolutionary violence in terms of the mystical mentality and the affective logic of crowds stimulated by their leaders. As he put it, 'the Jacobin is not a rationalist but a believer' (Le Bon 1912: 83). To pretend, however, that Le Bon, as well as the Italian school (Pareto, Mosca and Michels), are irrelevant because of their emphasis, unlike Weber and Durkheim, on human irrationalism is inappropriate because both perspectives are required to fully account for human behaviour.

Conclusion

I shall start this closing section with a controversial passage from Svend Ranulf (1939). Referring to Durkheim's *The Elementary Forms of Religious Life* (EFRL), he quotes from the conclusion the well-known passage in which Durkheim says:

The day will come when our societies will know again hours of creative effervescence, in the course of which new ideals will be born and new formulae emerge which will for a time serve as guide to humanity. (FEVR 1960: 611; Pickering 1975: 157)

Nowhere is Durkheim explicit as to which institutional forms will effect the salvation, and Ranulf asks rhetorically: 'is not the rise of fascism an event which, in due logic, Durkheim ought to have welcomed as that salvation from individualism for which he had been trying rather grippingly to prepare the way?' (Ranulf 1939: 31). This comment could be easily dismissed suggesting that it reflects the musings of a disgruntled, unemployed Scandinavian sociologist. However, what is fascinating is that in the article Ranulf refers to, and quotes from, two letters that Marcel Mauss had addressed to him. In the first letter (November 1936) Mauss writes as follows:

Durkheim and I were the founders of the theory of the authority of the *représentation collective*. That great modern societies, which had more or less emerged from the Middle Ages, could be the subject to suggestion as Australians are by their dances, and made to turn around like children in a ring, is something that we had not really foreseen. We did not put our minds to this return to primitivism. We were satisfied with a few allusions to the state of the crowds, when something quite different was at stake. (Gane 1992: 214)

In another letter (May 1939), Mauss concludes:

I think that all this is a real tragedy for us, an unwelcome verification of the things we had been suggesting and the proof that we should perhaps have expected this verification in the bad case rather than a verification in the good. (Gane 1992: 214–5)

In the light of these texts by Durkheim and Mauss, it is perhaps pertinent to ask: what was the meaning of the future effervescence that Durkheim had in mind? We know what Ranulf had to say. Mauss's letters are highly ambiguous, suggesting, on the one hand that, that the Durkheimian School had discovered in collective effervescence an important social mechanism, but, on the other hand, that this could be put to rather obnoxious use by modern totalitarian states.

Another Durkheimian, Bouglé, writing in the late 1930s, interprets Durkheim's reference to the future in a rather different, perhaps more positive way. He suggests that when Durkheim refers to a rejuvenating faith he is thinking essentially of socialism. And that, like Sorel, he presents socialism as a faith, and not as a science (Bouglé 1938: 34–5).

The same Machiavellian role in relation to the origins of modern totalitarianism has been attributed to the work of Le Bon. Hence, it is time to turn now to Le Bon and Durkheim's theory of collective effervescence. There is enough evidence to suggest that Durkheim, in his lifetime, insisted on distancing himself from Le Bon's sociological approach, denying him any scientificity. In spite of this negative attitude, the international sociological establishment accepted Le Bon as a *bona fide* sociologist (or at least social psychologist) and his theories were discussed in most history of sociology textbooks until well entered the 1950s. As we have pointed out in the 'Introduction', Le Bon was taken seriously by a variety of scholars including Freud, Weber, McDougall, Adorno, Michels and Sorokin.

Part of the problem, of course, has to do with the problematic relations between sociology and psychology in the Durkheimian School. Daniel Essertier wrote in 1927 that 'crowd phenomena play a preponderant role in Durkheim's EFRL; by a singular turn of events, books such as those of Dr. Le Bon, which in fact were subjected to criticism by Durkheim when he treated psychological explanation in sociology, explicitly or implicitly carry authority in the Durkheimian School' (Essertier 1927: 11). According to Essertier, this vulgar psychology, which Durkheim had rightly rejected, made a return in the EFRL.

In 1927 Marcel Mauss, reviewing Barnes's et al.'s *The History of the Social Sciences*, complained that Kimball Young had created a sociological category in which Durkheim, Le Bon and Sighele were placed together. The idea of an 'intensive collective psychology' to which Durkheim would belong he found it 'extremely abusive' (Mauss 1969: 285). In recent times both Lukes (1973) and Pickering (1984) have been critical of any attempts to insinuate that Durkheim's theory of collective effervescence was influenced by crowd psychology in general and Le Bon in particular.

Lukes is somewhat ambiguous in his presentation of the case. On the one hand, he admits that 'Durkheim was doubtedly affected by the crop of studies in crowd psychology' (1973: 462), but he adds that 'there is no evidence that he was specifically influenced by any of them'. And the reasons, in so far as Le Bon is concerned, are that 'Durkheim would have been the last person to regard Le Bon as a serious social scientist'. Pickering (1984) dedicates two chapters (21 and 22) to the topic of effervescent assembly, but it is in Chapter 22 that he focuses on the issue of crowd psychology. It is not easy to summarize his argument, which is detailed and complex, but he concludes that 'Durkheim does not see collective effervescence primarily, if indeed at all, in terms of crowd psychology' (1984: 402). In fact, neither Lukes nor Pickering engage in a detail analysis of Le Bon's *Psychologie des foules*, so we are left with the problem of comparing Durkheim with the ghost of Le Bon.

We have established that in the context of Durkheim's treatment of collective effervescence he never refers to the work of Le Bon. Both Lukes and Pickering refer to the only footnote in the EFRL (Durkheim 1960: 300) which can throw some light on the influence of crowd psychology on Durkheim's work. The reference is to a book by Otto Stoll entitled *Suggestion und Hypnotismus in der Völkerpsychologie*. Durkheim quotes from the second edition of 1904 (the first edition was in 1894). Now, who was Otto Stoll? We know that he was a medical doctor by training and a Professor of Geography and Ethnology at the University of Zürich. His area of ethnographic expertise was Central America. In addition to technical ethnographic books, in 1908 he published a more popular book entitled *Das Geschlechtsleben in der Völkerpsychologie* (which roughly translates as *Sexual Life of the Savages*).

His *Suggestion und Hypnotismus in der Völkerpsychologie* was meant as a sort of manual; it is essentially a descriptive text (both historically and ethnographically oriented), with very little analysis. The second edition was reviewed by Marcel Mauss in *L'Année Sociologique* (1903–4). Mauss *compte rendu* is generally positive, emphasizing 'la nature suggestive de la religion et l'influence suggestive de ses répresentations' (1903–4: 234). Perhaps the most interesting thing in Mauss's review is the reference to a book by Friedmann entitled *Über Wahnideen in Völkerleben* (*Hallucination in Primitive Society*) (1901). This text is perhaps the missing link in the crowd psychology saga of Durkheim. In it the author presents, according to Mauss, the idea that 'the *excitation psychologique* of the masses is in fact the most powerful moment of social life in general and of religious life in particular' (1903–4: 234).

Perhaps it does not matter so much whether Durkheim's theory of collective effervescence originated from crowd psychology or not. The crucial issue that seems to be at stake is the relationship between the social sciences and psychology. Durkheimians have always been reluctant to incorporate psychological explanations into their theoretical framework. It is against the *Rules*! On the other hand, a sociologist like Raymond Aron, when looking at the EFRL said that the phenomena of 'effervescence are the very paradigm of that psychological and social process in which religions are born' (Aron 1967: 355). That it is possible to read EFRL II.7 in the light of a theory which takes on board psychological and sociological elements we have the example of Moscocivi's *La Machine à faire des dieux* (1989).

–8–

The New Science of Anthroposociology and Eugenics: The Legacy of Vacher de Lapouge

Introduction

As Zeev Sternhell's *La droite révolutionnaire* (1978) has remarked, a new climate emerged in France in the 1890s. It was dominated by the influences of Gobineau and Darwin. Among the many sociological schools that flourished at the turn of the century, the anthroposociology of Vacher de Lapouge briefly caught the attention of philosophical and social-scientific circles in France and other countries. For a short time there was a kind of fascination with the bizarre and all-explaining doctrines of anthroposociology. Even Durkheim was not immune to such an appeal, and when in 1897 he was considering the first issue of *L'Année Sociologique* (hereafter AS), he asked Henri Muffang, a sympathizer of anthroposociology, to edit a subsection on the school.

In *L'Aryen* (1899: 511–12), Vacher de Lapouge salutes this New World:

> All human beings are related to each other and to all living beings. There are no specific human rights, like there are no bovine rights. Humans have lost their privileges of being apart, created at God's image; humans have no other rights than the rights of any other mammal. The very idea of right is a fiction. There is only force. Rights are conventions, transactions among equal or unequal powers. The right ceases when one of the contenders ceases to be powerful. Among the members of a society the law is that which is sanctioned by collective force. Among nations, this guarantee of stability is absent. Against force there is no right because the right is only the state created and maintained by force. All men are brothers, like all animals are brothers, but being a brother does not stop you being eaten. Fraternity is welcome, but God protect the vanquished! Life is maintained by death; to live it is necessary to eat, and to eat it is essential to kill.

There are three key ideological components that prepared the way to Nazism: the biological dogma of racial inequality, the moral nihilism invoking the 'struggle for existence' and the idea of the survival of the fittest as a universal law of nature. This chapter explores one of the crucial movements that prepared the path to Nazism: the turn of the century anthroposociological school represented by George Vacher de Lapouge. Vacher was a social Darwinist, socialist and craniologist who believed that it was possible to create a synthesis between Marx, Darwin and Gobineau. In other words, class struggle was a particular case of racial struggle. He upheld the superiority of the Aryan race, while supporting an anti-bourgeois sentiment and a theory of proletarian elitism (which Ludwig Woltmann, a German contemporary and colleague, called *Sozialaristokratie*). Among the German followers of Vacher de Lapouge the best known were Otto Ammon and Ludwig Woltmann. They were rather dilettantish but helped in the building of a German national consciousness on the basis of the racial idea. After World War I, the key influences which prepared the way to Nazism were the doctrines of H. S. Chamberlain; on the other hand, Hans F. K. Günther was an extremely influential anthropologist during Hitler's totalitarian regime. Both authors recognized Vacher de Lapouge's contribution to the new German *Weltanschauung*.

Aim and Scope of Anthroposociology

Not only was the term 'anthroposociology' coined by Vacher de Lapouge, but the very origins of the discipline can be traced back to lectures he delivered at the University of Montpellier from 1886 to 1892. In 1899 he could write:

> If the attempts made to stop my first developments had been successful, and if I have not written even a line, anthroposociology would have been established by Ammon in Karlshruhe in 1890, instead of being founded in Montepellier in 1886, but this science would be exactly the same at the time when these pages are printed. (Vacher de Lapouge 1899: 449)

Vacher de Lapouge recognized, however, that the true founder of the discipline was Gobineau, who was the first to have emphasized the importance of race in the evolution of peoples (Vacher de Lapouge: 545–6). Darwin's struggle for existence and Broca's craniology were also seen as important stepping stones in the development of anthroposociology.

Anthroposociology was established around the following premises: that human races are differently endowed in terms of intelligence and character, that the cephalic index is the concept with which to determine the capacity of the brain, that human behaviour is the result of the interaction between race and the social milieu, and that among human beings social selections predominate over natural selections. As a discipline, anthroposociology flourished in France (under Vacher de Lapouge) and Germany (under Ammon) at the turn of the century. There were also more or less faithful representatives in Italy (Livi), Spain (Oloriz), the United Kingdom (Beddoe) and the USA (Closson).

Georges Vacher de Lapouge, who lived between 1854 and 1936, was undoubtedly the most conspicuous representative of anthroposociology (Quilan 1998). He originally studied medicine and jurisprudence, before following a career as a librarian, first at the University of Montpellier and later in Rennes and Poitiers. Having come into contact with social Darwinism and craniology, he became an enthusiastic propagandist of these doctrines. By the mid-1880s he saw his task as the 'application of the conclusions of biology to the social sciences' (1886: 519). His wish to accede to an official position, as an anthropologist, was frustrated, although he taught unofficially (*courses libres*) for a number of years at the University of Montpellier. In addition to a good number of articles published in different professional journals, Lapouge published two major books based on his lectures, *Les sélections sociales* (1896) and *L'Aryen, son rôle social* (1899), as well as a collection of articles under the title *Race et milieu sociale* (1909). Perhaps the best known and most influential of his articles was 'Lois fondamentales de l'anthroposociologie' (1897), which was also published in Italian and English the same year. As a measure of his impact, Lapouge stated they existed more than 3000 references (mostly positive) to his work (1909: xix).

Otto Ammon's impact was perhaps more restricted to the German-speaking world, though some of his writings were translated into French and Italian, and his work was also commented upon worldwide. The monograph that established his anthropometric credentials was *Die natürliche Auslese beim Menschen. Auf Grund der anthropologische Untersuchen der Wehrpflichtigen in Baden* (1893), but it was in his *Gesellschaftsordnung und ihre natürlichen Grundlagen* (1895) (French translation 1900) that anthroposociology was presented as a new discipline. Internationally, the most cited of his writings was 'Histoire d'une idée. L'anthroposociologie' (1898). He also published *Zur Anthropologie der Badener* (1899).

As we shall see there are some differences between Lapouge and Ammon; for one thing, Lapouge was much more radical and pessimistic. An important dimension that can only be mentioned in passing is that Lapouge was a socialist who was trying to create a synthesis between Marx and Darwin; a severe critic of liberal democracy, he would maintain that:

> To the fiction of Fictions of Justice, Equality and Fraternity, scientific politics opposes the reality of Forces, Races and Evolution. Damned the peoples that waste their time on Dreams! (1896: 489)

In the context of this short *aperçu* on anthroposociology I shall only refer to two major thematic areas: social selections and the laws of anthroposociology.

Social Selectionism

An important issue was that Vacher de Lapouge was obsessed with the idea that the natural order of society had been dramatically changed due to the influence of social selections. Both the evolution of the species and of societies is the result of selections; and the latter can be due to death (struggle for existence) or to differential fertility (struggle for descendance). This section is based on Nagel (1975), but specially Bejin's (1982), contribution to the issue.

Social Darwinism was much less successful in France than in the UK or in Germany, perhaps because France was less developed both in terms of population and of industrial development. The strong dualism of Descartes' rationalism made France a place less propitious for the flourishing of social Darwinism. Neither Spencerian liberalism nor social democracy were firmly implanted. French culture was more favourable to the development of sociology of values centred on the ideas of consensus or social solidarity.

For Vacher de Lapouge all living beings were subjected to natural selection; mankind, in addition, is subjected to social selections, that is, the milieu created by it. The study of man comprises an additional branch of knowledge to that of the study of animals. This new discipline, named anthroposociology, has as its object the study of the reciprocal relations between race and social milieu (environment). The essential postulate of anthroposociology is that human actions are determined by a hereditary brain structure. Vacher proceeds in three stages.

In the first stage, he constructs ideal-types of the configurations of superior and inferior somatic and psychic types. These types spread or contract according to the hypotheses of natural selection, that is, without taking into account the influence of social selections. These hierarchical, ideal-typical configurations can be referred to as races. This concept is to be understood in a zoological, not a political sense. Vacher coined the term *ethnie* to refer to a community consisting of elements of different races but sharing the same culture and subjected to the same laws of selection.

Postulating the determination of human actions by a hereditary brain structure, anthroposociology maintains as a distinctive sign of races the cephalic index. This allows him to distinguish three types in the European population: *Homo Europeus, Homo Alpinus* and *Homo Contractus*.

In a second stage, Lapouge observes that social selections can produce an inversion of the natural order, allowing dysgenic elements to submerge eugenic ones. It is what he called the law of destruction of the perfects under the continued effect of selections. He referred to the following social selections:

1 *Military*. Modern wars eliminate the best men, while the dysgenic escape military conscription.
2 *Political*. The government of coteries and political parties favour the mediocre.
3 *Religious*. Priestly celibacy forbids a very good number of eugenics to reproduce themselves. Furthermore, religious persecutions often lead to the disappearance of elites.

4 *Moral.* Charity profits dysgenics.
5 *Legal.* The prohibition of polygamy works against eugenics.
6 *Economic.* Plutocracy favours the elimination of the intellectual aristocracy and leads to favour marriages dictated by financial reasons instead of eugenic ones.
7 *Professional.* The best-qualified individuals have generally low fertility.

Vacher's basic pessimism follows from the effects of these social selections. Progress, he insisted, is a human conception; in the realm of evolution there is no paradise, the best may not come. The power of science is limited; it only gives human beings consciousness, but has no effect on happiness.

The third stage involves a voluntaristic element. Systematic selection can allow men to remake human nature. Vacher believed that it was possible to use the formidable force of heredity to combat its own ravages, opposing a systematic selection to the destructive and unregulated selection that threatens mankind. Systematic selection seems more and more necessary, not only to ensure progress but also to prevent the impending deterioration of race. Theoretically and on its scientific or technical side, systematic selection is feasible. The difficulties, felt Vacher, were moral and social. However, he believed that these obstacles would become less formidable with ethnic changes in present populations, with the growth of different ethnic conceptions and with the advent of the new system of political, social and economic organization. Systematic selections may be directed towards the following ends:

1 To constitute a natural aristocracy among a given people.
2 To constitute specialized and distinct castes suited for different branches of work.
3 To transform a people as a whole in a given direction.
4 To form a universal dominant race.
5 To improve all humanity by using the most perfect local types.
6 To substitute for existing humanity a single, more perfect race.

To achieve its objectives systematic selection would have to proceed in two directions: to eliminate the degenerate, vicious and incapable elements and to increase and perfect the superior elements. Finally, if the individual initiative and moral pressure were not sufficient to succeed in these objectives, coercion would have to be exerted by the state.

As Taguieff (1994) has remarked, Vacher de Lapouge was concerned, particularly in his works *Selections sociales* and *L'Aryen,* with the selectionism and racialism of the future. As he put it rather bluntly, socialism would either be selectionist or nothing. Society must be organized in a hierarchical way, with specialized and separated castes. To achieve that end the state must intervene and this can only be achieved by a socialist state. Eugenics is a task that only an interventionist – that is, a socialist – can achieve. It is also the task of the state to transform society in such a way that individuals should all become perfect and equal.

As we have said, Vacher de Lapouge's aim was to create a world system of a socialist character. This is viewed as a long-term project, perhaps lasting a few centuries. An important feature of his socialist system is the fact that it will be based on selectionism. It is important to remember here that the present-day experience shows that social life is not favourable to the biologically healthier but rather the opposite. Future selectionism must change this pattern and favour the best people in terms of health and beauty.

In the last book that deals with the same topic (*Race et milieu social*, 1907), Vacher de Lapouge expressed vividly his ideas that the only way of marrying socialism and selectionism was with the abolition of democracy. He insisted that this attitude was a typically bourgeois prejudice. As to the peasant and workers, he believed that they were more sympathetic to his ideas. As to the government, it should definitely be in favour of the lower classes and used violence to repress the elites and the intelligentsia. An important element in the future policy of Vacher de Lapouge was his idea of biological improvement and, more specifically, a clearly biological interventionism of the state with radical proposals, specifically the sterilization (castration) of undesirable individuals. The author was well-aware that the basic obstacles to eugenicism were Christian morality and the plutocratic political regimes. In the first case, the explanation is easy to provide because it is well known that Christianity is in favour of genetically defective people. The same can be said for the plutocrats because their accumulation of money favours the reproduction of the people who are not necessarily intelligent.

Fundamental Laws of Anthroposociology

Before enunciating the fundamental laws of anthroposociology, it is important to introduce some basic concepts. Vacher de Lapouge describes what he called cephalic index as the ratio of the breadth of the head to its length. It is found by multiplying the maximum length of the head by 100 and dividing it by maximum breadth (Vacher de Lapouge 1897: 546). This allows for the distinction of two basic types: dolichocepalic or long-headed and brachycephalic or round-headed. On the basis of this it is possible to classify the European races in two major types: *Homo Europeus* and *Homo Alpinus*. A third European race, typical of southern Spain and Italy, is the *Homo Mediterraneus*, a mixed type.

According to Vacher de Lapouge, the *Homo Europeus* is, in addition of being dolichocephalic (long headed), tall, with light hair, blue eyes and long face. It is found in Great Britain, Scandinavia, North Germany and Holland. As to its key psychological features one can say that it is ambitious, energetic and courageous. As to its religion one can say that Protestantism is dominant. The *Homo Europeus* is enterprising, aggressive, domineering, self-reliant, a wealth generator, fore-sighted, a lover of liberty and individuality, adventurous, progressive and creative.

As to the *Homo Alpinus*, in addition of being brachycephalic (round headed), it is short, brunette and with a round face. It is found in France, Switzerland, South Germany, Poland, North Italy, Balkans, Asia Minor and the Caucasus. As to religion, those in Europe are mostly Catholic. Among its key psychological features, it is cautious, non-progressive and strongly attached to the native abode. Other features that are mentioned include that it is frugal, industrious gifted with common sense, and traditional; it absorbs rather than creates ideas, it is defensive, but normally a serf or a slave. As to the foresight it is limited to family life.

Finally, we must mention the *Homo Mediterraneus*. The most common type is short and dark, with a long face and head. He is found in the Mediterranean (Corsica, Sicily, Sardinia, South Italy, and parts of Spain). There is another type in which he is tall, but with a short face (Southern Spain and Kabylia in north Africa). As to the psychic characterization one can only say that it is rather varied.

According to Vacher de Lapouge (1898) the fundamental laws of anthro-posociology are as follows:

1 *Law of the distribution of wealth.* In countries inhabited jointly by *Homo Europeus* and *Homo Alpinus*, the former element possesses more than its proportionate share of wealth.
2 *Law of altitudes.* In regions inhabited jointly by *Homo Europeus* and *Homo Alpinus*, the former is concentrated in the less mountainous areas.
3 *Law of the localization of cities.* Important cities are almost always located in dolichocephalic regions and in the least brachycephalic parts of brachicephalic regions.
4 *Law of the urban indices.* The cephalic index of urban populations is lower than that of the surrounding rural populations. This law has a corollary: every city whose sphere of attraction embraces brachycephalic regions tends (other things being equal) to become more and more brachycephalic, although the migrants drawn to it are less brachycephalic than the average of the rural population.
5 *Law of emigration.* In a population in process of dissociation by displacement, it is the less brachycephalic element that emigrates.
6 *Law of marriages.* The cephalic index of the children of parents from two different regions is lower than the average between the indices of these regions. In other words, the dolichocephalic members of a community are more apt than the brachycephalic members to choose their spouses outside of residents of their own birthplace.

7 *Law of the concentration of the dolichoids*. In the dissociation of the elements of a population the migratory elements are attracted to the centres of dolichocephaly

8 *Law of urban elimination*. Urban life acts as an agency of selection in favour of the dolichoids and destroys or rejects the most brachycephalic elements.

9 *Law of stratification*. The cephalic index is lower and the proportion of dolichocephalics greater among the higher classes than among the lower classes in each community.

10 *Law of the intellectual classes*. Among intellectual workers the absolute dimensions of the head, and particularly the breadth, are greater than average.

11 *Law of epochs*. Since prehistoric times the cephalic index has everywhere and constantly tended to increase.

12 *Law of the greater activity of Homo Europeus*.

The Reception of the Anthroposociology in *l'Année Sociologique*

What was the rationale behind the Durkheimian idea of *L'Année Sociologique*? First and foremost, Durkheim thought that his journal should present a comprehensive picture of all the different sociological tendencies. Secondly, any sociologist would regard with suspicion a discipline like racial anthropology. The reason is that such an approach would make sociology, to a great extent, redundant in so far as it treated social facts as derivative. However, one should always keep in mind the fact that it is not always possible to foresee the results of a particular scientific trend.

Durkheim's 'honeymoon' with anthroposociology lasted three years. During this period Muffang edited a subsection of AS entitled 'Anthroposociologie' in which he reviewed (or rather summarized) articles and books on the topic. It published an average of thirteen pages a year, which was quite substantial, all things considered. In Volume IV (1900) Muffang's contribution disappeared and so did the subsection on anthroposociology as such. Subsequently, two of Durkheim's closest collaborators, Mauss and Hubert, reviewed writings related to race, national origins and prehistory, under the label 'Anthropologie et Sociologie'. However, after 1901, references to anthroposociology and allied topics were few and far between. A page had been closed in the Durkheimian sociological enterprise: that which dealt with the pretentions of racial science. The aim of the second part of this chapter is threefold: first, to provide an accurate description of the position of anthroposociology; secondly, to consider in some detail its reception in AS; and, finally, to compare Durkheim's attitude towards anthroposociology with that of his contemporaries, as well as to look at the fate of anthroposociology in the histories of sociology.

The least that one can say about the rubric 'anthroposociology' in AS is its miscellaneous, marginal and unstable character. As I have hinted in the introduction, the journal's honeymoon with anthroposociology was of short duration. It was only in the first three volumes that anthroposociology was accorded ample space and the sympathetic voice of Muffang. By Volumes IV and V, anthroposociology was being subjected to a sustained frontal assault by Henri Hubert and Marcel Mauss, who, as is well known, were both faithful Durkheimians. After that, and if we except the odd short review or reference, a curtain of heavy silence fell over anthroposociology.

It is interesting to note that Durkheim felt it necessary to write an introductory note to the first rubric on anthroposociology. The full text reads as follows:

> It has appeared at times that anthropology would render sociology useless. By attempting to explain historical phenomena by the sole characteristics of races, anthropology appeared to treat social facts as epiphenomena without life of their own and without specific action. Such tendencies could only awaken the suspicion of the sociologists. However, *L'Année sociologique* has as its primary objective to present to his readers a complete picture of all different tendencies within sociology. Furthermore, one never knows in advance the types of results that a scientific movement led to. It is for this reason that *l'AS* will take into consideration the research undertaken by anthroposociologists. And to that end, we have asked a follower of this school to collaborate with us. (*AS*, 1897, I: 519)

The correspondence between Durkheim and Bouglé illuminates some aspects of the place of anthroposociology in AS. In a letter of Durkheim to Bouglé (dated 15.7.1897), the future editor of the rubric on anthroposociology is mentioned as 'votre collègue Muffang' (Durkheim 1975, 2: 403). Durkheim referred also, and in favourable way, to an article that Bouglé had published recently (most probably Bouglé 1897). This paper, a critical review of the works of the leading representatives of anthroposociology (such as Ammon, Lapouge, Closson), was read by Durkheim with 'great interest', adding that 'I do not need to tell you that all these anthropological speculations leave us more than sceptic' (Durkheim 1975, 2: 403).

Although both Durkheim and Bouglé were critical of the pretensions and reductionism of anthroposociology, Durkheim, unlike Bouglé, was in favour of allowing Muffang to present the school in a descriptive way and in a favourable light. In another of his letters (dated 27 September 1897), Durkheim referred to Bouglé's intention of prefacing the rubric on anthroposociology with rather critical remarks and suggested a different approach:

> The preamble that you have written it seems to me a little too combative; I think that it is not appropriate to enter into arguments with the dogmatic problems generated by the anthropological method. We only have to indicate that our publication is an act of impartiality and its is done with reservation'. (1975, 2: 411)

In addition to this paragraph, Durkheim made some concrete suggestions for the improvement of Muffang's paper with the view of making it less repetitive, concluding: 'On the other hand, I am very happy with his contribution and his style is clear and interesting' (Durkheim 1975, 2: 412). By 1900, however, AS was run by a rather homogeneous team, much more so than Durkheim could have imagined when he started the journal. This meant the end of the rubric on anthroposociology, with which Durkheim and his team had lost sympathy. The reasons are obvious: anthroposociology was envisaged as reductionist, materialist, speculative and politically dangerous.

The first issue of AS introduced anthroposociology in some detail (15pp.). After Durkheim's short cautionary note reproduced above, there followed two substantial review articles that dealt with the works of Lapouge and Ammon respectively. Lapouge's *Les sélections sociales* (1896) was his first monograph, the transcript of a course that he taught at the University of Montpellier in 1888–9. Muffang celebrated the emergence of a new science, although he acknowledged that 'only the future will tell us which advantage can humanity extract from the laws acquired from anthroposociology' (AS, 1897, I: 525). Before reviewing *Les sélections sociales*, Muffang offered a brief *aperçu* of the development of the anthroposociological school, emphasizing Lapouge's early ideas about the superiority of the blonde, dolichocephalic race, that is, *Homo Europeus*.

The main focus of Lapouge's book is to show that human societies have instituted principles of social selection, which go against the grain of natural selection. Francis Galton had first mentioned this issue. As Muffang put it, while 'the natural selection generally assures the triumph of the strongest and the best, social selection too often assures the triumph of the mediocre and the feeble, and produces the elimination of the superior elements of the eugenic' (AS, 1897, I: 522). Muffang seemed to take the statistics provided by Vacher de Lapouge at face value, suggesting that 'the measurements provide here reliable data' (AS 1987, I: 522). He also seemed to be concerned with how one could contribute to the maximum possible diffusion of anthroposociological discoveries. He said that 'it is important to familiarise the masses with the ideas and the phenomena of inheritance, evolution and selection, and to determine a movement of opinion contrary to the marriage of the spoiled individuals and in accordance with the true duties towards each species' (AS, 1897, I: 524–25).

The second major item that received Muffang's attention was the work of Otto Ammon. Under review was an article entitled – 'Die Geschichte einer Idee' (1896), and a book, *Die Gesellschaftsordnung und ihre natürlichen Grundlagen* (1896). As in Lapouge's case, Muffang emphasized the importance of the anthropometric data that had been collected, which seemed to establish, without the shadow of a doubt, what is called Ammon's Law: 'la plus grand dolichocephalie des urbains' (AS, 1987, I: 526). If this happened it was because 'the dolicocephalic were attracted towards the cities as a result of their aptitudes and their physical features' (AS, 1987, I: 526). Interestingly, Muffang indicated that very different political conclusions can follow from the anthropometric data referred to; while 'for Lapouge the *social* selections act in a pejorative sense against the *natural* selection . . . for Ammon social selections and natural selections are identical' (AS, 1987, I: 527). Ammon insisted that a flexible class system was the best mechanism to ensure a progressive selection and social order.

The space dedicate to anthroposociology was slightly less (twelve pages) in the second volume of AS than in the previous year. Lapouge's 'Les lois de l'Anthroposociologie' (1897), published also in English (in America) and Italian occupied centre stage. After acknowledging the role played by Gobineau in the development of anthroposociology, the review reproduced the substance of the laws, more or less verbatim. Muffang also referred to certain other studies which seemed to confirm Lapouge's Laws. Of particular importance among these was a joint empirical study by Durand de Gros and Lapouge on the Aveyron area.

Livi's *Saggio di geografia del militarismo in Italia* (1897) seemed to confirm rather well the anthroposociological hypothesis that the economic and military aptitude is higher in those areas where *Homo Europeus* predominates. Although not quite favourable to the anthroposociological standpoint, Sergi's *I dati antropologici in sociologia* (1898), received a lengthy discussion of nearly three pages. Sergi put forward a racial classification different from that of Lapouge, based not on the cephalic index but on the shape of the skull. In any case, what Muffang welcomed was Sergi's conviction that what was required to make sense of the origins and stratification of the population was a joint anthropometric, archaeological and philological approach.

One issue that seemed to baffle many of the practitioners of anthroposociology was that the cephalic index proved insufficient in characterizing racial groupings. The fact that *Homo Mediterraneus* was dolichocephalic, but not tall and blonde was quite a puzzle. This issue taken up by Sergi was also mentioned in another item discussed by Muffang: Ripley's *The Racial Geography of Europe* (1897). The works of Fouillée and Winiarski, which were quite critical of Lapouge, were also mentioned, but not properly reviewed. On the other hand, Closson's 'The Hierarchy of European Races' (1897) attempted to confirm statistically that *Homo Europeus* was more economically active than *Homo Alpinus*. Muffang also mentioned other studies which suggested that Aryans were less criminally inclined than the other two European races.

In Volume III, dated 1898–9, thirteen pages were dedicated to 'Anthroposociologie'. Muffang's main emphasis (five pages) was on Ammon's long study (*Zur Anthropologie der Badener*, 1899). This book had been in the making for more than ten years and was meant to be a powerful empirical demonstration of the major tenets of anthroposociology. Two major conclusions seemed to emerge from

Ammon's study: a worrying historical tendency towards an increase in the cephalic index (in other words, a progressive increase of brachicephalic populations), and a strong correlation between race and class (the predominance of the dolichocephalic element in the upper classes).

As I said already said, the rubric 'Anthroposociologie' and its editor Muffang disappeared from AS from Volume IV onwards, Hubert and Mauss taking over the section, but under a different label. In addition, the tone of the commentaries became very different. For example, while Muffang's review of Vacher de Lapouge's *Les sélections sociales* (1896) was extremely favourable, if bland, Hubert's review of Lapouge's next book, *L'Aryen, son role social* (1899), was rather negative. Anthroposociology was depicted as a false science, while Vacher de Lapouge was presented as a rabid prophet of Aryanism. Most damaging was Hubert's dismantling of Lapouge's basic principles and his emphasis on the unreliability of his statistics. Finally, there was the political sub-text; for Hubert the whole anthroposociological exercise had no other outcome than creating a dangerous Aryan mythology.

It is intriguing that the subsection 'Anthroposociologie' should have disappeared to be substituted by a more neutral term – 'Anthropologie et Sociologie' – which in practice covered the same ground, a mere nine pages being dedicated to the subject matter. In terms of space J. Deniker's *Les races et les peuples de la terre* (1900) was the main item of interest (four pages). Marcel Mauss, who reviewed this longish book considered it 'an excellent ethnographic and anthropological text' (AS, 1900, IV: 139). One thing was clear in Mauss's mind: the difficulty of establishing clear racial categories. Deniker proposed a new concept, that of a people, which was defined by its *'caractères ethniques'*; Mauss, however, found this concept rather unsatisfactory because of its vagueness (it referred to physical, social and linguistic features alike). In the final resort, the only things that existed for Mauss were societies, that is, 'groups defined by their distribution in a specific habitat' (AS, 1900, IV: 141). Nonetheless, Mauss recognized the usefulness of the data on races and peoples. Deniker's book was, he concluded, a work that 'constituted a very rich repertory of facts' (AS, 1900, IV: 143).

I have already indicated that in his review of Lapouge's *L'Aryen. Son rôle social* (1899), Henri Hubert was rather dismissive and caustic, embracing many of the criticisms that had been put forward by L. Manouvrier in his 'L'indice céphalique et la pseudosociologie' (1899). This two-part article was also reviewed by Hubert, who heralded it as a defence of 'sociology against the alleged sociologists' (AS, 1900, IV: 143) as Vacher de Lapouge. Manouvrier accused the anthroposociological school of being essentially pseudoscientific and of being fixated on a concept – that of the cephalic index – which explained nothing.

Hubert's conclusion to the review of Lapouge's book emphasises an essential Durkheimian standpoint: sociology does not depend on anthropology. As he put it:

Mister de Lapouge suppresses sociology by absorbing it. Perhaps he is right. We do not know for sure that races have special intellectual aptitudes, and that these correspond to certain physical features. These propositions should be studied in an infinitely careful and complex way. In any case, it is not our task We will continue to investigate the social causes of social facts. We will carefully register what will be said of their anthropological effects, but the study of the anthropological factors that effect the evolution of our society is completely beyond our critique. (AS, 1900, IV: 146)

In this long quotation it is worth noting that Hubert's rejection of anthroposociology is essentially on methodological grounds. In other words, sociology must stand on its own. Another important point is that the possibility of racial explanations is not rejected; what is condemned is the superficiality and shoddiness of anthroposociology. In a nutshell, what Hubert is reasserting is a different conception of sociological practice. While Lapouge gives explanatory primacy to the biological concept of inheritance, the Durkheimian vision consists in assuming that social facts can be explained by reference to social causes. So-called 'anthropological factors' fall outside the remit of sociology, even though they may be relevant in the course of social evolution. This position is not without contradiction, though; on the one hand, the autonomy of the social domain is one of the key defining features of the Durkheimian endeavour, on the other hand, the possibility of anthroposociology is not altogether denied. But is it not the case that if biological facts can account for social ones, then sociology is to a great extent irrelevant? Part of the problem arises from the concept of race used in the literature of the time. Race is both a biological and a cultural concept, hence the confusion between race and peoples or nations. As I mentioned in the 'Introduction', Vol. IV decided the destiny of anthroposociology in AS for good; in the forthcoming volumes, the space dedicated to it was minimal and extremely critical.

The Fate of Anthroposociology

It is not my intention to produce an exhaustive survey of all the reactions to anthroposociology. I have only chosen a few representative items. Generally speaking, the ranges of opinions oscillate from cautious reservation to all-out condemnation. If we except a few recognized followers like Muffang and Closson, most sociologists, anthropologists and social philosophers were weary of the craniological and racial determinism of the new school, but they were also baffled by the pretended scientificity of the mountain of statistics thrown at them. Until the contradictions arising from the data were uncovered, anthroposociology enjoyed a certain appeal.

One of the first long book reviews of Lapouge's *Les selections sociales* was published in the prestigious *Revue scientifique*. The author, the philosopher F. Paulhan (1896: 13), found the text:

> An interesting book, with a real value . . . The theories of the author are bold and strongly presented, and their consequences have a great impact. In spite the reserves and restrictions of the book, it is important for anybody who is interested in scientific sociology.

After this introduction, Paulhan provides the reader with a long summary of Lapouge's main ideas. Special emphasis is placed on the concept of social selection and its deleterious effects on modern European society. Paulhan was also interested in the applied side of Lapouge's ideas, in particular the eugenic possibilities, which were rather limited. Undoubtedly, a book of such a revolutionary scope was bound to elicit numerous objections, particularly among the sentimental *bien-pensants*. In any case, Lapouge's theses were not proven, but rather speculative. Nonetheless, we are in the presence of a precious book, 'fertile in audacious ideas, in interesting verifications, in fruitful suggestions and in free and long-range perspectives' (Paulhan 1896: 18).

Among Durkheim's best-known contemporaries, it was perhaps the philosopher and social scientist Alfred Fouillée who devoted the greatest attention to anthroposociology. The 'Introduction' to his *Psychologie du peuple français* (1898a) is largely a presentation and discussion of the anthroposociological theses. This led Otto Ammon to consider Fouillée 'among the partisans of the anthroposociological theory which have converted race in the most important factor of history, have attributed a great importance to the dolichoides and have lamented the universal rise of the brachicephalics' (Ammon 1898: 168–9). This conclusion was rather far-fetched; what happened, insisted Fouillée, was that 'Ammon has taken for a formal adhesion the existence of a number of passages where I only present such a theory' (Fouillée 1898b: 369).

Fouillée was, in fact, dubious about both the principles and the conclusions of anthroposociology, while admitting that the data were interesting, though inconclusive. Any attempt at creating a philosophy of history on the basis of the statistics collected by anthroposociology was bound to fail. In conclusion, Fouillée insisted that 'without taking into account certain physical characteristics from the point of view of anthropology and of the distinction between the different human varieties, it is impossible to recognise the psychic, moral and social importance that the anthroposociologists attribute to it' (Fouillée 1898b: 371).

The same *Revue International de Sociologie* that published Ammon and Fouillée had the previous year (1897) published a short review of Lapouge's *Les sélections sociales*. The editor, Renée Worms, after a brief summary of the book asked himself: *'Que veut cette théorie?'* His answer was rather positive, while acknowledging that many specialists rejected its anthropological basis. In short, a book 'full of interest, which is also full of fertile suggestions. Practically all pages present interesting facts and original ideas' (Worms 1897: 330).

A very different, much more politically inspired article was that of Bouglé (1897). Reviewing works by Ammon, Lapouge and Closson, the crucial question that Bouglé believed lay at the core of the anthroposociological quest was 'the idea of the inequality of the human race' (Bouglé 1897: 448). This doctrine tried to provide an 'biological explanation of the expansion of the egalitarian ideas' (Bouglé 1987: 448), that is, of the triumph of democracy. What was at stake for Bouglé was not so much the accuracy of the theories, which he nonetheless disputed, but rather ethical issues. Hence his conclusion:

> If it is true that declaring that humans are equal we carry a judgement not over the way that nature created them, but on the way in which society must treat them, the most precise craneometries can neither gives us wrongness nor reason. Believing that it is up to scientific observations to judge in the last resort the value of this practical idea, anthropology forgets that social questions are not only factual questions, but also and especially questions of principle. (Bouglé 1987: 461)

A more favourable, though not uncritical review article was Mazel's (1899). Vacher de Lapouge was saluted as a 'rigorous scholar, armed with statistics and data, cephalic indices and anthropometric measurements' (Mazel 1899: 666). For Mazel, Lapouge's description of the ways in which social selections operate in society to thwart natural selection were perfectly reasonable. The book should be compulsory reading for social scientists, 'because, on the one hand, they will profit from a vast number of excellent suggestions and, on the other hand, if they deserve to be called sociologists, they will be protected from the standard idea of anthroposociology' (Mazel 1899: 672). In conclusion, anthroposociology cannot stand up to the sociological ideal. The existence of inequalities in society cannot be justified on biological grounds. None the less, Mazel believed that the ideas of Ammon and Lapouge were useful to 'guarantee against the obvious exaggerations of the egalitarian spirit' (Mazel 1899: 675).

The extremely negative tone of Manouvrier's long review of anthroposociology (1999) made quite an impact in the scientific opinion of the time. He insisted that Ammon's and Lapouge's obsession for the cephalic index was surprising in the extreme. By fetishizing it, they left unconsidered other, perhaps more relevant, anthropological data. Had they taken them into account, they would not find themselves in the odd position of having to explain why the city attracted dark-eyed, dark-complexioned individuals and why they survived better than the blondes. In addition, the putative correlation between head form and psychological features was not demonstrated.

Except for his *Race et milieu social* (1909), that is a collection of his papers, Lapouge's contributions to anthroposociology in the 1900s were published in German in the *Politisch-Anthropologisch Revue*, edited by Ludwig Woltmann. The

French journals, Lapouge often complained, had lost interest in the new discipline. Perhaps the final, most devastating review of anthroposociology came from Belgium (Houzé 1906). For Houzé, anthroposociology should be rejected because, as Manouvrier had noted, it is a pseudo-science that cannot account for the complex phenomena of society. The Aryan hypothesis, for example, fails to distinguish between linguistic and ethnic facts: there may be an Indo-European language, but there is no Indo-European ethnic group. In his detailed study Houzé showed that intelligence did not depend on the brain alone but also on other organs. Furthermore, at birth the brain was a virgin organ, which only developed with education. Only basic 'aptitudes' were transmitted. Houzé also rejected the idea of social selection defended by Lapouge (following Broca and Galton), that is, the conviction that natural selection ceased the moment the human brain developed.

Houzé was, on the whole, very critical of the scientific pretensions of anthroposociology, and he went to great lengths to dismantle its intellectual pretensions. He insisted on the spurious character of the distinction between dolichocephalics and brachycephalics; in fact, the population was so mixed that the classification made no sense at all, even without bringing in *Homo Mediterrraneus* to complicate things. As to Lapouge's laws, the least that could be said was that they were contradicted by facts everywhere. Houzé concluded that Lapouge suffered from delusions of grandeur when he asserted that his school was appreciated worldwide.

It would be wrong, however, to conclude that the social scientific establishment rejected anthroposociology tout court; or to be more specific, that race had ceased to be an explanatory variable. If we take, for example, the attitude of the leading American anthropologist of the period, Franz Boas, it is clear that he was critical but circumspect concerning the explanatory power of race. The main point to be emphasised here is that his thought on racial matters evolved slowly over a long period of time from a position in the 1890s in which he believed that mental differences between races were not negligible, to a total rejection of racial formalism in the 1930s. By 1911, when the first edition of *The Mind of Primitive Man* was published, Boas was still struggling to accommodate the role of the racial variable in the anthropological scheme of things (Stocking 1968, 1974).

How did anthroposociology fare in the histories of sociology of the first quarter of the twentieth century? It is interesting that as late as 1915, in the context of writing a short but panoramic article on French sociology, Durkheim referred very briefly to anthroposociology, although this school did not have an 'influence déterminable' (Durkheim 1975, I: 116). Vacher de Lapouge's theses are depicted as '*très aventureuses*' and in need of being '*plus solidement établies*'. Of course, Durkheim did not fail to mention that anthroposociology had the pretension of '*résorber la sociologie dans l'anthropologie*' (Durkheim 1975, I: 116)).

It is perhaps appropriate to conclude this brief survey of the impact of anthroposociology on the social sciences by considering Pitirim Sorokin's *Contemporary*

Sociological Theories, which was published in 1928. He certainly gave a prominent place to anthroposociology in his text. In a book of nearly 800 pages, he dedicated 100 pages to the different authors who fell under the label 'Anthroporacial, Selectionist and Hereditarist School'. His general opinion of the school is that 'it has been one of the most important and valuable schools in sociology, in spite of its one-sidedness, fallacies and exaggerations' (Sorokin 1928: 308). As to the work of Lapouge, he believed it to be 'stamped with originality, independence and erudition' (Sorokin 1928: 234). After providing a detailed exposition of the work of Gobineau, Chamberlain, Lapouge, Ammon, Galton, Pearson and others, Sorokin proceeded to a careful but balanced criticism of the school. He rejected as not proven a number of hypotheses, such as the polygenetic origins of mankind and the superiority of the Aryan race. Many of the so-called Lapouge-Ammon laws also came under heavy criticism, mostly on the basis that both historical and anthropometric data were rather contradictory. Sorokin insisted, however, that the school had proved a number of principles, particularly the existence of 'innate differences between races, social classes and individuals' (Sorokin 1928: 279), the idea that the differences are due to environmental and hereditary factors, and the theory of social selection (in a modified form, with positive effects).

In 1948, when H. E. Barnes edited a 1000-page volume entitled *An Introduction to the History of Sociology*, there were four chapters devoted to French sociology, focusing on Fouillée, Tarde, Le Bon and Durkheim. Neither anthroposociology nor Lapouge were mentioned. Ammon was briefly referred to as a Darwinist who 'made an honest effort to work out a theory of social evolution in terms of the principles of heredity, selection, variation, the struggle for existence and the survival of the fittest' (Barnes 1948: 211). More recent general histories have at best totally ignored anthroposociology or at worst produced one liners that make Lapouge the object of an infantile but politically correct derision.

Conclusion

It is difficult to assess the real impact that Lapouge's work had on the ideological foundations of Nazi Germany (Hecht 2000). There is little doubt that anthroposociology made an impression in German as well as Nordic and Anglo-Saxon circles. As Sternell (1978) has noted, anthroposociology is one of the many components that found a place in the making of the Nazi ideological brew. An obvious impact, or at least convergence, exists between Vacher de Lapouge and Ludwig Woltmann – an author to whom will refer in the 'conclusion' of the book. Suffice it to say that Vacher de Lapouge and Woltmann were in favour of what they called 'aristocratic socialism'. They also defended a selectionist and Aryanist socialism that involved the creation of a new morality. They envisaged Christianity as a dysgenic religion and put forward a vitalist and cosmic religion inspired by Darwinian-Galtonian presuppositions.

Vacher did not always agree with the use that was made of his ideas in Germany. For example he criticized Houston Stewart Chamberlain's utilisation of anthroposociology to justify German expansionism. Nor did he have much sympathy for German Romantic nationalism. Although in the social scientific circles anthroposociology was practically dead by the beginning of the twentieth century and Vacher became an entomologist, he still kept defending his pessimistic views about humanity; in particular, the social evils brought about by racial hybridity and dysgenic practices like World War I. American eugenicists and Aryanists like Charles Davenport and Madison Grant acknowledged the role of Vacher.

During the late 1920s, and until his death in 1936, Lapouge was in contact with a number of German authors, and in particular with the Volkish theorist Hans Günther who acknowledged his intellectual affiliation with the founder of anthroposociology. Vacher contributed a number of articles on race and eugenics to Günther's journal *Die Sonne* (The Sun). During the war years Vacher de Lapouge became the *maitre à penser* of the official Vichian anthropology. In Germany, Alfred Rosenberg, *Reichsleiter* and author of the Nazi Bible, *The Myth of the Twentieth Century*, highlighted the importance of both Gobineau and Vacher de Lapouge in the making of modern racial theories.

–9–

The Idea of Revolutionary Violence:
The Legacy of Sorel

Introduction

Georges Sorel is a rather enigmatic and much maligned figure; an engineer by profession, he was a jack of all ideological trades. In his lifelong ideological meandering, he moved from Catholicism to Marxism, from Marxism to syndicalism, from syndicalism to nationalism, from nationalism to proto-fascism and from the latter to Leninism (Curtis 1959; Roth 1980; Kolakowski 1981; Stanley 1981; Juillard and Sand; Charzat 1986; Jennings 1985; Ohana 1986; Steven 1990; Guchet 2001). Underneath this incessant change lied a constant search for the new ethical principles that could change the morally corrupt and declining bourgeois society in which he was forced to live. His *Reflections on Violence* (1906) correspond to the syndicalist period. Mussolini very openly and Lenin more discretely were admirers of the work of Sorel. The German sociologist Karl Manheim saw him as a scientific precursor of the kind of *Weltanschäuung* that generated fascism. For its part, Hannah Arendt asserted that Sorel was somebody who glorified violence as a way of overthrowing bourgeois society.

Although Sorel has often been presented as a Marxist (at least a *sui generis* Marxist), there are many differences between Marxism and Sorelism. One that is particularly relevant to our endeavours is the role of religion and morality. While Marx and Engels tended to see these concepts in epiphenomenal terms, Sorel believed that they had to be treated as important categories of social life. What is at stake here is that Sorel asserts the centrality of human will; the idea that it is conscious human action that changes society. His socialism is hence much more volontaristic than that of Marx.

It was in the context of labouring on the issue of working-class consciousness that Sorel developed the idea of revolutionary images as myths. Myths, which were to be carefully distinguished from utopias (or intellectual constructions), were conceived as 'the expressions of a will to act on reality so as to change it' (Portis 1980: 57). For the proletariat the myth of modern times was the general strike. And the vision or a goal towards which the proletariat was working was the revolution. In a nutshell, Sorel described the general strike as 'the myth within which all of socialism is contained; that is, it involves a complex of images capable of naturally evoking all the feelings which are raised in the struggle of the socialist movement against contemporary society' (Portis 1980: 46).

When assessing the validity of myths, Sorel believed that they were only effective if they encouraged morality, action and creativity. Myths are conveyed by means of symbols that appeal to the imagination and emotions. For Sorel, symbols are the objectification of a myth, that is, a word or a thing representing something else. Symbols are forms of expressing a mythical content. The only symbols that Sorel discusses are the spoken words; in his work there is no reference to signs, emblems, posters, etc. Speech is essential for the man of action because it is evocative, inspiring and stirs up emotions. In *Reflections on Violence*, Sorel mentions as examples of valid myths the following historical examples: Homeric myths and heroism, Christianity's Second Coming and moral progress, the French Revolution and the will to victory and, in modern times, the proletariat's myth of the general strike (Gross 1982: 108).

Marx and Engels on Violence

Was Sorel a Marxist? What was the impact of Marx and Engels on Sorel's idea of violence? At the end of the *Communist Manifesto* Marx and Engels wrote: 'The communists openly declare that their ends can be attained only by the forcible overthrow of all existing conditions'. Two conclusions seem to follow from this statement:

1 That the existing social and political system is to be changed by a revolution.
2 That a social revolution is to be identified with an overthrow of that existing social system.

Other texts could be presented to justify the stance that Marx and Engels believed that the state machine could only be smashed by revolutionary means, which by definition have to be violent. It is possible however, to find many texts in which they referred to a peaceful revolution, that is, one attained by a class struggle without violence. In other words, Marx and Engels distinguished the concept of social revolution from the paths it may take (violent or peaceful) depending upon the presence of democratic political possibilities (Schaff 1973; Hook 1973).

A distinction should be made social revolution in the broadest and in the narrower sense. In the broader sense, social revolution means just a change in the social formation – a change in the infrastructure and in the superstructure; that is, a total change, a substantial change. Here we are referring to a radical change, irrespective of whether it is peaceful or violent. In the narrower sense, social revolution is connected with rapid, violent change, which is a peaceful development brought about by an accumulation of quantitative changes. Class struggle is perfectly compatible with evolutionary change.

Marx and Engels were influenced by the French Revolution and the revolutionary struggles of the nineteenth century (specially the Commune). Marx saw the need for armed revolution, of opposing revolutionary force to reactionary force; in other words, seeing violence as the culmination of the class struggle. He was not afraid of the prospects of an armed struggle for power, and he did not shun it. However, he did not glorify violence for the sake of violence, and he never said that violence was the only path to proletarian victory. Furthermore, he emphasized that a peaceful transition was possible and even desirable.

Both Marx and Engels saw different possibilities of peaceful transition to socialism; for example, they saw the United States as a possible case. In a letter to Kugelmann, in 1871, Marx asserted that due to the weakness of the military and bureaucratic structure of the United States a non-violent transition was possible there, while this was much more unlikely in continental Europe where the state machinery was all too powerful and had to be destroyed prior to a socialist era.

Equally, England was a Marx and Engels candidate for a peaceful revolution. In the *Preface* to the English edition of *Capital* (1886), three years after Marx's own death, Engels wrote that Marx was convinced that the English transition to socialism might take place exclusively by peaceful and legal means, but he urged the neutralization of the ruling classes, who would hardly submit without a fight. As early as 1871, after the French Commune, Marx suggested that the working classes of England could obtain their objectives by means other than rebellion.

Marx's attitude was pragmatic. Wherever a peaceful overthrow of the old order was possible, peaceful means should be used, but wherever the machinery of the state was well entrenched and aggressive other means would have to be used, including armed struggle. After the Hague Congress of the International in 1872, Marx insisted on the workers taking over the political apparatus in order to build a new labour organization. However, he carefully emphasized the need to device specific strategies for specific situations. This would depend on the institutions, manners and traditions of various countries. At this stage he indicated that the workers of in the US, England and perhaps Holland could achieve their objectives by peaceful means.

One factor that enhanced the chances of a peaceful transition was the existence of a parliamentary system, and that is why Engels in 1891 admitted that in addition to England and the US, France could also have a peaceful road to socialism. An issue worth raising is that of whether adopting of a peaceful strategy for transition to socialism necessarily means the adoption of a reformist standpoint that, by nature, would betray the goal of the social revolution. Here the crux of the matter is whether social reforms are the sole objective of the programme or not. If they are, then this seems to go against the Marxist perspective of overthrowing of the old social order.

The Second International, led by Eduard Bernstein, discarded the notion of social revolution and settled down for gradual reforms. He stated that the final goal meant nothing; that the important thing was the movement towards the goal. This may explain the attitude of Sorel against reformism and may help to account for his theory of violence. The attitude of Lenin and Stalin concerning violence was unclear. On the whole, they discovered Marx's conviction that socialism could be arrived at peacefully in the advanced countries of the West. However, Lenin and Stalin were in favour of an organization of illegal cadres and the rule of armed insurrection even for England and the US. There was a shift also from Marx to Lenin in that the former was concerned with democracy and the latter with power (dictatorship of the proletariat) (Cohen-Almagor 1993). And this is the context in which Georges Sorel appeared within the socialist movement.

The Intellectual Milieu of Sorel and his Concept of Social Myth

Sorel is much more open than Durkheim in admitting intellectual influences in his work. The idea of myth as an instinctive unconscious process is central to Sorel's work, and in particular to his *Reflections on Violence*. The sources of this concept can be traced back to a variety of authors: Vico's *ricorsi*, Bergson's *élan vital*, Le Bon's crowd psychology, Tarde's imitation, and so on. As we have seen in Chapter 7, all attempts to pin down Durkheim's concept of effervescence to the influence of Le Bon, and generally of so-called crowd psychology, have been spurned. As to Bergsonian influences, the issue has been hardly touched upon. Last but not least, one could raise the issue of Sorel's possible influence on Durkheim. However, my aim in the next section is more modest: to detect parallelisms between Sorel and Durkheim and to explore their common intellectual sources.

Sorel became interested in Marx at the same time that he became interested in Vico, and it would be fair to say that Sorel looked at Marx through Vichian eyes. Sorel long study on Vico was published in the socialist journal *Le Devenir Social* in 1896. At a general level, Sorel emphasizes two key Vichian ideas: 'History has to be understood as the history of human ideas and history has to be seen as the history of human creation (hence the centrality of ethics)' (Jennings 1983: 330). As a result of Vico's influence, Sorel tended to envisage Marx's law of the collapse of capitalism in metaphysical terms, that is, as social poetry, as social myth. Although Sorel's idea of myth stems from a long tradition (which most probably includes Durkheim), his most immediate and relevant source is Vico. For Vico myth is a 'source of non-rational human motivation' (Jennings 1985: 122).

This myth as a form of consciousness is typical of the primitive beginnings, that is, what Vico calls ideal history. According to Vico, in the rudimentary forms of society, that is, among savages and barbarians, there is no solution of continuity between the past (a domain in which affectivity dominates) and the future (a domain in which activity dominates). 'Myth, which is a fragment of human history transfigured by primitive thought, transforms itself naturally into a *réprésentation* of the future, that is, into a mobilising image' (Juillard 1990: VII). What Sorel borrowed from Vico was a description of the 'psychological evolution of the human intellect and, in particular, from the idea that at the beginning of this evolution man thought instinctively and practically, not rationally' (Jennings 1985: 122).

Jennings remarks that, at this early stage in Sorel's intellectual evolution, there is no influence of Bergson, but that by the time Sorel came to write *Reflections on Violence* (1906) Bergsonian notions were superimposed on Sorel's Vichian concept of myth. Another important influence of Vico on Sorel was the reassessment of the role of religious beliefs in society. As a consequence of it, Sorel came to accept the social legitimacy of religion. It no longer made sense to him whether religion was true or false; the important matter was that religious beliefs were the result of deep-seated convictions (Jennings 1983: 335). Vico's famous cyclical theory of decline and rebirth (*ricorsi*) could provide an adequate explanation for the continued existence of Christianity. However, what mattered most to Sorel were the characteristics of early Christianity – a period in which religion was quasi-instinctive because the early Christians thought in terms of myths (austerity, heroism, revolt, and so forth). As Jennings remarked 'all qualities ascribed to early Christianity were subsequently attributed by Sorel to the merging syndicalist movement' (Jennings 1983: 337).

To sum up. Sorel is critical of Marx's conviction that 'religion must disappear in the face of science . . . Religion always find elements of rejuvenation in the mystical' (Jennings 1983: 336). At a wider level, it is obvious that what Sorel rejects in Marx, and specially in his followers, is economic determinism. To explain ideas and sentiments one must refer to the psychological evolution of society; to how the ideas of duty, conscience and reason evolve. As a revolutionary syndicalist, Sorel will say with Vico that a *ricorso* can only take place 'when the popular soul returns to a primitive state, when everything is instinctive, creative, poetic' (Sorel 1905: 273). In this context, it is possible to say that strikes engender sentiments of fraternity, of union, of heroism; they represent the victory of the instinctive over bourgeois intellectualism (Jennings 1983: 340).

I have mentioned in passing that by the time Sorel came to write *Reflections on Violence* the influence of Bergson was quite visible. Neither Sorel nor Bergson made a secret out of that, and although Bergson never endorsed Sorel's politics he admitted that Sorel was a good interpreter of his work, and that he also admired him intellectually. As Horowitz has put it: 'Both were responding to a cultural milieu, and both did a great deal to shape the specifics of this milieu while drawing sustenance from each other' (Horowitz 1961: 43).

Bergson' *Essai sur les donnés immédiates de la conscience* (1889) (*Time and Free Will*) was an important influence on a Sorel who was concerned with mobilizing the working class. The point was how to convince men to change the world. In the myth of the general strike he found a source of energy which would maintain the tension against the established, bourgeois order, and in the final resort would contribute to its downfall. In 1907 Bergson published *L'évolution créatrice* (*Creative Evolution*) in which he 'postulated the existence of an all-pervading *élan vital* (vital impulse) that carries life, by more and more complex forms, to higher and higher destinies' (Jennings 1983: 139). Sorel applied Bergson's ideas to human activity, to the purposes of groups. Sorel saw the Bergsonian concept of intuition as relevant to the description of the modern socialist movement, although he rejected Bergson's attempts to use biology to explain social facts. On the other hand, Sorel saw sympathetically the Bergsonian idea of religious (or rather spiritual) renaissance, and his rejection of rationalism and scientism.

For Sorel, following Bergson, 'both religion and revolutionary myths occupy the profounder region of our mental life' (Nye 1973: 428). Sorel envisaged the 'apotheosis of the general strike as a moral purification of the world, as an end in itself; this typifies his chialistic (millenarian) attitude' (Sonn 1989: 271). It would be inappropriate, however, to extract the wrong conclusions from these statements; in spite of the analogies between religion and socialism (and particularly of the symbolic force of both Christianity and religion), Sorel suggests that each has unique psychological characteristics (Sorel 1990: 84–5).

Perhaps it would be useful to illustrate Sorel's subtle position concerning the comparison between religion and socialism. Pareto said that Sorel was a believer, at least for a while, in the divinity of the proletariat. Sorel had observed that both early Christianity and the French Revolution had

> derived their dynamic force from myths that aroused in their adherents a self-sacrificing enthusiasm capable of transcending the ordinary difficulties standing in the way of cooperation among individuals, so Sorel thought that the myth of the general strike might offer the proletariat a similar basis for a common inspiration and purpose arising from needs already manifested among the workers themselves. By giving to these needs an epic character, Sorel believed that the syndicalist myth with its militant conception of a violent class war might very well engender qualities of personal responsibility and personal significance. (Humphrey 1951: 209)

As I said above, for Sorel it may not be valid to trace socialism and religion back to the same psychological forces, but the evolution of both movements produces similar effects in society, and hence makes the comparison interesting.

Celestin Bouglé, a member of the Durkheimian School, coined the term 'Bergsonian syndicalism' to refer to the impact of Bergson's doctrines on Sorel and his colleagues during the first decade of this century. Paramount among Bergson's ideas in this context is his rejection of intellectualism. In the able hands of the Bergsonian syndicalists the concept of *élan vital* transforms itself into the concept of *élan ouvrier*. As pragmatists of sorts, they give primacy to action. It is interesting to mention in passing, that the 'Jamesian impact came at a late stage in Sorel's life' (Horowitz 1961: 43). His book *L'utilité du pragmatisme* (1921) can be seen as 'a statement of staunch support for James at the expense of Bergson' (Horowitz 1961: 43). According to Bouglé it is plain that Sorel preaches the separation of the working class from the rest of society as a means to enhance class authenticity; only in this way can the working class give rise to a new morality. As we know, myth is the precondition for the existence of action; but a myth is 'not a description of things but an expression of will'. Bouglé, of course, points out that Sorel never asks the question of how society will be reorganized; only the creation of heroism matters (Bouglé 1909: 412).

The Bergsonian element is also present in Sorel's call to the synthesis of dynamic images. As he put it: 'strikes have created in the proletariat the most noble and dynamic sentiments. The general strike has a unifying effect and increases the intensity of the group; it also rememorates the most telling images. What is obtained is an instantaneous intuition of socialism that language could not offer in a clear way. This is the equivalent of the perfect knowledge of Bergsonian philosophy' (Bouglé 1909: 413). Bouglé concludes that the weakness of Sorel's perspective is that a society is not a factory and that the new society cannot be constituted by an assemblage of factories. In a critique to one of Sorel's colleagues – Lagardelle – Durkheim had insisted that classes cannot be cut off from the national milieu. What is missing, then, in Sorel is a proper sociological perspective. However, one of the merits of the Bergsonian syndicalists is that they have emphasized the importance of morality, purity and freedom, and these are essential characteristics in any socialist movement (Bouglé 1909: 415).

In addition to Vico and Bergson, Sorel also took an early interest in Le Bon, which he kept for the rest of his life. A correspondence between the two authors took place over approximately twenty years (Charzat 1986). In spite of the ideological differences (Le Bon was always opposed to socialism) they both appreciated each other's work; in 1901 Le Bon's considered Sorel as the 'most erudite of French socialists', while Sorel referred to Le Bon, in 1911, as 'the greatest psychologist that we have in France' (Sand 1986: 166–7). In 1895 Sorel reviewed Le Bon's *Psychologie des foules* (1895) for *Le devenir social*. Although Sorel found in the book interesting information and ingenious remarks, the review is rather short and critical of crowd psychology, and in particular of Le Bon's equating crowds to nations, sects, social classes, and so forth. Furthermore, Sorel doubted the degree of scientificity that could be attached to categories such as suggestion, contagion, and so on, which constituted Le Bon's main explanatory conceptual arsenal (Sand 1986: 167–8). A few years later, in a review of Le Bon's *La psychologie du socialisme* (1898), Sorel (1899) agreed that socialism was essentially a mental state, and that a parallelism could be established between the history of socialism and the history of Christianity. Le Bon insisted in 'the notion of socialism as a religious phenomenon, appealing to the affective, dreamlike and chimerical qualities of human nature' (Nye 1973: 427).

By the time Sorel was writing *Reflections on Violence*, that is, 1905–6, his attitude towards Le Bon was much more positive, even concerning Le Bon's idea of the spontaneity of the masses. Although it is perhaps still true that his idea of myth owes more to Vico and Bergson than to Le Bon, it is plain that Le Bon's *idées images* inspired Sorel's definition of the myth as 'an organisation of images capable of evoking instinctively all sentiments that correspond to the different manifestations of the war of socialism against modern society' (Sand 1986: 171). Furthermore, Le Bon insisted in the idea that images have to be taken as a whole, that is, they cannot be broken into their component parts; a point that Sorel shared concerning myths. As he put it: 'It is myth in its entirety which is alone important' (Sorel 1999: 117).

It could be said that there still is quite a conceptual gap between Le Bon and Sorel; after all, if Le Bon's main focus is the crowd, Sorel's main interest is class confrontation. Although both collective groups are characterised by irrational states of conscience, classes and crowds are very different; in the former members preserve their individuality, while in the latter they are dissolved in the mass. Certain psychological mechanisms of crowd behaviour (hatred, revenge and jealousy), are not appropriate to characterize classes which are meant to exhibit class consciousness (Sand 1986: 171–2). On the other hand, after 1908 Sorel seems to agree with Croce that socialism is dead. There follows the so-called nationalist period of Sorel in which he sustains that the only reservoirs of moral force are the nation and tradition.

We can now bring together the different strands that converge in Sorel's *Reflections on Violence*. Sorel is interested in the nature of symbolic images and their effect on political action. His main contribution to this field is to have pointed out that human behaviour is far from being rational; that a number of spontaneous and emotive elements are part and parcel of political motivation. If we focus on his idea of myth he defines it 'as an emotionally charged artificial construct, which though perhaps inaccurate or absurd, reaches people at a deeply conscious level and inspires them to action' (Gross 1982: 104). This author, in a remarkable article, provides us with a number of key points concerning Sorel's treatment of myth (Gross 1982: 104–5):

First, 'myths cannot be cognitively understood, because they operate in some pre-reflexive area of the mind where intuitions and beliefs are also stimulated'.

Second, 'myths are frequently objectifications of the convictions of a group, that is, an expression, in the form of images, of the goals and aspirations of an entire collectivity'.

Third, 'myths are too amorphous and volatile to be subjected to scientific study'.

Fourth, 'myths are neither true nor false, nor can they be separated in its component parts. Only the consequences of a myth can reveal its validity'.

Fifth, 'myths, as action-images, cannot be refuted; the power of a myth (or a belief) rests on faith, which is not open to rational analysis'.

Sixth, 'it is because they are undemonstrable that myths have such a powerful appeal for the masses. People want and need to believe: myths seize the imagination with great force and provoke emotions and qualities of sacrifice and struggle which allow for heroic deeds'.

Seventh, 'myths tap a vital part of the psyche which would be otherwise inactivated'.

Eighth, 'myths are not lies, propaganda or ideology in the modern sense of these words. They are not cynically manufactured either. Myths are already present, in a latent form, within the mass itself. They are already anchored in the collective unconscious' (Jung).

Durkheim and Sorel

In the context of this chapter it is perhaps appropriate to mention to the reader that fate has handed me down a crooked deal in the form of an historical play in which the two main characters refuse to talk to each other. Because a play consisting mainly of monologues and asides could be extremely boring, I have decided to spice it up with what I believe are plausible dialogues.

The first, and foremost, personage of our drama is, of course, Emile Durkheim or rather, more specifically, the Durkheim of the *Les formes élémentaires de la vie religieuse* (EFRL). Now, I see the EFRL as a book for all seasons. This is well justified because, after all, Durkheim's most important objective in the book was: 'Comprendre la nature religieuse de l'homme, c'est à dire à révéler un aspect essentiel et permanent de l'humanité' (Durkheim 1960: 2) ('clarifying the religious nature of man, that is to say, of revealing an essential and permanent aspect of humanity', Durkheim 1975: 102).

If what really concerns Durkheim is modern man, then, the text, dealing with the most primitive religion of mankind, is crying out loud to be applied to modern times. This is far from being a revolutionary innovation in the reading of the EFRL; indeed, much of the inspiration for my endeavour stems from Jeffrey Alexander's (1988) collection and, generally speaking, from Norbert Bellah's studies on civil religion (Bellah 1970). In the conclusion to the EFRL Durkheim remarks that all societies, if they want to survive, must maintain their unity and specific characteristics, and that the way to do that is by periodical gatherings in which individuals come together and through ceremonies and rituals strongly reassert their common sentiments. It is irrelevant whether the assembly celebrates a strictly religious belief or an important event in the life of the nation (Durkheim 1960: 610). This statement, we might say, tells us how societies keep together, how social order and solidarity is maintained.

The problem with *le lieu et le moment*, which constituted Durkheim's social milieu was that, in his view and that of many of his contemporaries, it lacked moral fibre; it was a period of malaise and mediocrity. Durkheim, however, was confident that *'un jour viendra où nos sociétés connaîtront à nouveau des heures d'effervescence créatrice . . . au cours desquelles de nouveaux idéaux surgiront, pendant un temp qui serviront de guide a l'humanité'* (Durkheim 1960: 611) ('the day will come when our societies will know once again hours of creative effervescence in which new ideals will be born and new formulae will emerge which will for a time serve as a guide to humanity', Durkheim 1975: 157)

This statement provides a framework for the explanation of how societies change. At this point it is perhaps appropriate to introduce the second personage of my historical play, and this is no other than the enigmatic and much-maligned figure of Georges Sorel. My main purpose in this paper is to elicit the common ground between Durkheim's EFRL and Sorel's *Reflections on Violence*. This may seem a rather tall order or a chimerical enterprise because no two texts could apparently be more dissimilar than Sorel's *Réflexions sur la violence* (1906/1908) and Durkheim's *Les formes élémentaire de la vie religieuse* (1912). Sorel's book unashamedly presents itself, as we have seen, as a political tract aimed at creating a new proletarian morality centred on the idea of revolutionary violence; the avowed objective of the text is to annihilate the mediocre and decadent bourgeois society that surrounds him, and in the same motion create a rejuvenated, socialist society. Durkheim's book, it is well known, focuses essentially on the religion of the most primitive of societies – the Australian Aborigines.

What I maintain in this chapter is that, if there is a common guiding thread through *Reflections* and the *Elementary Forms* or, even more generally, between the political projects of Sorel and Durkheim is their moral concern. In fact, what characterizes and gives unity to the work of both men is the search for a new morality. This is a point that, in the case of Durkheim needs no belabouring; as to Sorel, his life-long ideological meandering, as we have indicated, hide, among other things, a constant search for new ethical principles that can change the morally corrupt and declining bourgeois society in which he was forced to live.

Hans Joas (1993: 23) has remarked that there exist affinities between Sorel and Durkheim, but they can only be found if one places both authors in the proper intellectual scene of turn of the century France. And this means, among other things, to be prepared to accept that Sorel and Durkheim drew at times from the same philosophical sources. Peter Nijhoff (1985: 263–4) has suggested that there are convergences and divergences between the works of Sorel and Durkheim. According to him it is possible to present these relationships in four major stages:

1   *1894–5*. There is an attempt by both authors to reject a morality based on an individualist philosophy and to reconstruct morality on the basis of social life. It is what Durkheim calls to treat the facts of moral life from a scientific perspective, while Sorel also emphasizes the fact that ethical ideas have social origins. There is, however, a difference in method. Durkheim favours a rational reconstruction on the basis of technical progress. As he put it: 'Not only does the division of labour exhibit that character by which we define morality, but it increasingly tends to become the essential condition for social solidarity' (Durkheim 1984: 332). Under the joint influence of W. James and H. Bergson it is possible to observe that Sorel takes a line based on what could be called 'pragmatic activism'.

2   *1895–1900*. Both Durkheim and Sorel express a concern for the 'moral malaise' which is typical of the *fin de siècle*. It is not just a matter of highlighting the moral problem of modernity, which for many thinkers is a chronic problem. There is an urgency about this moral malaise. Implicit in that attitude is a critique of all kind of mechanical and deterministic conceptions of human ideas. What we see in both authors is that they accord a 'growing significance to the relative autonomy of mental constructions' (Nijhoff 1985: 263). In *Suicide*, Durkheim refers to the fact that social life consists of representations; Sorel refers also to representations, that is, collective moral sentiments. Socialist ethics is the result of the progressive organization of the socialist movement. Later on the key word for Sorel will be 'myth'.

3   *1900–8*. This stage could be superficially described as one of antagonism between Durkhein and Sorel. It is a period in which sociology is institutionalized by Durkheim; the discipline also becomes more politicized. There follows a more unitary and doctrinaire conception of sociology. Sorel denounces sociologists as 'professionals of a secular cult'. He rejects the idea of a sociological school (and

the Durkheimian School in particular), and favours a more diverse and independent approach. However, during this period there is a progressive spiritualization of the social question in Durkheim. He places successively his hopes in industrial development, the development of professional corporations and education. As to Sorel, his faith in revolutionary syndicalism is no obstacle for a commitment to the role of ideas and emotions as motors of history.

4   *1908–14*. In this period Durkheim pursues his evolutionary tendency towards giving prominent attention to the social function of religion. This culminates in the publication of EFRS in 1912. Sorel, for his part, discovers new reasons for thinking that certitude emanates from both religious experience and scientific experimentation, but believes that these two activities cannot take place inside the centralized and hierarchical structures of, respectively, the Church and the university. What is required is an asceticism that is only found among those who have withdrawn from the official world.

Conclusion

I think it will be appropriate to conclude this chapter by referring to what Marcel Mauss thought about Sorel and about the relationship between Sorel and Durkheim. Writing in 1925 Mauss showed sympathy for some of the characteristics of the Russian Revolution; in particular, the *soviets* (as professional organizations in which property and political functions were vested) corresponded to the moral, political and economic conclusions that Durkheim had reached in *La division du travail social* and other texts. In a somewhat cavalier fashion, Mauss attributed the affinity between Durkheim's theory and *soviet* praxis to the role of George Sorel, who having borrowed these ideas from Durkheim, then influenced Lenin (Mauss 1925). Quite a far-fetched genealogy!

Ten years later, in 1936, and with the hindsight of fascist regimes in existence, Mauss's attitude towards Bolshevism changed and he tended to see strong affinities between communism and fascism – the latter tyranny deriving from the former. In a letter to Elie Halévy he wrote the following:

> 'The basic doctrine from which all of this is deduced is that of the *minorités agissantes* (active minorities) as it was called in Parisian anarcho-syndicalist circles, and particularly as it was developed by Sorel . . . The same doctrine of the minority, of violence and the same corporativism, have spread in my lifetime from Sorel to Lenin and Mussolini. All three recognise it. Let me add that Sorel's corporatism was halfways between that of Pouget and that of Durkheim, and eventually came for Sorel to correspond to a reactionary view of the past of our societies'. (Mauss *in* Gane 1992: 213)

If anything, this passage puts a lot of weight on the impact of Sorel's doctrines, but with the rather curious and implicit objective of handing a compliment to Durkheim as the originator of the corporativist doctrines. Sorel is obviously the fall man, taking the blame for the emergence of the tyrannies of the twentieth century. Durkheim is left in the background, with his honour intact.

There can never be a convincing answer to the question of the extent to which Durkheim was influenced by Sorel or Le Bon. And the simple reason is that in the EFRL Durkheim does not cite them. So, what is the point of the whole exercise? Essentially, to recover the richness and complexity of the turn-of-the-century social scientific (and in a wider sense intellectual) scene. Both Sorel and Le Bon played an important part in it; if we lose them, our inheritance, our sociological capital (to use Bourdieu's expression) is diminished. And this has also an impact on our contemporary, current sociological endeavours. If in addition to that it can help to clarify or enlighten certain aspects of Durkheim's work, all the better.

–10–

The Origins of Nazi Ideology

Introduction

To suggest that Hitler's philosophy of history was an outlandish and crazy conception of man based on the supremacy of the principles of hierarchy, subordination and inequality, is not accurate (Lukacs 1997; Kershaw 1998, 2000). The point to emphasize is that, from the late nineteenth century, there was a major development of the ideas that characterized the four main thinkers considered in this book (Mosse 1964, 1966, 1978a, 1978b; Burleigh 1996). As I have already mentioned in the preface, it is not my pretension to suggest that Gobineau, Le Bon, Vacher de Lapouge and Sorel are the sole culprits in the making of the *Weltanschauung* of the Nazi Germany. Their influence is important but not exclusive or predominant.

One could always insist that social Darwinism, which must be interpreted as a sort of misapplied Darwinism, is perhaps the key feature of the late nineteenth-century German's way of thinking. Who are the guilty parties in these events? Darwin was open to a great number of interpretations, left and right, democratic and authoritarian, and so forth. It does not make sense, however, to refer to a continuity between Darwin and Hitler! As to the role of Darwin's nephew, Francis Galton, with his invention and development of eugenics, it is perhaps more controversial, but no decidedly one-sided. In any case, the crucial element is the fact that Nazi Germany exhibited a rigid and powerful combination of the *ideés-force* of racism, crowds, eugenics and violence. There is little doubt that these *idées-force* were the most powerful building blocks of Nazi ideology, although perhaps there were also others.

The main purpose of this last chapter is to present a number of German thinkers who, between the 1890s and the 1930s constitute the kind of continuity that accounts for the appearance of Nazi ideology. The intellectual background of these thinkers is varied, but their ideas are connected with the four French thinkers that we have considered in detail. In so far as the last thinker in the series, Alfred Rosenberg, played a key role in shaping Hitler's ideology, the main purpose the intellectual demonstration is achieved. This is not to say, of course, that we are suggesting that Hitler was familiar with the four authors that we have considered, although Gobineau and Le Bon were possibly known to him, albeit superficially and indirectly. On the other hand, by introducing at the beginning of the process the contribution of Houston Stewart Chamberlain, a Germanified Englishman, in whom all the major elements of German racism, social Darwinism and eugenics converged, and who was, partly inspired by Gobineau, extremely influential in offering a solid basis for the building of Nazi ideology. In so far as Gobineau and Chamberlain were the two key inspirers of Nazism, it is interesting to emphasize that they were not German, but French and English, respectively; of course, Darwin was of English extraction.

To start at the beginning of the intellectual process of Nazi ideological form-ation, we must refer to the impact that Ernst Haeckel had on German thought. It is important to remember that a profoundly devalued social Darwinism became the essential component of National Socialism. Darwin's expression 'the survival of the fittest' was transformed into an ideological component that incorporated racial inequality and struggle for existence. This explosive combination encouraged, under Hitler, a policy not only of eliminating the racially inferior people, but selecting also the racially superior ones.

A crucial point to be made about Ernst Haeckel (Stein 1988; Weindling 1989; Zmarzlik 1972) is that be became an extremely popular writer among the Germans. Suffice it to say that his *Die Welträtsel* (*The Riddle of the Universe*) published originally in 1899, had sold half a million copies by 1933. His first influence was on the liberal bourgeoisie, but from the beginning of the twentieth century his main impact was on the semi-literate people, that is, the working class, the *declassé* petty bourgeoisie and the youth of all classes. Both socialists and nationalists were very appealed by the book. What is interesting about *Die Welträtsel* is not the main message, but the package of a number of things: scientism, belief in progress, anticlericalism and anti-Christianity.

Haeckel saw in Darwin's theory the chance to provide a unified theory of physical, biological and psychological phenomena; in practice, this meant a universal, speculative philosophy. Perhaps the most distinctive aspect of his philosophy was the duty of self-preservation and self-assertion according to the natural law of struggle for life. That there are clear differences between the existing human races is a point emphasized by Haeckel following Gobineau's conception. It is obvious that there is an abyss, he would say, between the Hottentots and the Germans. Some important social consequences, in the sense of the life-value assigned to each race, followed from this conception. For Haeckle the future could not be conceived in terms of freedom but in a rather deterministic way, that is, following the laws of nature. The population programme conceived by Haeckel was essentially eugenic in nature: from biological selection at birth to the elimi-nation of the grown-up incurables. Furthermore, pernicious criminals should be eliminated. At another level, the idea of spreading the German *Lebensraum*, or vital space, was essential; the idea of an expansion towards the East was essential. It is obvious that the National Socialist bio-policy, as Michel Foucault (1997) would call it, was well inaugurated by Haeckel, and indeed followed by many others. In this sense, Hitler 'did not invent national socialist bio-policy' (Stein 1988: 51), but took it from the Haeckels and converted it into a down to earth treatise, as *Mein Kampf* should be perceived.

There were, of course, others pretentiously scientific writers who represented also a contribution to the socially Darwinistic National Socialism. If we are referring to Otto Ammon, and particularly Ludwig Woltmann, who were present at the turn of the century, the role of their colleague Vacher de Lapouge, becomes obvious. Otto Ammon, as I have mentioned in Chapter 8 was the joint founder, with Vacher de Lapouge, of anthroposociology. From our present perspective, what is essential to recall is the idea of racial superiority of the Aryans.

The racial theories of Ludwig Woltmannn

From a presentist perspective it is difficult to explain the irresistible appeal that racial theories of history had for a good number of social scientists at the turn of the nineteenth century. Woltmann was certainly not alone in embracing 'race' as a key anthropological concept, but what is somewhat puzzling is that his 'Aryanism' was preceded, in his intellectual biography, by an attempt to reconcile Marx and Darwin in the light of a sort of Kantian categorical imperative. He stated very clearly that his work was, at least in part, the result of seriously considering the ethical implications of Darwinist theory. There is little doubt that these conse-quences appear to bring him closer to what we would call social Darwinism, although Woltmann's original concern was to make possible a synthesis of the cognitive, biological and social motivations of moral life.

The transition from Darwinism to Social Darwinism is not so difficult to explain, and certainly both Darwin and Spencer contributed to such an equation. The impact of Darwinism and Social Darwinism in Western European social-anthropological thought was so pervasive that socialist parties were in no position to resist it. Furthermore, the fact that Marx and Engels had praised Darwin lavishly was an additional factor that explains the appearance of what could be referred as Marxism-Darwinism. Woltmann, as a member of the German Social-Democratic Party and contributor to *Die Neue Zeit*, was certainly not the first to underline the convergences between Darwin and Marx, but in his case Darwin came soon to be viewed through a Nietzschean angle, with all its implications (from the re-evaluation of all values to the idea of superman).

It appears, then, that if the influence of Kant, Marx and Darwin did not disap-pear completely from Woltmann's work, towards the end of his life and particularly in his contributions to the journal that he edited (*Politisch-Anthropologisch Revue*), social Darwinism and Nietzscheanism seem to take over. This would also explain Woltmann's sudden interest in racial hygiene and related issues. It is in the context of this journal that one can observe how Woltmann's conceptions are more and more influenced by the racial literature of the period, and particularly by the work of Gobineau, Galton, Le Bon, Lapouge, Ammon, Chamberlain and others. As a result of this series of influences Woltmann's historical perspective changed. The natural history of human races became the foundation for the theory of the history of the state. There was a sort of move from a Marxian economism to a special kind of idealism in so far as ideas for Woltmann meant basically the organ that produced them – the brain. The power of ideas referred to certain races and individuals that possessed them, and were in a position to spread them – a resonance of the French social scientist Tarde? The task of anthropology was for Woltmann eminently 'political' in that it was meant to enquire how the biological features of human races influenced the political development of the different peoples (*Völker*).

Woltmann's discovery of 'Aryanism' led him into a predictable path: the belief that the Nordic race was the carrier of world civilization. There followed a frantic attempt to illustrate this thesis by reference to the presence of the Germanic race in all the major civilizations in Western Europe (particularly France and Italy). His last book includes the discovery of the 'physical type of genius', and it was thorough iconographic procedures that he tried to demonstrate the Germanic presence in the civilizational work of Renaissance Italy. After much ideological meandering Woltmann, like many other *fin de siècle* thinkers, found in the category of race an absolute, overarching concept that could explain the rise and fall of civilizations. It is difficult to assess the influence of Woltmann in Germany, though Lukacs has insisted that it was minimal. Woltmann's tragic death in 1907, at the age of 36, makes it difficult to put forward any conjecture concerning its possible intellectual and political evolution. That he became a sort of *Völkish* thinker there is little doubt, though the lack of anti-semitic elements in his writings indicates that he was not a proto-Nazi.

The Ideological Impact of H. S. Chamberlain

I have already mentioned the central importance of H. S. Chamberlain in the development of Nazi ideology. His book *The Foundations of the Nineteenth Century* (1899) became the key text of German racism, offering what became a model for Nazi philosophy. Chamberlain was an English aristocrat, but was brought up in the Prussian style. He was influenced by Wagner and Schenman, which would explain his penchant for Gobineau's ideas, which his friends had espoused. In his foundational text he updated Gobineau with anthropo-sociology and social Darwinism. However, a crucial distinction is the one he made between the Teutons and the Jews over the heritage of the ancient world and the survival of Christianity. As Biddis has pointed out, Chamberlain emphasized two essentially racist perspectives:

> First, that the races of man are not merely different from one another, but are also arranged according to a hierarchy of talent and value, wherein the Aryan peoples are supreme; secondly, that the interplay of these unequal races is the fundamental key for the explanation of social and political phenomena in all their complexity'. (Biddis 1969: 12)

According to Chamberlain nineteenth-century culture was the result of six fundamental influences:

1 Hellenic art, literature and philosophy
2 Roman law and state-craft organisation
3 Revelation of Christ, with a redeeming power, at a world-level.
4 A chaos resulting from the collapse of the Roman Empire
5 The negative and destructive influence of the Jews.
6 The creative and regenerative character of the Aryan race, specially of the Teutons or Germans.

It is relevant to emphasize that Chamberlain contemplated the past as the development of cultural periods that were dominated by different racial types. In so far as the modern period was concerned, the role of the Germanic race had been dominant since the Renaissance. Chamberlain made a rather unusual statement concerning Christ: he was not Jewish, but probably Aryan. For him, Judaism was a materialist system of beliefs, whereas Christianity was an idealist religion. No doubt, the birth of Christianity was the most important event in world history. As for Judaism, it was plain that it was a social and political danger from time immemorial. In modern times it was identified with wealth, capitalism and war. Religion was not the real feature of Judaism; in fact, instead Chamberlain thought that the Jews have no aptitude for religious thought. At the social level they are intolerant and against Western civilization. It may be the case that Chamberlain had a personal animosity against Judaism, but it is a well-known fact that anti-Judaism was a crucial feature of Nazism.

An important point that I have made is that Chamberlain's *The Foundations of the Nineteenth Century* transformed into a prophet of race for reasonably well-educated Germans. It is not, however, that he used a precise concept of race; sometimes he used a biological definition of race, sometimes he used a cultural one. To say that he presented an intuitive experience of race is perhaps the most appropriate way of formulating his thesis. If one examines the racial history offered in Chamberlain's text, it is obviously a rather complex and comprehensive vision that is presented to explore the formation of the German conception of race. For the sake of the argument, I would suggest the following key elements that explain the Germanic way of thinking (Field 1981: 223) and that also suggest at the foreign influence of both French and English thinkers:

1 *Aryan supremacy*. The idea of its superiority was essentially put forward by Gobineau, but also Renan. It is important to emphasize, however, that Chamberlain rejected Gobineau's pessimist belief about the extinction of the Aryans through miscegenation.

2 *Anti-semitism*. There is a an obvious reference to Vacher de Lapouge's expression of a 'crude hatred of the Jews'.

3 *Messianic and mystical notions of race*. These are perhaps essentially Germanic notions.

4 *Social Darwinism*. The origins are naturally in Darwin, though according to Chamberlain Darwin's conception of race was vague and contradictory.

5 *Eugenics*. He emphasizes the fact that Francis Galton's *Hereditary Genius* (1869) signifies the appearance of eugenics. The idea of racial hygiene (socially guided selection) was to be introduced to substitute natural selection.

6 *Anthropo-sociology*. In so far as Vacher de Lapouge, and Otto Ammon, established a correlation between size of skulls and religious beliefs, urbanization and statistics for wealth in Europe, a racial classification followed.

The idea of a 'noble race' was behind Chamberlain's objective. To that end, the existence of a number of elements was essential:

1 Having a good racial material.
2 Practising endogamy and avoiding foreign blood.
3 Practising natural selection.
4 Controlling interbreeding.

A final point. One must refer to the future of Germany as conceived by Chamberlain. He wanted an expansion of the country; and to that end it had to be based on a racial and national unity. He was very critical of a number of movements of his time: socialism, liberalism, materialism and Catholicism. He was in favour of an authoritarian and conservative monarchy, solidly based on *Volkish* appeals for a political consensus, hence transcending the barriers formed by ideas or classes.

For what it is worth, Hitler attended his funeral in 1927. Perhaps more important, however, is the fact that he influenced directly and massively two coming ideologists of Nazism examined below: H. F .K. Günther and Alfred Rosenberg.

The Influence of an Anthropologist: H. F. K. Günther

There is little doubt that the key thinker of the German racial politics under Nazism was H. F .K. Günther (Conte and Essner 1995). His inspirers were his compatriots whom we have mentioned, Otto Ammon and Ludwig Woltmann, as well as the obscure French author Georges Vacher de Lapouge. Günther was a professor of anthropology at Iena in 1930, Berlin in 1935 and Freiburg in 1939. He was the author of an extremely successful book entitled *Raciology of the German People* (1922), which sold about 125,000 exemplars. He was racially prejudiced, defending the importance of the Nordic man, which was presented with spiritual qualities. At the low level of school teaching, his ideas were presented according to the following principles.

Human beings, Günther stated, consist of different races, which produce different cultures. The Nordic race is the most impressive because it exhibits the highest intellectual and spiritual characteristics. Mixing the different races is considered dangerous. Racial features tend to persist in human beings for a long historical period. In Germany there are different races, but the Nordic is by far the best – tall, blue-eyed, courageous, decisive, free and active. The inhabitants of the south are brown, war-oriented and concerned with the sentiment of honour. The Jews are strange to the land – a pure race, but feeble, tarnished and defective. It should be obvious that any mixture of the Nordic with the Jews is a crime and defilement. It is obvious that the state has to protect the family. Racially pure people should marry among themselves and encourage the survival of the healthy children.

It is interesting to note that the key ideas of Günther were taken into the Nazi practice that consisted in the juridical and/or physical elimination of the so-called enemies of the German/Aryan race and the application of a strict eugenicist policy. In 1933 a number of measures were promulgated: a law against the propagation of hereditary illnesses, law compelling the sterilization of mentally ill people and serious criminals. A couple of years later, in 1935, the law of healthy marriages was introduced. It meant that people who were either psychologically or physically ill were not allowed to marry. Finally, in 1939, the principle of euthanasia was introduced, killing mentally ill and old people; the same principle applied to the wounded soldiers and others. Generally speaking, in the late 1930s Jews, Gypsies and Slavs were marginalized; during the Second World War many of them were eliminated.

Alfred Rosenberg: Hitler's Main Ideologist

We are coming now to our last author, Alfred Rosenberg, who undoubtedly played a key role in the shaping of Hitler's ideology and was the main ideologist of the Nazi Party, with all the implications that he had for the evil of the system. It is not an exaggeration to say that Rosenberg's *The Myth of the Twentieth Century* (1930) was the most important book, if we exclude Hitler's *Mein Kampf*. The book combines a variety of ideas: anti-Judaism and anti-Catholicism, Kantianism and Hinduism, Zoroastrianism and Nordic religion. At the best level, the Germanic virtues are emphasized: honour, loyalty, courage, and truthfulness. A regeneration and expansion of Germany is sketched; not surprisingly, the culture of the Aryan race is emphasized. His text was undoubtedly very influential, perverting the youth at a grand scale.

Alfred Rosenberg was born in the Baltic, went to school in Riga and studied in Moscow. In 1920 he had already joined the National Socialist German Worker's Party (Nazi Party). He was successively the editor of the *Völkischer Beobachter* (from 1921) and the *Nationalsozialistische Monatshefte* (from 1930). He was very active Nazi member from the very beginning of the movement. In 1924, when Hitler was imprisoned, he became the leader of the Party. As a leader and organizer of the *Kampfbund für Deutsche Kultur* (Combat League for German Culture), he formulated a literary vision of Nazism (Lixfeld 1994).

Rosenberg became acquainted with Chamberlain's *Foundations of the Nineteenth Century* in his youth. He believed that Chamberlain's book was electrifying and impressive. It can be said that on the basis of a racial theory inherited by Chamberlain from Gobineau, Rosenberg developed an idea of Germanic superiority. As we have pointed out, there is a clear trajectory from Gobineau to Wagner and from this latter and Woltmann to Chamberlain that provides an idea of the formation of a racial theory which shaped the viewpoints of Rosenberg and Hitler. In fact, part of Rosenberg's conceptions were the result of imitating Gobineau's ideas. As George Mosse (1964) has suggested concepts like Aryan, racial purity, racial bastardization, and so forth, were the result of such influence.

One of the important criticisms made by Robert Cecil (1972) was that one of the horrendous assumptions sustained by Nazism for many years was that the Slavs were an inferior race and the Jews a race totally alien to humanity. In spite of that, Rosenberg always felt that his ideology was noble. However, it would be appropriate to see Gobineau and Rosenberg as upholding doctrines that, in the words of Alexis de Tocqueville, were evil and produced 'inequality, pride, violence, contempt for one's fellow men, tyranny and vileness in all its forms' (Tocqueville 1980: 322). No doubt, anti-Semitism was an essential feature of Rosenberg's doctrine. The Jews were perceived as perpetrators of deicide, usurers, criminals, intolerant, materialistic and unspiritual who had to be criticized, attacked and eliminated. However, Rosenberg always believed that his thinking was intellectually noble. Condemned to death by the war tribunal in 1946, he nonetheless remained alien to his guilt – a way of reasoning that he could not understand and that hence kept him out of the non-Nazi reality.

Conclusion

I would like to conclude by reiterating that my objective or attitude in this book is not to blame Gobineau, Le Bon, Vacher de Lapouge and Sorel (and even less Maistre and Galton) as the principal guilty characters behind the tragic political realities of the twentieth century, Nazism (or fascism) and communism. That they wrote texts that could be, and were, used by totalitarian movements is undoubtedly true. They are, of course, not the sole authors, but certainly representatives of the four main ideological contributions to totalitarianism: race, crowd, eugenics and violence.

I should like to emphasize, once again, that what constitutes Nazi ideology is an articulation of these four basic elements. It seems to me that this combination is particularly appropriate to deal with Nazism, and while crowds and violence are crucial to account for all totalitarian movements, race and eugenics are particularly applicable to the Nazi experience (Burleigh and Wipperman 1991; Burleigh 1994, 2000; Proctor 1999; Weindling 1989).

Bibliography

Acosta, J. de (1590) (1989) *Historia natural y moral de las Indias.* México: Fondo de Cultura Económica.

Adams, M. (1990) *The Wellborn Science: Eugenics in Germany, France, Brazil and Russia.* Oxford: OUP.

Alexander, J. (1988) (ed.) *Durkhemian Sociology: Cultural Studies.* Cambridge: CUP.

Alibert, J. (1990) *Etat et religion.* Paris: Tequi.

Allport, G. W. (1968) 'The Historical Background of Modern Social Psychology', in Lindzey, G. et al. *The Handbook of Social Psychology*, vol. 1. New York: Dover.

Almog, S. (ed.) (1988) *Antisemitism Through the Ages.* Oxford: Pergamon.

Ammon, O. (1893) *Die natürliche Auslese beim Menschen.* Jena: Fischer.

Ammon, O. (1895) *Die Gesellschaftsordnung und ihre natürlichen Grundlagen.* Jena: Fischer.

Ammon, O. (1898) 'Histoire d'une idée. L'anthroposociologie', *Revue International de Sociologie*, 6(1): 145–81.

Ammon, O. (1899) *Zur Anthropologie der Badener.* Jena: Fischer.

Amselle, J. L. (1997) 'Michel Foucault et la guerre des races', *Critique*, 606: 787–800.

Arendt, H. (1944) 'Race-Thinking Before Racism', *Review of Politics,* 6: 36–73.

Arendt, H. (1951) *The Origins Of Totalitarianism.* New York: Harcourt Brace.

Arendt, H. (1969) *On Violence.* New York: Harcourt Brace.

Arnulf, S. (1939) "Scholarly Forerunners of Fascism", *Ethics*, 1939, 50: 16–34.

Aron, R. (1967) (1989) *Les étapes de la pensée sociologique.* Paris: Gallimard. (tr. *Main Currents in Sociological Thought*, 2 vols. New York: Anchor Books).

Augstein, H. F. (1996) *Race. The Origins of an Idea, 1760–1850.* Bristol: Thoemmes Press.

Baker, J. R. (1974) *Race.* London: Oxford University Press.

Bannister, R. C. (1979) *Social Darwinism. Science and Myth in Anglo-American Thought.* Philadelphia: Temple University Press.

Banton, M. (1977) *The Idea of Race.* London: Tavistock

Banton, M. (1983) *Racial and Ethnic Competition.* Cambridge: Cambridge University Press.

Banton, M. (1987) 'The Classification of Races in Europe and North-America: 1700–1850', *International Social Sciences Journal*, 111: 45–60.

Banton, M. (1987) (1998) *Racial Theories*. Cambridge: Cambridge University Press (2nd edition).

Barker, A. J. (1978) *The African Link. British Attitude to the Negroes in the Era of the Atlantic Slave Trade, 1550–1807*. London: Cass.

Barnes, H. E. (1920) 'A Psychology of Modern Social Problems and of Contemporary History: A Survey of the Contribution of Gustave Le Bon to Social Psychology', *American Journal of Psychology*, 32: 333–69.

Barnes, H. E. (1925) 'Representative Biological Theories of Society', *Sociological Review*, XVII: 120–30; 182–94; 294–300.

Barnes, H. E. (1948) *An Introduction to the History of Sociology*. Chicago, IL: Chicago University Press.

Barrows, S. (1981) *Distorting Mirrors*. New Haven: Yale University Press.

Barzun, J. (1932) *The French Race*. New York: Columbia University Press.

Barzun, J. (1938) *Race. A Study in Modern Superstition*. New York: Little, Brown.

Barzun, J. (1941) (1958) *Darwin, Marx and Wagner*. New York: Doubleday Anchor (2nd edition).

Bastide, R. (1967) 'Colour, Racism and Christianity', *Daedalus,* 96: 312–27.

Beauchard, J. (1985) *La puissance des foules*. Paris; PUF.

Becker, H. and Barnes, H.E. (1961) *Social Thought: Lore to Science*, vol. 2. New York: Dover.

Bejin, A. (1982) 'Le sang, le sens et le travail: Georges Vacher de Lapouge darwiniste social et fondateur de l'anthroposociologie', *Cahiers Internationaux de Sociologie*, LXXII: 323–43.

Bejin, A. (1985) 'De Malthus à la sociobiologie', *Revue européenne des sciences sociales*, XXIII (69): 121–37.

Bellah, R. (1970) *Beyond Belief*. Berkeley: University of California Press.

Bellomy, D. C. (1984) *'Social Darwinism' Revisited*. Perspectives in American History, N. S., 1: 1–129.

Benassar, B. (1975) *The Spanish Character*. Berkeley: University of California Press.

Bendyshe, J. (1863–4) *The History of Anthropology*. Anthropological Society of London, Memoirs, I: 335–458

Berenbaum, M. (ed.) (1990) *A Mosaic of Victims*. Princeton: Princeton University Press.

Bergson, H. (1889) (1993) *Essai sur les donnés immédiates de la conscience*. Paris: Presses Universitaires de France.

Bergson, H. (1907) (1985) *L'évolution créatrice*. Paris; Presses Universitaires de France.

Berlin, I. (1979) *Against the Current*. London: Hogarth Press.

Berlin, I. (1991) 'Joseph de Maistre and the Origins of Fascism' in *The Crooked Timber of Humanity*. London: Fontana Press, pp. 91–174.

Berlin, I. (1994) 'Introduction' to Maistre's *Considerations on France*. Cambridge: Cambridge University Press.

Bernardini, J. M. (1997) *Le darwinisme social en France (1859–1918)*. Paris: Centre Nationale de la Recherche Scientifique.

Bessel, R. (1984) *Political Violence and the Rise of Nazism*. Oxford: Oxford University Press.

Best, G. (1988) *The Permanent Revolution*. London: Fontana.

Biddiss, M. (1966) 'Gobineau and the Aryan Myth', *History Today*, 16: 572–8.

Biddiss, M. (1969) 'Houston Stewart Chamberlain. Prophet of Tourism'. *History Today*, 19: 10–17.

Biddiss, M. (1970a) 'Prophecy and Pragmatism: Gobineau's Confrontation with Tocqueville', *The Historical Journal*, 13: 611–33.

Biddiss, M. (1970b) *Father of Racist Ideology*. London: Weidenfeld & Nicolson.

Biddiss, M. (1977) *The Age of the Masses*. London: Penguin.

Biddiss, M. (1979) (ed.) *Images of Race*. Leicester: Victorian Library.

Biddiss, M (1986) 'Arthur de Gobineau and the Illussions of Progress', in Hall, J. (ed.) *Rediscoveries*. Oxford: OUP.

Blanckaert, C. (1988) 'On the Origins of French Ethnology: W. Edwards and the Doctrine of Race' in Stocking, G. W. (ed.) *History of Anthropology*, vol. 5: 18–55.

Bloch, M. (1940–5) 'Sur les grandes invasions', *Revue de Synthèse*, 19: 55–81.

Boas, F. (1911) *The Mind of Primitive Man*, New York: Macmillan.

Boas, G. (1973) 'Primitivism', *Dictionary of the History of Ideas*. New York: Scribner, vol. III: 577–79.

Bocock, R. (1976) *Freud and Modern Society*. London: Routledge.

Boissel, J. (1967) *Gobineau polémiste. Les races et la republique*. Paris: Pauvert.

Boissel, J. (1972) *Victor Courtet de L'Isle*. Paris: PUF.

Boissel, J. (1973) *Gobineau, l'Orient et l'Iran*. Paris: Klincksieck.

Boissel. J (1981) *Gobineau*. Paris: Hachette.

Boissel, J. (1993) *Gobineau, biographie. Mythes et realité*. Paris; Berg.

Bouglé, C. (1897) 'Anthropologie et démocratie', *Revue de métaphysique et de morale*, 5: 443–61.

Bouglé, C. (1909) 'Syndicalistes et Bergsoniens', *Revue du Mois*, 7: 403–16.

Bowler, P. (1976) 'Malthus, Darwin and the Concept of Struggle', *Journal of the History of the Behavioural Sciences,* 37: 631–50.

Bowler, P. (1984) *Evolution*. Los Angeles: California University Press.

Bracher, K. (1969) *The German Dictatorship*. Hardmonsworth: Penguin.

Bramson, L. (1961) *The Political Context of Sociology*. Princeton: Princeton University Press.

Breitman, R. (1991) *The Architect of Genocide*. London: Grafton.

Bridenthal, R., Grosmann, A. and Kaplan, A. (eds.) (1984) *When Biology Became Destiny: Women in Weimar and Nazi Germany*. New York: Monthly Review.

Broberg, G. (1983) 'Homo sapiens. Linnaeus's Classification of Man' in Frängsmyr, T. (ed.) *Linnaeus. The Man and his Work*. Berkeley: University of California Press.

Buenzod, J. (1967) *La formation de la pensée de Gobineau*. Paris: Nizet.

Buffon, G. L. (1971) *De l'homme*. Paris: Maspero.

Bullock, A. (1951) *Hitler, A Study in Tyranny*. London: Penguin

Burke, E. (1790) (1969) *Reflections on the Revolution in France*. London: Penguin.

Burleigh, M., Wippermann, W. (1991) *The German Racial State, 1933–1945*. Cambridge: Cambridge University Press.

Burleigh, M. (1991) 'Euthanasia in the Third Reich', *Social History of Medicine*, 4: 317–28.

Burleigh, M. (1994) *Death and Deliverance. 'Euthanasia' in Germany 1900–1945*. Cambridge: Cambridge University Press.

Burleigh, M. (1997) *Ethics and Extermination*. Cambridge: Cambridge University Press.

Burleigh, M. (2000) *The Third Reich. A New History*. London: Macmillan

Burnham, J. (1943) *The Machiavellians: Defenders of Freedom*. Washington: Gateway.

Burrow, J. W. (1968a) *Evolution and Society*. Cambridge: Cambridge University Press.

Burrow, J. W. (1968b) 'Introduction' to Darwin's *The Origin of the Species*. London: Penguin.

Burrus, E. J. (1984) 'Alonso de la Vera Cruz, Pioneer Defender of the American Indians', *The Catholic Historical Review*, 70 (4): 531–46.

Canetti, E. (1960) *Crowds and Power*. London: Penguin.

Caro-Baroja, J. (1978) *Los judios en la España moderna y contemporánea*, 3 vols. Madrid: Istmo.

Carol, A. (1995) *Histoire de l'eugénisme en France*. Paris: Seuil.

Castillo-Urbano, F. (1992) *El pensamiento de Francisco de Vitoria. Filosofía política e Indio americano*. Barcelona: Anthropos.

Castradori, F. (1991) *Le radici dell'odio. Il Conte de Gobineau è le origini del razzismo*. Milano: Xenia.

Cecil, R. (1972) *The Myth of the Master Race. A Rosenberg and Nazi Ideology*. London: Batsford

Chamberlain, J. E. and Gilman, S. L. (1985) *Degeneration: The Dark Side of Progress*. New York: Columbia University Press.

Charzat, M. (1977) *Georges Sorel et la révolution du XXe siècle*. Paris: Hachette.

Charzat, M. (ed.) (1986) *Cahier Georges Sorel*. Paris: L'Herne (No. 53).

Chase, A. (1977) *The Legacy of Malthus*. New York: Knopf.

Chorover, S. L. (1979) *From Genesis to Genocide*. Cambridge, MA: MIT

Churchill, W. F. (1974) *The Influence of the Enlightenment on the French Revolution*. London: Heath.

Cioran, E. M. (1991) *Anathemas and Admirations*. London: Arcade.

Claeys, G. (2000) 'The "Survival of the Fittest" and the Origins of Social Darwinism', *Journal of the History of Ideas*, 61(2): 223–40.

Clark, L. (1984) *Social Darwinism in France*. University, AL: University of Alabama Press.

Cohen, W. B. (1980) *The French Encounter with Africans (1530–1880)*. Bloomington: University of Alabama Press.

Cohen-Almagor, R. (1993) 'Marx, Engels, Lenin and Violence', *Terrorism and Political Violence,* 3(2): 1–24.

Coleman, W. (1964) *Georges Cuvier, Zoologist*. Cambridge, MA: Harvard University Press.

Conte, E. and Essner, C. (1995) *La Quête de la Race. Une Anthropologie du Nazisme*. Paris: Hachette.

Count, E. (1950) *This is Race*. New York: Schuman

Cowan, R. W. (1977) 'Nature and Nurture: The Interplay of Biology and Politics in the Work of Francis Galton', *Studies in the History of Biology*, 1: 133–208.

Crocker, L. G. (1968) *Rousseau's Social Contract*. Cleveland, Ohio: The Press of Case Western Reserve University.

Curtin, P. D. (1964) *The Image of Africa*. Madison, WI: University of Wisconsin Press.

Curtis, M. (1959) *Three Against the Third Republic: Sorel, Barres and Maurras*. Princeton: Princeton University Press

Daline, V. (1973) 'Marx et Gobineau', *Recherches Internationales à la Lumière du Marxism*, 4: 1–15.

Darcel, J. L. (1976) 'Introduction' to Josep de Maistre's *De l'état de nature, Etudes Maistriennes*, 2, Chambery, Savoie

Darwin, C. (1968) *The Origin of Species*. London: Penguin,

Darwin, C. (1981) *The Descent of Man*. Princeton University Press.

Darwin, C. (1974) *Autobiography*. Oxford : Oxford University Press.

Davis, B. D. (1966) (1988) *The Problem of Slavery in Western Culture*. Hardmonsworth: Penguin.

Davis, B. D. (1986) *Slavery and Human Progress*. New York: Oxford University Press.

Defourneaux, M. (1966). *La vie quotidienne dans l'Espagne du siècle d'Or*. Paris: Hachette.

Degler, C. (1959) 'Slavery and the Genesis of American Race Prejudice', *Comparative Studies in Society and History*, 2: 49–66; 488–95.

Delacampagne, C. (1983) *L'invention du racisme*. Paris: Fayard.

Delacampagne, C. (1990) 'Racism and the West: From Praxis to Logos' in Goldberg, D. T. (ed.) *Anatomy of Racism*. Oxford: Blackwell.

Desmond, A. and Moore, J. (1991) *Darwin*. London: Penguin..

Dominguez-Ortiz, A. (1963 and 1970). *La sociedad española en el siglo XVII*, 2 vols. Madrid: Centro Superior de Investigaciones Científicas.

Drouard, A. (1999) *L'eugénisme en question*. Paris: Ellipses.

Dumont, L. (1986) *Essays on Individualism*. Chicago: University of Chicago Press.

Dupeux, L. (1989) *Histoire culturelle de l'Allemagne (1919–1960)*. Paris: Presses Universitaires de France.

Durkheim, E. (1912) (1960) *Les Formes élémentaires de la vie religieuse*. Paris: Presses Universitaires de France.

Durkheim, E. (1975a) *Durkheim on Religion*. Edited by W.S.E. Pickering. London: Routledge & Kegan Paul.

Durkheim, E. (1975b) *Textes*, 3 vols. Paris: Minuit.

Durkheim, E (1976) 'Lettres', *Revue Française de sociologie*, 17(2): 174

Durkheim, E. (1978) 'Review of Schaeffle's Bau und Leben des Sozialen Körpers' in E. Durkheim, *On Institutional Analysis*. Chicago: University of Chicago Press, pp. 93–114.

Duvernay-Bolens, J. (1995) 'L'Homme zoologique. Races et racisme chez les naturalistes de la première moitié du XIXe siècle', *L'Homme*, 133: 9–32.

Eatwell, R. and O'Sullivan, N. (eds) (1989) *The Nature of the Right*. London: Pinter.

Eddy, J. H. (1984) 'Buffon, Organic Alterations and Man', *Studies in the History of Biology*, 7: 1–45.

Eiseley, L (1968) *Darwin's Century*. New York: Anchor Books.

Essertier, D. (1927) *Psychologie et Sociologie*. Paris: Alcan.

Eugene, E. (1998) *Wagner et Gobineau*. Paris: La Cherche Midi.

Evans, W. M. (1980) 'From the Land of Canaan to the Land of Guinea: The Strange Odyssey of the Sons of Ham', *American Historical Review*, 85: 15–43.

Fancher, R. (1979) *Pioneers of Psychology*. New York: Norton.

Fancher, R. (1983a) 'Francis Galton's African Ethnography and its Role in the Development of Psychology', *The British Journal for the History of Science*, 16: 67–79.

Fancher, R. (1983b) 'Alphonse de Candolle, Francis Galton and the Early History of the Nature-Nurture Controversy', *Journal of the History of the Behavioural Sciences*, 19: 341–52.

Faust, D. F. (ed.) (1981) *The Ideology of Slavery*. Baton Rouge: Louisiana University Press.

Fenton, C. S. (1980) 'Race, Class and Politics in The Work of E. Durkheim', in O'Callaghan, M. (ed.) *Race and Colonialism*. Cambridge: Cambridge University Press.

Fernandez-Santamaria, J. A. (1977) *The State, War and Peace*. Cambridge: Cambridge University Press.

Field, G. (1981) *Evangelist of Race. The Germanic Vision of H. S. Chamberlain*. New York: Columbia University Press.

Finley, M. (1980) *Ancient Slavery and Modern Ideology*. London: Chatto.

Fisichella, D. (1993) *Il pensiero politico di de Maistre*. Roma: Laterza.

Foucault, M. (1966) (2001) *The Order of Thing* .London: Routledge.

Foucault, M. (1997) *Il faut défendre la société*. Paris: Gallimard/Seuil.

Fouillée, A. (1898a). *Psychologie du peuple français*. Paris: Alcan.

Fouillée, A. (1898b). 'L'anthroposociologie', *Revue Internationale de Sociologie*, 6(1): 368–71

Frank, F. (1956) 'From Equality to Organicism', *Journal of the History of Ideas*, 17: 54–69.

Frangsmyr, T. (1983) *Linnaeus*. Berkeley: University of California Press.

Freeman, D. (1974) 'The Evolutionary Theories of Darwin and Spencer', *Current Anthropology*, 15: 211–37.

Freud, S. (1921) (1985) *Group Psychology and the Analysis of Ego*. London: Penguin.

Frost, F. (1990) 'Fair Women, Dark Men: The Forgotten Roots of Colour Prejudice', *History of European Ideas*, 5: 669–79.

Futuyma, D (1995) *Science on Trial*. Sunderland: Sinauer.

Gager, J. (1983) *The Origins of Anti-Semitism*. New York.: Oxford University Press.

Gale, B. (1972) 'Darwin and the Concept of Struggle for Existence', *Isis*, 63, 321–344.

Galton, Francis (1904) 'Eugenics: Its Definition, Scope, and Aim', *Sociological Papers*, pp. 46–99

Galton, Francis (1908) *Memories of my Life*. London: Methuen.

Galton, Francis (1909) *Essays in Eugenics*. London: The Eugenics Education Society (New York: Garland, 1985)

Gane, M. (1992) *The Radical Sociology of Durkheim and Mauss*. London: Routledge.

Gardiner, P. (1959) *Theories of History*. Glencoe, Ill.: Free Press.

Gasman, D. (1971) *The Scientific Origins of National-Socialism*. London: Elsevier.

Gaulmier, J. (1965) *Spectre de Gobineau*. Paris: Pauvert

Geiger, R. (1977) 'Democracy and the Crowd: the Social History of an Idea in France and Italy, 1890–1915', *Societas*, 7: 47–71.

Gelatelly, R. (1990) *The Gestapo and German Society: Enforcing Racial Policy 1933–1945*. Oxford: Oxford University Press.

George, K. (1958) 'The Civilised West Looks at Primitive Africa: A Study in Ethnocentrism', *Isis*, 49: 62–72.

George, W. (1982) *Darwin*. London: Fontana Masters.

Gergen, K. (1967) 'The Significance of Skin Colour in Human Relations', *Daedalus*, 96: 390–406.

Giddens, A. (1989) *Sociology*. Cambridge: Polity Press.

Gillham, N. W. (2001) *A Life of Sir Francis Galton. From an African Exploration to the Birth of Eugenics*. Oxford: Oxford University Press.

Gervasoni, M. (1997) *Georges Sorel, una biografia intellectuale*. Milan: Unicopoli.

Giner, S. (1976) *Mass Society*. London: Martin Robertson.

Ginneken, J. van (1985) 'The 1895 Debate on the Origins of Crowd Psychology', *Journal of the History of the Behavioural Sciences*, 21: 375–82.

Ginneken, J. van (1992) *Crowd, Psychology and Politics, 1871–1899*. Cambridge: Cambridge University Press.

Ginsberg, M. (1921) *The Psychology of the Crowd*. London: Routledge.

Girard, R. (1977) *Violence and the Sacred*. Baltimore, Mar.: The Johns Hopkins University Press.

Gobineau, J. A. (1970) *Selected Political Writings*. London: Jonathan Cape.

Gobineau, J. A. (1983) *Oeuvres*, 3 vols . Paris: Gallimard.

Goldstein, M. (1998) *The People in French Counter-Revolutionary Thought* London: Lang.

Goodman, D. (1980) *Buffon's Natural History*. Milton Keynes: The Open University Press.

Goriely, G. (1982) 'Georges Sorel et l'idée de révolution', *Revue de l'Institut de Sociologie*, 1–2: 7–22.

Gossett, T. F. (1963) *Race. The History of an Idea in America*. Dallas: Southern Methodist University Press.

Gould, S. J. (1980) *Even since Darwin*. London: Penguin.

Gould, S. J. (1981) *The Mismeasure of Man*. London: Penguin

Gould, S. J. (1985) *The Flamingo Smile*. New York: Norton.

Graham, H. (1977) 'Science and Values: The Eugenics Movement in Germany and Russia in the 1920s', *American Historical Review*, 82: 1133–64.

Graumann, C. and Moscovici, S. (eds) (1986) *Changing Conceptions of Crowd Mind and Behaviour*. New York: Springer

Graumann, C and Moscovici, S. (eds) (1986) *Changing Conception of Leadership*. New York: Springer.

Greece, J. C. (1954) 'The American Debate on the Negro's Place in Nature, 1780–1815', *Journal of the History of Ideas*, 15: 385–96.

Greene, J. C. (1954) 'Some Speculations on the Origin of Human Races', *American Anthropologist*, 56: 31–41.

Greene, J. C. (1959) *The Death of Adam*. Ames, IA: Iowa State University Press.

Greene, J. C. (1981) *Science, Ideology and World View*. Berkeley: University of California Press.

Greil, A. L. (1981) *Georges Sorel and the Sociology of Virtue*. Washington DC: University Press of America.

Gross, D. (1982) 'Myth and Symbol in Georges Sorel' in Drescher, S., Sabean, D. and Sharlin, A. (eds) *Political Symbolism in Modern Europe*. New York.: Transaction.

Gruber, H. E. (1974) *Darwin on Man*. New York: Wildwood House.

Guchet, I. (2001) *Georges Sorel, 1847–1922. Serviteur désinteréssé du proletariat*. Paris: L'Harmattan.

Guillaumin, C. (1967) 'Aspects latents du racisme chez Gobineau', *Cahiers Internationaux de Sociologie*, 42: 145–58.

Haller, J. S. (1971a) *Outcasts from Evolution: Scientific Attitudes of Racial Inferiority, 1859–1900*. New York: McGraw-Hill.

Haller, J. S. (1971b) 'Race and the Concept of Progress in Nineteenth Century Anthropology', *American Anthropologist*, 73: 710–24.

Haller, J. S. (1995) *Outcast from Evolution. Scientific Attitudes to Racial Inferiority, 1859–1900*. Carbondale: Southern Illinois University Press.

Halliday, R. J. (1971) 'Social Darwinism', *Victorian Studies*, 14: 389–409.

Hammond, M. (1980) 'Anthropology as a Weapon of Social Combat in Late Nineteenth Century France', *Journal of the History of the Behavioural Sciences*, 16: 118–32.

Hanke, L. (1951) *Bartolomé de las Casas*. The Hague: Nijhoff.

Hanke, L. (1959) (1970) *Aristotle and the American Indians*. Urbana: Indiana University Press.

Hannaford, I. (1996) *Race. The History of an Idea in the West*. Washington: Woodrow Wilson.

Harris, M. (1968) *The Rise of Anthropological Theory*. New York: Crowell.

Hawkins, M. J. (1980) 'Traditionalism and Organicism in Durkhheim's Early Writings', *Journal of the History of the Behavioural Sciences*, 16: 31–44.

Hawkins, M. J. (1997) *Social Darwinism in European and American Thought, 1860–1945*. New York: Cambridge University Press.

Hayes, P. (1992) *The People and the Mob*. Wesport, Conn.: Praeger.

Hayward, J. E .S. (1963) 'Solidarity and the Reformist Sociology of Alfred Fouillée', *American Journal of Economics and Sociology*, 22: 205–22; 303–12.

Hayward, J. E. S. (1991) *After the French Revolution*. London: Harvester

Hecht, J. M. (1999) 'The Solvency of Metaphysics. The Debate over Racial Science and Moral Philosophy in France (1890–1919)', *Isis*, 90: 1–24.

Hecht, J. M. (2000) 'Vacher de Lapouge and the Rise of Nazi Science', *Journal of the History of Ideas,* 61(2): 285–304.

Heilke, T. (1990) *Voegelin on the Idea of Race*. Baton Rouge: Louisiana State University Press.

Himmelfarb, G. (1959) *Darwin and the Darwinian Revolution*. London: Norton.

Himmelfarb, G. (1968) 'Varieties of Social Darwinism', in *Victorian Minds* London: Weidenfeld.

Hobbes, T. (1651) *Leviathan*. London: Penguin.

Hodgen, M. (1964) *Early Anthropology in the Sixteenth and Seventeenth Centuries*. Philadelphia: University of Pennsylvania Press.

Hofstadter, R. (1944) *Social Darwinism in American Thought*. New York: Beacon Press.

Holt, N. R. (1975) 'Monists and Nazis: A Question of Scientific Responsibility', *The Hastings Centre Report*, 5: 37–43.

Holton, R. J. (1978) 'The Crowd in History: Some Problems of Theory and Method', *Social History*, 3: 219–33.

Hook, S. (1973) 'Myth and Fact in the Marxist Theory of Revolution and Violence', *Journal of the History of Ideas*, 34: 271–80.

Horowitz, A. (1990) 'Law and Customs: Rousseau's Historical Anthropology', *The Review of Politics,* 152(2): 215–41.

Horowitz, I. L. (1961) *Radicalism and the Revolt Against Reason. The Social Theories of G. Sorel*. Carbondale: Southern Illinois University Press.

Horsman, R. (1976) 'Origins of Anglo-Saxonism in Great Britain', *Journal of the History of Ideas*, 37: 387–410.

Horsman, R. (1981) *Race and Manifest Destiny*. Cambridge, MA: Harvard University Press.

Houzé, E. (1906). *L'Aryen et l'Anthroposociologie: Etude critique*. Bruxelles: Institut Solvay.

Hughes, H. S. (1979) *Consciousness and Society*. London: MacGibbon and Kee.

Hume, D. (1748) (1985) *Essays*. Indianapolis, IN: Liberty.

Humphrey, R. (1951) *G. Sorel. Prophet Without Honour*. Cambridge: Harvard University Press.

Hunter, G. K. (1967) 'Othello and Colour Prejudice', *Proceedings of the British Academy*, 53: 139–63.

Huxley, T. H. (1959) *Man's Place in Nature*. Ann Arbor, MI: University of Michigan Press.

Janson, H. W. (1952) *Apes and Ape-Lore in the Middle Ages and the Renaissance*. London: Warburg Institute.

Jarvie, I. C. (1989) 'Recent Work in the History of Anthropology and Its Historiographic Problems', *Philosophy of the Social Sciences*, 19: 345–75.

Jennings, J. R. (1983) 'Sorel, Vico and Ethics' in Tagliacozzo, G. ed. *Vico and Marx*. New Jersey: Humanities.

Jennings, J. R. (1985) *Georges Sorel. The Character and Development of his Thought*. London: Macmillan.

Joas, H. (1993) 'Durkheim's Intellectual Development: the Problem of Emergence of a New Morality and New Institutions as a Leitmotif in Durkheim's Oeuvre', in Turner, S. (ed.), *Emile Durkheim. Sociologist and Moralist*. London: Routledge, pp. 229–45.

Jones, G. (1980) *Social Darwinism in English Thought*. London: Harvester Press.

Jordan, W. D. (1974) *The White's Man Burden*. New York: Oxford University Press.

Jouanna, A. (1981) *L'idée de race en France au XVI siècle at au début du XVII*, 2 vols. Montpellier: Presses d'Impremerie de Recherche Universitaire Paul Valery.

Juillard, J. and Sand, S. (1985) *Georges Sorel en son temps*. Paris: Seuil.

Juillard, J. (1990) 'A risque de penser' in Sorel, G. *Réflexions sur la violence*. Paris: Seuil, pp. I–XVI.

Kamen, H. (1965) (1985) *Inquisition and Society in Spain*. London: Weidenfeld.

Kaye, H. L. (1986) *The Social Meanings of Modern Biology*. London: Harvester.

Kelly, A. (1981) *The Descent of Darwin. Popularization of Darwin in Germany*. Chapel Hill NC: North Carolina University Press.

Kelly, A. (1981) *The Descent of Darwin. Popularization of Darwin in Germany*. Chapel Hill: The University of North Carolina Press.

Kennedy, P. and Nicholls, A. (eds) (1981) *Nationalist and Racialist Movements in Britain and Germany before 1914*. London: Macmillan.

Kershaw, I. (2000) *Hitler*, 2 vols. London: Allen Lane.

Kevles, F. (1985) *In the Name of Eugenics*. London: Penguin.

Keynes, M. (ed.) (1993) *Sir Francis Galton*. London: Macmillan.

King, E. G. (1990) *Crowd Theory as a Psychology and the Leader and the Led*. Lewiston: Edwin Mellen Press.

Klineberg, O. (1940) (1962) *Social Psychology*. New York: Holt, Rinehart and Winston.

Kolakowski, L. (1981) *Main Currents of Marxism*, 3 vols. Oxford: Oxford University Press.

Krausnick, H. and Broszat, M. (1970) *Anatomy of the SS State*. London: Paladin.

Kristeller, P. O. (1972) *Renaissance Concepts of Man*. New York: Harper & Bros.

Kropotkin, P. (1955) *Mutual Aid*. New York: Dover.

Kuper, A. (1991) 'Anthropologists and the History of Anthropology', *Critique of Anthropology*, 11: 125–42.

Las Casas, B. (1971) *Selection of his Writings*. New York: Knopf.

Le Bon, G. (1894) *Les lois psychologiques de l'évolution des peuples*. Paris: Alcan

Le Bon, G. (1895) *Psychologie des foules*. Paris: Alcan

Le Bon, G. (1895) (1960) *The Crowd*. London: Penguin

Le Bon, G. (1912) (1980) *The French Revolution and the Psychology of Revolution*. New Brunswick, NJ: Transaction Books.

Lebrun, R. (1965) *Throne and Altar*. Ottawa: University of Ottawa Press.

Lebrun, R. (1972) 'J. de Maistre and Rousseau', *Studies on Voltaire and the Eighteenth Century*, 88: 881–98.

Lebrun, R. (1988) *Joseph de Maistre. An Intellectual Militant*. Montreal: McGill-Queen University Press.

Lemonon, M. (1972) *Le rayonnement de Gobineau en Allemagne* (thesis, 4 vols., Université de Strasbourg).

Lemonon, M. (1982) 'Gobineau, père du racisme? La diffusion en Allemagne des idées de Gobineau sur les races', *Recherches Germaniques,* 12: 78–108.

Lévi-Strauss, C. (1960) (1967) *The Scope of Anthropology*. London: Cape.

Lewis, B. (1970) 'Race and Colour in Islam', *Encounter*, 35(2); 18–36.

Lewis, B. (1971) *Race and Colour in Islam*. New York: Harper.

Lewis, B. (1986) *Semites and Anti-Semites*. London: Weidenfeld.

Lewis, B. (1990) *Race and Slavery in the Middle East*. Oxford: Oxford University Press.

Lewontin, R. C. (1986) 'Review Symposium', *Isis*, 77, 2: 314–17.

Lifton, J. (1986) *The Nazi Doctors*. New York: Basic Books.

Lively, J. (1965) 'Introduction' to *The Works of Joseph de Maistre*. London: G. Allen.

Lixfeld, H. (1994) *Folklore and Fascism. The Reich Institute for German Volkskunde*. Bloomington, IN: Indiana University Press.

Llobera, J. R. (1977) 'The History of the Social Sciences as a Problem', *Critique of Anthropology*, 2(7): 17–42.

Llobera, J. R. (1988) 'The Dark Side of Modernity', *Critique of Anthropology*, 8(2): 71–6.

Llobera, J. R. (1989) 'Alfred Fouillée and the *psychologie des peuples* in turn of the century France' (Ms) (Sp. tr. in *Caminos discordantes*. Barcelona: Anagrama).

Locke, J. (1994) *Two Treatises of Government*. London: Everyman.

Logue, W. (1983) *From Philosophy to Sociology*. DeKalb, IL: Northern Illinois University Press.

Lorimer, D. (1978) *Colour, Class and the Victorians*. Leicester: Leicester University Press.

Lovejoy, A. (1948) *Essays in the History of Ideas*. Baltimore: Johns Hopkins Press.

Lovejoy, A. O. (1968) 'Buffon and the Problem of the Species' in Glass, B., Temkin, O. and Strauss, L. W. (eds) *Forerunners of Darwin*. Baltimore: Johns Hopkins.

Luhrmann, T. M. (1990) 'Our Master, Our Brother: Levi-Strauss's Debt to Rousseau', *Cultural Anthropology*, 5: 396–413.

Lukacs, J. (1997) *The Hitler of History*. London: Phoenix.

Lukes, S. (1973) *E. Durkheim. His Life and Work*. Hardmonsworth: Penguin.

MacDougall, H. (1982) *Racial Myth in English History*. Montreal: Harvest House.

McGuire, G. R. (1987) 'Pathological Subconsciousand Irrational Determinism in the Social Psychology of the Crowd', *Current Issues in Theoretical Psychology*, 13: 201–17.

MacPherson, C. B. (1962) *The Political Theory of Possessive Individualism*. Oxford: Oxford University Press.

Mahn-Lot, M. (1999) *Las Casas moraliste. Culture et foi*. Paris: Cerf.

Maistre, J. de (1965) *The Works of Joseph de Maistre*. London: Allen & Unwin.

Maistre, J. de (1974) *Considerations on France*. Montreal: Mc-Gill-Queen's University Press.

Maistre, J. de (1993) *Saint Pétersburg Dialogues*. Montreal: McGill.

Maistre, J. de (1977) *Letters on the Spanish Inquisition*. New York: Scholar Reprints.

Malefijt, A. de W. (1968) 'Homo Monstruosus', *Scientific American*, 219(4): 112–18.

Malthus, R. (1973) *An Essay on the Principle of Population*. London: Dent.

Mann, G. et al. (eds) (1973) *Biologismus um 19. Jahrhundert in Deutschland*. Stuttgart: Enke.

Mann, G. (ed.) (1990) *Die Natur des Menchen*. Stuttgart: Fisher.

Mannheim, K. (1971) *From Karl Mannheim*. Oxford: Oxford University Press.

Mannheim. K. (1986) *Conservatism*. London: Routledge

Manouvrier, L. (1899) 'L'indice céphalique et la pseudosociologie', *La Revue de l'Ecole d'Anthropologie*, 9: 233–59, 280–96.

Manuel, F. M. (1956) 'From Equality to Organicism', *Journal of the History of Ideas*, 17: 54–69.

Marino, L. (ed.) (1975) *Joseph de Maistre tra Illuminismo e Ristaurazione*. Torino: Centro Studi Piemontesi.

Marpeau, B. (2000) *Gustave Le Bon. Parcours d'un intellectuelle, 1841–1931*. Paris: CNRS Editions.

Maser, W. (1970) *Hitler's Mein Kampf*. London: Faber.

Mauss, M. (1903–4) 'Review of O. Stoll's Suggestion und Hypnotismus in der Völkerpsychologie', *L'Année Sociologique*, 1903–4, 8: 233–4.

Mazel, H. (1899) 'Sociologues contemporaines. Vacher de Lapouge', *Mercure de France*, 29: 662–75.

Mazundar, P. E. (1992) *Eugenics, Human Genetics and Human Failings*. New York: Routledge, Chapman & Hall.

McClelland, J. S. (1970) *The French Right (From Maistre to Maurras)*. London: Jonathan Cape.

McClelland, J. S. (1989) *The Crowd and the Mob*. London: Unwin.

McDougall, W. (1920) *The Group Mind*. Cambridge: Cambridge University Press.

Mechoulan, H. (1979) *Le sang de l'autre ou l'honneur de Dieu*. Paris: Fayard.

Merquior, J. G. 'Virtue and Progress: The Radicalism of George Sorel', in J. Hall *Rediscoveries*. Oxford: Oxford University Press, pp. 123–37.

Merton, R. K. (1960) 'The Ambivalences of Le Bon's *The Crowd*', in introduction to Le Bon's *The Crowd*. New York: Penguin Books

Metraux, A. (1982) "French Crowd Psychology", in Woodward, W. and Ash, M., (eds), *The Problematic Science*. New York: Prager, pp. 276–99.

Michel, F. (1847) (1983) *Histoire des races maudites de la France et de l'Espagne*. Donostia: Elkar.

Mommsen, W. and Hirschfeld, G. (1982*) Social Protest, Violence and Terror in Nineteenth and Twentieth Century Europe*. London: Macmillan.

Montagu, A. (1974) *Man's Most Dangerous Myth: The Fallacy of Race*. Walnut Creek: Altamira Press.

Montesquieu, C. (1989) *The Spirit of the Law*. Cambridge: Cambridge University Press.

Montaigne, M. (1991) *The Complete Essays*. London: Allen Lane.

Moore, B. (1958) *Political Power and Social Theory*. Cambridge: Harvard University Press.

Moscovici, S. (1985) *The Age of the Crowd*. Cambridge: Cambridge University Press.

Moscovici, S. (1989) *La Machine à faire des dieux*. Paris: Fayard.

Mosse, G. L. (1961) *The Culture of Western Europe*. London: John Murray.

Mosse, G. L. (1964) *The Crisis of German Ideology*. New York: Schocken Books.

Mosse, G. L. (1981) *Nazi Culture. A Documentary History*. New York: Schocken Books.

Mosse, G. L. (1991) *The Nationalization of the Masses*. Ithaca, N.Y: Cornell University Press.

Mosse, G. L. (1978a) *Nazism. A Historical and Comparative Analysis of National Socialism*. Oxford: Blackwell

Mosse, G. L. (1978b). *Towards the Final Solution. A History of European Racism*. New York: Fertig.

Mosse, G. L. (1980) *Masses and Man. Nationalism and Fascist Perceptions of Reality*. New York: Fertig.

Muller-Hill, B. (1988) *Murderous Science: Elimination by Scientific Selection of Jews, Gipsies and Others, Germany 1933–1945*. Oxford: Oxford University Press.

Murard, L. and Zylberman, P. (1983) 'L'enfer tonique (Malthus et Gobineau)', *History of European Ideas*, 4(2): 151–82.

Nagel, G. (1975) *Georges Vacher de Lapouge: ein Beitrag zur Geschichtem des Sozialdarwinismus in Frankreich*. Freiburg: Schulz.

Nef, J. (1963) 'Truth, Belief and Civilisation: Tocqueville and Gobineau', *Review of Politics*, 25, 4: 65–78.

Nijhoff, P. (1985) 'Georges Sorel et Émile Durkheim: convergences et divergences, 1894–1899' in Juillard, J. and Sand, S. (eds) *Georges Sorel et son temps*. Paris: Editions du Seuil, pp. 263–85.

Nisbet, R. (1952) 'Conservatism and Sociology', *American Journal of Sociology*, 58; 167–75.

Nisbet, R. (1962) *Social Change and History*. New York: Oxford University Press.

Nisbet, R. (1986) *Conservatism*. Keynes: Open University.

Noakes, J. (1984) 'Nazism and Eugenics. The Background to the Nazi Sterilization Law of 14 July 1933', in Bullen, R. et al (eds) *Ideas into Politics*. London: Croom Helm, pp. 75–94.

Nolte, E. (1965) *Three Faces of Fascism*. London: Weidenfeld.

Nouvelle Revue Française, La (1991) *Hommage a Gobineau*. Paris: Gallimard.

Nye, R. A. (1973) 'Two Paths to the Psychology of Action: Le Bon and Sorel', *Journal of Modern History*, 45: 411–38.

Nye, R. A. (1975) *The Origins of Crowd Psychology*. London: Sage.

Nye, R. (1977) *The Anti-Democratic Sources of Elite Theory*. London: Sage.

Odom, H. H. (1967) 'Generalisations on Race in Nineteenth Century Anthropology', *Isis*, 58: 5–18.

Ohana, D. (1986) 'The Role of Myth in History: F. Nietzsche and G. Sorel' in *Religion, Ideology and Nationalism*. Jerusalem: The Historical Society of Israel.

Ohana, D. (1991) 'Georges Sorel and the Rise of Political Myth', *History of European Ideas*, 13(6) 733–46.

Oldroyd, D. R. (1980) *Darwinian Impacts*. Keynes: Open University

Olender, M. (1981) *Le racisme. Mythes et sciences*. Paris: Complexe.

Ortega y Gasset, J. (1930) (1984) *The Revolt of the Masses*. New York: Norton.

Pagden, A. (1982) *The Fall of Natural Man*. Cambridge: CUP.

Pagden, A. (1993) *European Encounters with the New World*. New Haven: Yale University Press.

Pagliaro, H. (ed.) (1973) *Racism in the Eighteenth Century*. New York: Fress Press.

Paul, D. (1984) 'Eugenics and the Left', *Journal of the History of Ideas*, 45: 567–90.

Pauly, P. J. (1993) 'Essay Review: The Eugenics Industry', *Journal of the History of Biology*, 26(1): 131–45.

Paulhan, F. (1896) 'Les selections sociales d'après un livre récent', *Revue Scientifique*, 33(6): 13–18.

Peel, J. D. Y. (1968) *H. Spencer*. London: Heinemann.

Pennington, K. (1970) 'Bartolomé de las Casas and the Tradition of Medieval Law', *Church History*, 39: 149–61.

Pichot, A. (2000) *La société pure. De Darwin à Hitler*. Paris: Flammarion.

Pickering, W. S .F. (1975) *Durkheim on Religion*. London: RKP.

Pickering, W. S .F. (1984) *Durkheim's Sociology of Religion*. London: RKP.

Pieterse, J. (1990) 'Empire and Race' in Pieterse, J. *Empire and Emancipation*. New York: Praeger.

Plamenatz, J. (1963) *Man and Society*. London: Routledge

Pois, R. (ed.) (1970) *Alfred Rosenberg. Selected Writings*. London: Jonathan Cape.

Poliakov, L. (1966) *History of Anti-Semitism*, 2 vols. London: Elek Books.

Poliakov, L. (1971) 'Les idées anthropologiques des philosophes du Siècle des Lumières', *Revue française d'Histoire d'Outre-Mer*, 212: 255–78.

Poliakov, L. (1974) *The Aryan Myth*. New York: Basic Books

Poliakov, L. (1976) *Le racisme*. Paris: Seghers.

Popkin, R. (1974) 'Bible Criticism and Social Science', in R. S. Cohen and M. Wartofsky (eds) *Methodological and Historical Essays on the Natural and Social Sciences,* Dordrecht: Reidel, pp. 339–60

Portis, L. (1980) *G. Sorel*. London: Pluto Press.

Proctor, R. (1988) 'From Anthropologie to Rassenkunde in the German Anthropological Tradition', in *History of Anthropology*, 5: 138–79.

Proctor, R. (1988) *Racial Hygiene. Medicine under the Nazis*. Harvard: Harvard University Press.

Pulzer, P. G. J. (1964) *The Roots of Political Anti-Semitism in Germany*. New York: John Wiley.

Quinlan, S. (1999) 'The Racial Imagery of Degeneration and Depopulation: Georges Vacher de Lapouge and Anthroposociology in "Fin-de Siècle" France', *History of European Ideas*, 24(6): 393–413.

Rainger, R. (1978) 'Race, Politics and Science: The Anthropological Society of London in the 1860s', *Victorian Studies*, Autumn 1978, pp. 51–70.

Raverea, M. (1986) *Joseph de Maistre, pensatore dell'origine*. Milano: Mursia.

Ready, W. J. (1995) 'The Traditional Critique of Individualism in Post' *History of Political Thought*, 1: 49–75.

Rey, P. L. (1981) *L'universe romanesque de Gobineau*. Paris: Gallimard.

Richards, J. R. (2000) *Human Nature after Darwin*. London: Routledge.

Richter, M. (1958) 'The Study of Man – A Debate on Race: The Tocqueville-Gobineau Correspondence', *Commentary*, 25: 151–60.

Roger, J. (1970) 'Buffon' in *Dictionary of Scientific Biography*, 2: 576–82. New York: Scribners.

Roger, J. (1989) *Les sciences de la vie dans la pensée française du XVIII siècle*. Paris: Armand Colin.

Rogers, J. A. (1972) 'Darwinism and Social Darwinism', *Journal of the History of Ideas*, 32: 265–80.

Röhrich, W. (1982) 'Georges Sorel and the Myth of Violence', in Mommsen, W. and Hirschfeld, G. (eds) *Social Protest, Violence and Terror in Nineteenth and Twentieth Centuries Europe*, London: Macmillan, pp. 245–56.

Ross, R. (ed.) (1982) *Racism and Colonialism*. The Hague: Nijhoff.

Roth, J. (1967) 'The Roots of Italian Fascism: Sorel and Sorelismo', *The Journal of Modern History*, 39: 30–45.

Roth, J. (1980) *The Cult of Violence: Sorel and the Sorelians*. Berkeley: University of California Press.

Rousseau, J. J. (1755) (1984) *A Discourse on Inequality*. London: Pelican.

Rouvrier, C. (1986) *Les idées politiques de Gustave LeBon*. Paris: PUF

Rude, G. (1959) *The Crowd in the French Revolution*. Oxford: Clarendon Press.

Rude, G. (1981) *The Crowd in History*. London: Lawrence and Wishart.

Rule, J. (1988) *Theories of Civil Violence*. Berkeley: University of California Press.

Rupp, L. (1977) 'Mothers of the Volk: The Image of Women in Nazi Ideology',
Signs, 3(2): 362–79.

Ruse, M. (1974) *The Darwinian Revolution*. Chicago: Chicago University Press.

Ruse, M. (1980) 'Social Darwinism: Two Sources', *Albion*, 12: 23–36.

Russell-Wood, A. J .R. (1978) 'Iberian Expansion and the Issue of Black Slavery:
Changing Portuguese Attitudes', *American Historical Review*, 83: 16–42.

Sand, S. (1985) *L'illussion du politique*. Paris: La Découverte.

Sand, S. (1986) 'Psychologie des classes et psychologie des foules', *Cahiers de
l'Herne*, 1986, 53: 165–82.

Sellière, E. (1903) *Le comte de Gobineau et l'aryanisme historique*. Paris: Plon.

Sellière, E. (1918) *H. S. Chamberlain, le plus recent philosophe du panger-
manisme mystique*. Paris: La renaissance du livre.

Schaf, A. (1973) 'Marxist Theory on Revolution and Violence', *Journal of the
History of Ideas*, 34: 263–70.

Schecter, D. (1990) 'Two Views of the Revolution: Gramsci and Sorel', *History of
European Ideas*, 12(5): 637–53.

Schiller, F. (1993) *Paul Broca. Founder of French Anthropology*. New York: Oxford
University Press.

Schneider, W. H. (1982) 'Towards the Improvement of the Human Race. The
History of Eugenics in France', *Journal of Modern History*, 54: 268–91.

Scott, J. A. (1951) *Republican Ideas and the Liberal Tradition in France*. New
York: Columbia University Press.

See, H. (1933) 'Philosophies racistes de l'histoire: Gobineau, Vacher de Lapouge,
H. S. Chamberlain', *La Grande Revue (Pages Libres)*, 785: 65–84.

Seliger, M. (1958) 'Race-Thinking during the Restoration', *Journal of the History
of Ideas*, 19: 273–82.

Seliger, M. (1960) 'The Idea of Conquest and Race Thinking during the Restoration', *Review of Politics*, 22: 545–67.

Sellière, E. (1903) *Le comte de Gobineau et l'aryanisme historique*. Paris: Plon.

Sellière, E. (1918) *H. S. Chamberlain, le plus recent philosophe du panger-
manisme mystique*. Paris: La Renaissance du Livre.

Semmel, B. (1959) 'Karl Pearson, Socialist and Darwinist', *British Journal of
Sociology*, 9: 111–25.

Sièyes, E. (1982) *Qu'est-ce que le Tiers Etat?* Paris: Presses Universitaires de
France.

Simon, W. (1960) 'Herbert Spencer and Social Organism', *Journal of the History
of Ideas*, 21: 294–9.

Smith, A. (1984) *Gobineau et l'historie naturelle*. Gèneve: Droz.

Smith, S. S. (1995) *An Essay on the Cause of the Variety of Complexion and Figure in the Human Species*. Bristol: Thoemmes.

Snowden, F. (1970) *Blacks in Antiquity*. Cambridge MA: Harvard University Press.

Snyder, L. L. (1962) *The Idea of Racialism. Its Meaning and History*. Princeton, NJ: D. van Nostrand.

Sonn, R. (1989) *Anarchism and Cultural Politics in the Fin de Siècle France*. Lincoln: University of Nebraska Press.

Sorel, G. (1905) 'Le Syndicalisme révolutionnaire', *Le Mouvement socialiste*, 17: 265–280.

Sorel, G. (1999) *Reflections on Violence*. Cambridge: Cambridge University Press.

Sorokin, P. (1928) *Contemporary Sociological Theories*, New York: Harper.

Spencer, H. (1890) *Essays*, 3 vols. London: Williams & Norgate.

Stanley, J. L. (1982) *The Sociology of Virtue: The Political and Social Theories of Georges Sorel*. Berkeley: University of California Press.

Stanton, W. (1960) *The Leopards' Spots. Scientific Attitudes towards Race in America*. Chicago IL: Chicago University Press.

Stark, W. (1962) *The Fundamental Forms of Social Thought*. London: Routledge Kegan Paul.

Stein, A. (1955) 'Adolf Hitler und Gustave Le Bon', *Geschichte im Wissenschaft und Unterricht*, 6: 362–8.

Stein, G. J. (1988) 'Biological Science and the Roots of Nazism', *American Scientist*, 76(1): 50–8.

Steinberg, D. L. (1992) 'Genes and Racial Hygiene. Studies of Science under National Socialism', *Science as Culture*, 14: 116–29.

Stepan, N. (1980) *The Idea of Race in Science: Great Britain 1800–1960*. London: Macmillan.

Stern, F. (1961) *The Politics of Cultural Despair*. Berkeley: University of California Press.

Sternhell, Z. (1978) *La droite révolutionnaire*. Paris: Seuil.

Sternhell, Z (1983) *Ni droite ni gauche. L'ideologie fasciste en France*. Paris: Complexe (English tr. *Neither Left Nor Right*). Princeton, NJ: Princeton University Press, 1986).

Sternhell, Z. (1989) *Naissance de l'idéologie fasciste*. Paris: Gallimard. (with M. Sznajder and M. Ashéri) (English tr., *The Birth of Fascist Ideology*), Princeton, NJ: Princeton University Press, 1994).

Stocking, G. (1968) *Race, Culture and Evolution*. Chicago: Chicago University Press.

Stocking, G. W. (1973) 'From Chronology to Ethnology: J.C. Prichard and British Anthropology' in Prichard, J. C., *Researches into the Physical History of Man*. Chicago, IL: Chicago University Press.

Stocking, G. W. (1974) *The Shaping of American Anthropology. A Franz Boas Reader*. Chicago, Ill.: Chicago University Press.

Stocking, G. W. (1987) *Victorian Anthropology*. New York: Free Press.

Strauss, L. (1963) *The Political Philosophy of Hobbes*. Chicago IL: Phoenix Books.

Taguieff, P. A. (1995) *Les Fins de l'antiracisme*. Paris: Michalon.

Taguieff, P. A. (1998) *La couleur et le sang. Doctrines racistes à la française*. Paris: Mille et une nuits.

Taine, H. (1986) *Les origines de la France contemporaine*, 2 vols. Paris: Robert Laffont.

Talmon, J. (1970) 'The Legacy of Georges Sorel: Marxism, Violence and Fascism', *Encounter*, 34(2): 47–60.

Thiec, I. J. (1981) 'Gustave Le Bon, prophète de l'irrationalisme de masse', *Revue Française de Sociologie*, 22: 409–28.

Thuillier, G. (1977) 'Un anarchiste positiviste: Geroges Vacher de Lapouge' in Guireal, P. and Temime, E. (eds) *L'idée de race dans la pensée politique française contemporaine*. Paris: Centre Nationale de la Recherche Scientifique.

Tocqueville, A. de (1959) 'Correspondance d'Alexis de Tocqueville et d'Arthur de Gobineau' in *Oeuvres complètes*, vol. IX. Paris: Gallimard.

Tocqueville, A. de (1980) *On Democracy, Revolution and Society*. Chicago: University of Chicago Press.

Todorov, T. (1984) *The Conquest of America*. New York: Harper & Row.

Todorov, T. (1994) *On Human Diversity. Nationalism, Racism and Exoticism in French Thought*. Harvard: Harvard University Press.

Todorov, T. (1995) *The Morals of History*. Minneapolis: University of Minnesota Press.

Vacher de Lapouge, G. (1886) 'L'Heredité', *Revue d'Anthropologie*, vol. I: 212–25.

Vacher de Lapouge, G. (1896) *Les sélections sociales*, Paris: Fontemoing.

Vacher de Lapouge, G. (1897) 'Les lois fondamentales de L'Anthropo-sociologie', *Revue Scientifique*, 8(18): 545–52.

Vacher de Lapouge, G. (1899) *L'Aryen, son rôle social*. Paris: Fontemoig.

Vacher de Lapouge, G. (1909) *Race et milieu social*. Paris: Rivière.

Vanderpool, H. (ed.) (1973) *Darwin and Darwinism*. London: Heath

Vernon, R. (1973) 'Rationalism and Commitment in Sorel', *Journal of the History of Ideas*, 34: 405–20.

Vernon, R. (1978) *Commitment and Change*. Toronto: University of Toronto Press.

Vincent, K. S. (1990) 'Interpreting Georges Sorel: Defender of Virtues or Apostle of Violence?', *History of European Ideas*, 12: 239–57.

Vitoria, F. de (1991) *Political Writings*. Cambridge: Cambridge University Press.

Voegelin, E. (1933) *Die Rassenidee in der Geschichte. Von Ray bis Carus*. Berlin: Junker und Dünnhaupt.

Voegelin, E. (1940) 'The Growth of the Race Idea', *Review of Politics*, 2: 283–317.

Von Fritz, K. (1973) 'The Influence of Ideas on Ancient Greek Historiography', *Dictionary of the History of Ideas*, vol. II. New York: Scribner.

Vorzimmer, P. (1969) 'Darwin, Malthus and the Theory of Natural Selection', *Journal of the History of Ideas*, 30: 527–42.

Vout, M. and Wilde, L. (1987) 'Socialism and Myth: The Case of Bergson and Sorel', *Radical Philosophy*, 46: 2–7

Walicki, A. (1979) *A History of Russian Thought*. Stanford, CA.: Stanford University Press.

Walton, R. C. (1994) 'The Holocaust: Conversion to Racism through Scientific Materialism', *History of European Ideas,* 19: 787–94.

Weindling, P. (1985) 'Weimar Eugenics', *Annals of Science*, 42: 303–18.

Weindling, P. (1989) *Health, Race, and German Politics between National Unification and Nazism, 1870–1945*. Cambridge: Cambridge University Press.

Weindling, P. (1991) *Darwinism and Social Darwinism in Imperial Germany*. Stuttgart: Fisher.

Weingart, P. (1987) 'The Rationalisation of Sexual Behaviour: The Institutionalisation of Eugenics in Germany', *Journal of the History of Biology*, 20: 159–93.

Weiss, S. F. (1985) 'The Race Hygiene Movement in Germany', *Osiris*, 3: 193–236.

Weiss, S. F. (1987) *Race Hygiene and National Efficiency. The Eugenics of W. Schallmayer*. Berkeley: University of California Press.

Wells, K.D. (1973) 'William Charles Wells and the Races of Man', *Isis*, 64: 215–25

Whisker, J. B. (1982) *The Social, Political and Religious Thought of Alfred Rosenberg*. Washington: University Press of America.

Wilde, L. (1986) 'Sorel and the French Right', *History of Political Thought*, 7: 361–74.

Williams, D. O. (1982) 'Racial Ideas in Victorian England', *Ethnic and Racial Studies,* 5: 196–212.

Williams, E. A. (1985) 'Anthropological Institutions in Nineteenth Century France', *Isis*, 76: 331–48.

Williams, E. (1944) *Slavery and Capitalism*. Cambridge: Cambridge University Press.

Wokler, R. (1976) 'Tyson and Buffon on the Orang-utan', *Studies on Voltaire*, 155: 2301–19.

Wokler, R. (1980) 'The Apes in the Enlightenment Anthropology', *Studies on Voltaire*, 192: 1164–75.

Wokler, R. (1982) 'From the Orang-utan to the Vampire: Towards an Anthropology of Rousseau', in Leigh, R. A. (ed.) *Rousseau after 200 Years*. Cambridge: Cambridge University Press.

Woodroffe, M. (1981) 'Racial Theories of History and Politics: The Example of H. S. Chamberlain', in Kennedy, P. and Nicholls, A. (eds) *Nationalist and Racialist Movements in Britain and Germany before 1914*. London: Macmillan.

Worms, R. (1897) Review of Vacher de Lapouge (1896), *Revue International de Sociologie*, 5(1): 329–30.

Yolton, J. (1970) *Locke and the Compass of Human Understanding*. London: Cambridge University Press.

Young, E. (1968) *Gobineau und der Rassismus*. Meisenheim: Hain

Young, R. M. (1985) *Darwin's Metaphor*. Cambridge: Cambridge University Press.

Zmarzlik, H. G. (1972) 'Social Darwinism in Germany' in Holborn, H. (ed.) *Republic to Reich. The Making of the Nazi Revolution*. New York: Pantheon.

Index

Acosta, Joseph de 27
Adam (biblical figure) 28, 30, 63, 74
adaptation 75
Adorno, Theodor 101
Africa, Africans 12–3, 24, 29, 36–8
  dehumanization of 30–3
  mental inferiority of 39–40
  slavery 33
Alembert, Jean le Rond d' 37
Alexander, Jeffrey 130
Alexander VI (pope) 21
Allport, Gordon 94
Alpines 10
America, Americans 36
  blacks and 30
  discovery of 17–8, 22
  mental inferiority of 39
  monstrous races and 27
  terrestrial paradise in 27
American Indians 2
  Christianity and 25
  origin of 27
  homunculi 25
  infidel 20
  simple-minded 20
  tutelage of 21
Ammon, Otto 4, 104–5, 112, 116–17, 119,
    137–8, 140–1
  *Anatomy of a Pygmie Compared with that
    of a Monkey, an Ape and a Man* (Tyson)
    28–9
L'ancien régime (Tocqueville) 67
Anglo-Saxon
  see England
anthropology
  Le Bon on 88
  Vacher de Lapouge on 108–10
  Woltmann on 138
anthroposociology 10, 104–6, 108–19, 138,
    140

anti-Semitism
  Chamberlain on 139–40
  Kant on 34
  Medieval Spain and 14–5
  Rosenberg on 142
apes 13
  Africans and 32
  human beings and 28–9, 34, 39
Apologetic History (Las Casas) 23
Apologia (Ginés de Sépulveda) 24
Aquinas, Thomas 21, 25
Arendt, Hanna 87, 121
Aristotle 10, 19–20, 25, 28
Aron, Raymond 67, 102
Aryans, Aryan race, Aryanism 3, 10, 61, 64, 70,
    113–4, 118–9, 137–40, 142
Asia, Asian 27, 36–7, 39
Australian Aborigines 130
Augustinian 17–8
Aztecs 18, 25, 62

Barnes, Harry Elmer 1101, 119
Barrows, Susanna 96
Barzun, Jacques 42
Baer, Karl von 79
Bayle, Pierre 25
Bejin, André 106
Bellah, Norbert 130
Bergson, Henri 124–6, 131
Bergsonian syndicalism 127
Berlin, Isaiah 2, 41, 50–1, 53–6, 87
Berlioz, Louis Hector 45
Bernier, François 29
Bernstein, Eduard 124
Bible 11–2, 27–8, 30–1, 37, 54, 65, 74
Biddis, Michael 57, 139
biology 75
black colour 13, 30–3
black race 63, 98
Bloch, Marc 42, 44–5

Boas, Franz 118
Bodin, Jean 43
Boissel, Jean 58, 60–1
Bonald, Louis de 47–8
Bonaparte, Napoleon 96
Bouglé, Célestin 100, 111, 117, 127
Boulanviliiers, Henry de 41, 43–5
Boulanger, Georges 95
Bourdieu, Pierre 133
brachycephalic 10, 108–10, 114, 118
Broca, Paul 88, 118
Buckle, Henry Thomas 67
Buenzod, Janine 60
Buffon, George Louis 2, 31, 34, 37–9
Bultmann, Rudolph 12
Burgess, Ernst 87
Burke, Edmund 47–8, 51

Camper, Peter 10
Cannibals, On the (Montaigne) 28
Capital I (Marx) 75, 123
Caro-Baroja, Julio 14
Caribbean, Caribbeans 20, 28
Catholicism 121
    French Revolution against 47
    Maistre as defender of 51, 53
    Sixteenth century Spain and 18
Cecil, Robert 142
Celts 11
Chamberlain, Houston Steward 4, 104, 119–20,
    136, 138–40, 142
Charles V, Emperor, 19, 21, 23
chimpanzees
    Africans and 31
    humans beings and 29
    monkeys and 29
Christ
    see Jesus Christ
Christianity, Christian 8, 12–15, 27, 119–20
    anthroposociology and 119–20
    eugenicism and 108
    Holy Inquisition and 26
    Chamberlain on 139
    valid myth 122, 125, 128
civil slavery 19
Cioran, Emil Michael 53–4
Civilisations de l'Inde (Le Bon) 88
Civilisation des Arabes, La (Le Bon) 88

civilizations 63, 92
class
    consciousness 128
    struggle 123
Clausewitz, Karl Marie von 42
Closson, Carlos 104, 11, 113, 115, 117
collective effervescence 100–2, 124
colonialist ideology 89
colour prejudice
    early modern English literature on 30
Columbus, Christopher 27
communism 69, 143
comparative anatomy 28
Comte, Auguste 48, 69
Condorcet, Marquis de 77
conservatism 48–9, 51
Contemporary Sociological Theories (Sorokin)
    118–9
Copernicus, Nicolaus 73
Course (Comte) 69
Courtet de l'Isle, Victor 61
Cousin, Victor 45
craniometry 10
Critical and Historical Dictionary (Bayle) 28
    conservatism 47, 51
Crocker, Leslie G. 47–8
crowd 2–4, 86, 95–7, 100–2, 128, 135, 143
    psychology 85, 101–2, 124
Crowd, The (Le Bon) 85–6, 94
Curtin, Philip 32, 38
Cuvier, Georges 2, 39–40

Darwin, Charles 3, 73–81, 83, 88, 104–5,
    135–7, 140
Darwinism, Darwinian 74–5, 89, 119–20, 137
Das Geschlechten under Völkerpsychologie
    (Stoll) 102
Davenport, Charles 120
De Indis (Vitoria) 20–2
De la démocracie en Amérique (Tocqueville)
    67
De l'Esprit des lois (Montesquieu) 34
De l'état de nature (Maistre) 51–2
Democrates secundus (Sepúlveda) 23
Deniker, Joseph 114
Descartes, René 106
Descent of Man, The (Darwin) 75, 78
Dictionnaire de la langue française (Littré) 69

Index

Diderot, Denis 37
Die natürliche Auslese beim Menschen
   (Ammon) 105
Die WelttrÄtsel (Haeckel) 136
dolichocephalics 10, 108–10, 112, 114, 118
Dreyfus Affair 95
Dubos, Jean-Baptiste 44–5
Durand de Gros, Joseph Pierre 113
Durkheim, Emile 3, 48, 87, 94, 97, 99–103,
   110, 116, 118–9, 124, 127, 129–33
Durkheimian School 87, 99, 101, 11, 132

effervescence
   see collective effervescence
EFLR
   see Elementary Forms of Religious Life
      (Durkheim)
egalitarianism 117
élan vital (vital impulse) 124, 127
Elementary Forms of Religious Life, The
   (Durkheim) 99, 129–30, 132
elitism 90
encomienda 22–3
Encyclopédie (Diderot and D'Alembert) 37
Engels, Friedrich 121–3, 137
England, English
   early perception of the blacks 30–3
   eugenics in 84
   racial superiority81
   social Darwinism 106
Enlightenment 5, 30, 33–4, 46–8, 50, 54
Essay on the Principle of Population, An
   (Malthus) 77
Essai sur les moeurs et l'esprit des nations
   (Voltaire) 34
Essai sur la psychologie des foules (Fournial)
   85
*Essai sur les donnés immédiates de la
   conscience* (Bergson) 126
Essai sur l'inegalité des races humaines
   (Gobineau) 3, 7, 57–61, 65
Essais et mélanges sociologiques (Tarde) 85
Essays (Spencer) 77
Essays in Eugenics (Galton) 82
Essertier, Daniel 101
Ethiopian
   see African
ethnie 106

Études sur les barbares et le Moyen Age
   (Littré) 69
eugenics, eugenicism 2–4, 80–4, 108, 120,
   135–6, 140–1, 143
Eurocentrism 34
Europe, Europeans, 27, 29, 36–8
European superiority 40
Eve (biblical figure) 28, 30
evolution, evolutionism 38–9, 74–5, 79

fascism
   see totalitarianism
Ferdinand (King of Aragon) 17–8
Final Solution 7
Finley, Moses 10
Foucault, Michel 42–3, 137
Fouillée, Alfred 90, 113, 116, 119
Foundations of the Nineteenth Century, The
   (Chamberlain) 138–9, 142
Fournial, Henry 85
France, French
   impact of social Darwinism in 106
   sixteenth and seventeenth centuries idea of
      race 41–5
   Third Republic
Franks 41–2, 44–5, 61
French races 42–3, 45
French Revolution 4, 41, 45–51, 54, 58, 67, 75,
   95–6, 122–3, 126
Freud, Sigmund 73, 86, 101
Friedmann, Wilhelm 102
Fromm, Erich 87
Fustel de Coulanges, Numa Denis 45
Futuyma, Douglas J. 80

Gager, John 12
Galen, Claudius 23
Galileo (Galileo Galilei) 73
Gallics, Gauls 42, 44–5
Gallo-Romans 44–5, 61
Galton, Francis 3–4, 76, 81–3, 118–19, 135,
   138, 140, 143
Gaulle, Charles de 87
Gaulmier, Jean 58
general strike 121, 125, 127
Germany, Germans 22
   eugenics in 84
   Nazi 135, 142

racism in 136, 139
social Darwinism in 106
totalitarianism in 4
Gesellschaftsordnung und ihre natürlichen Grundlagen (Ammon) 105, 112
Giddens, Anthony 57, 94
Ginés de Sepúlveda, Juan 19
Ginnekan, Gaap van 87, 89–90
Gobineau, Joseph Arthur 3, 5–6, 9, 45, 57–71, 104, 119–20, 135–6, 138, 142–3
Gobineau, Father of Racist Ideology (Biddis) 57
God 28, 37, 49, 52
    Darwin's idea of 74
    Maistre's idea of 54–5
Goethe, Johann Wolfgang 37
'Good Savage'
    criticized by Maistre 52
gorilla 29
Gould, Stephen Jay 73
Grant, Madison 120
Greco-Roman world 2, 9–13
Greece (ancient)
    concept of race in 11
    ethnocentrism in 10
    Gobineau on 62, 65
    race and climate in 9
Greene, John C. 34, 76, 79
Group Mind, The (MacDougall)
Guizot, François 45
Günther, Hans F.K. 104, 120, 141
Gypsies
    extermination by Nazis 71, 141

Haeckle, Ernst 136–7
Halévy, Elie 132
Ham (biblical name) 11–2, 31
Hegel, Georg Wilhelm Friedrich 9
Herder, Johann Gotfried von 9, 37
Hereditary Genius (Galton) 140
Herodotus 65
Herzl, Theodor 87
Hippocrates 9
Histoire de l'Ancien Gouvernement de la France (Boulainvilliers) 43
Histoire des institutions politiques de l'ancienne France (Fustel de Coulanges) 45
Histoire des Perses (Gobineau) 60
Histoire d'Ottar Jarl (Gobineau) 60

Histoire naturelle (Buffon) 37–8
Historia natural y moral de las Indias (Acosta) 27
historical sociology 6
History and Description of Africa (Africanus) 32
History of Civilization in England (Buckle) 67
History of the Indies (Las Casas) 22
History of the Social Sciences, The (Barnes) 101
Hitler, Adolf 9, 70, 87, 99, 104–5, 135, 137, 141–2
Holy Inquisition 26
Holland, Dutch 123
    early perception of the blacks 33
Homer 65
Homo Alpinus 106, 108–9, 113
Homo Europeus 106, 108–10, 112–3
Homo Mediterraneus 106, 108–9, 118
Homo sapiens 35–6
Homo troglodytes 36
homunculi 25
Horace 11
Horowitz, Irving Louis 126
Hotman, François 43
Houzé, Emile 118
Hubert, Henri 11, 114–5
Human Faculty (Galton) 81
human nature
    Darwin and 74
    Galton and 81
    Rousseau and 85
    Taine and 85
human species, unity of, 39–40
Hume, David 28, 33–4
Huxley, Thomas H. 75

Iberian peninsula
    see Spain
Il faut défendre la société (Foucault) 42
Image of Africa, The (Curtin) 38
Incas 25
India
    compared with Europe 88
Indies
    see America
inheritance
    acquired characteristics 80

biological concept 115
Inquisition 52–3
Inquisition in Spain (Kamen) 15
intelligence
  size of the skull and 88
Inter caetera (papal bull) 20
Introduction to the Histyory of Anthropology,
  An (Barnes) 119
Ireland, Irish 78
Isabella (Queen of Castile) 17–8
Islam 13, 17
  black slavery and 32
Israel 27
  ancient 11–2
Italy, Italians 22, 97
  early perception of blacks 33
ius gentium 22

James, William 127, 131
Japhet (biblical figure) 11–2
Jefferson, Thomas 13
Jennings, Jeremy 125
Jesus (Christ) 12, 27, 71, 99
  as non-Jewish 139
Jews, Judaism
  see also anti-Semitism
  alien race in Nazi Germany 142
  burning in early modern Spain 26
  extermination by the Nazis 71, 141
  Israel, Ancient, 11–2, 28
  medieval Europe and 13–15
  seen by Chamberlain 139
Joas, Hans 131
Jordan, Winthrop 30–2, 36
Jouanna, Arlette 41

Kant, Kantian 33–4, 137, 142
Khaldum, Ibn 32
Kamen, henry 15
kin selection 79
Kropotkin, Peter 87
Kugelman, Ludwig 123

La division du travail social (Durkheim) 132
La droite révolutionnaire (Sternhell) 103
La folla delinquente (Sighele) 85
La Foule (Le Bon) 3
La machine à faire des dieux (Moscovici) 102

La psychologie du socialisme (Le Bon) 128
La science politique fondé sur la science de
  l'homme (Courtet de l'Isle) 61
Lagardelle, Hubert 127
Lamarck, Jean-Louis 78, 88
Lamarckian, Lamarckism 78–80, 89
L'Année Sociologique (journal) 110–115
Lapouge
  see Vacher de Lapouge
L'Aryen. Son rôle social (Vacher de Lapouge)
  103, 105, 107, 114
Las Casas, Bartolomé 19–25
Le Bon, Gustave 3, 5, 85–101, 119, 124,
  127–8, 135, 138, 143
leader(s) 86, 97
lecherousness
  applied to Africa 32
Lebensraum (vital space) 136
Lebrun, Richard 47, 50
Lenin, Vladimir Ilyich 87, 99, 124, 132
Leninism 121
Les formes élémentaires de la vie religieuse
  (Durkheim)
  see *Elementary Forms of Religious Life, The*
Les origines de la France contemporaine
  (Taine) 85
Les lois psychologiques de l'évolution des
  peuples (Le Bon) 90
Les Premières Civilisations (Le Bon) 88
Les races et les peuples de la terre (Deniker)
  114
Les selections sociales (Vacher de Lapouge) 4,
  105, 107, 112, 114–6
Les soirés de Saint-Pétersbourg (Maistre) 54
L'évolution créatrice (Bergson) 126
Lesseps, Ferdinand de 95
Lévi-Strauss, Claude 6, 57
L'Homme et les Sociétés (Le Bon) 88–9
L'opinion et la foule (Tarde) 85
L'origine de l'inégalité parmi les hommes
  (Rousseau) 52
Linnaeus, Carolus 2, 34–7
Littré, Emile 69
Lukes, Steve 101
Livi, Ridolfo 113
L'utilité du pragmatisme (Sorel) 127
Luther, Martin 9, 12, 71
Lyell, Charles 79

Mably, Abbé 44
MacDougall, William 86, 101
Machiavelli, Niccolo 18
Machiavellian 100
Maistre, Joseph de 2, 41, 47–56, 87, 143
Malthus, Thomas Robert 77–8, 88
Manheim, Karl 121
Man's Place in Nature (Huxley) 75
Marcion 12
Marpean, Benoit 87
Manouvrier, Léonce-Pierre 114
Marx, Karl 60, 68–9, 71, 73, 75, 81, 194–5, 121–5, 137
Marxism 121–2, 138
Marxism-Darwinism 137
Massenpsychologie und Ich-Analyse (Freud) 86
Maupertois, Pierre 38
Mauss, Marcel 100–2, 110, 114, 132
Mayas 25
Mazel, Henri 117
Mein Kampf (Hitler) 142
Memoirs of my Life (Galton) 82
Merton, Robert K. 93–5, 99
mestizo 29
Method of Attracting all People to the True Faith (Las Casas) 23
Mexico 20
Michelet, Jules 45
Michels, Robert 99, 101
Middle Ages 13–5
Mill, John Stuart 67
Mind of Primitive Man, The (Boas) 118
mob 85
Mohammed 99
modernity
    crisis of 5
    'dark side' of 6
Mongolian
    see Asian
monkey 29
monogenism 34
Montague, Ashley 29
Montaigne, Michel de 28
Montesquieu, Charles de Secondat 10, 33–5, 41, 45
Moore, Barrington 26
Moors, Moriscos 8, 13, 17, 26, 53
Mosca, Gaetano 87, 99

Moscovici, Serge 94, 102
Mosse, George 142
Muffong, Henri 110–15
Muqaddimah (Khaldum) 32
mulatto 29
Mutual Aid (Kropotkin) 81
Myth of the Twentieth Century, The (Rosenberg) 120, 142
myths 5–6, 121–2, 124–5, 127–8, 131

Napoleonic Era 95
nation, nationalism 90
'National Character, Of' (Hume) 34
natural selection 74–5, 78, 80, 83, 106, 113, 140
natural slavery 19
Nazi Germany
    see Germany and Nazism
Nazism, Nazis 4, 6, 9, 71–2, 81, 103–4, 119–20, 135, 141–3
Nerval, Gérard de 45
Nagel, Günther 106
Neumann, Franz 87
Newton, Issac 73
Nietzsche, Nietzschean 9, 71, 137–8
Nijhoff, Peter 131
Nisbert, Robert 48
Noah (biblical figure) 11, 28
'noble race'
    defined by Chamberlain 140
'noble savage'
    see primitivism
Normans 43
Notes on Virginia (Jefferson) 13

Orang-utan 29
Oriental civilizations 65
Origin of Species, The (Darwin) 73–5, 80
original sin 55
Ortega y Gasset, José 87

Pagden, Anthony 24
Pareto, Vilfredo 87, 99, 126
Park, Robert 87
Pasquier, Étienne 43
Paul, Saint 12
Paul III (pope) 18
Paulhan, Jean 115–6

Pearson, Karl 119
people(s) 90
Persia, Persians 9, 62
Peru 20
Peyrère, Isaac La 28
Phoenicians 11
Pickering, William S.F. 101
physical anthropology 88
Plato 11, 71
Poliakov, Leon 9, 11, 13, 219, 33
political myth(s) 90
Politisch-Anthropologish Revue (journal) 117,
    137
Politics (Aristotle) 19
Polo, Marco 13
polygenism 28, 34
Portugal, Portuguese 18, 24
    early perception of black people 33
postmodernists 1
Pre-Adamite (Peyrère) 28
Prichard, james Cowles 61
'primitivism' 27
Principles of Political Economy (Mill) 67
proletariat 121, 127
Protestantism 17
Psycholgoie des foules (Le Bon) 85, 94–5, 97,
    101
Psychologie du peuple Français (Fouillé) 116
purity of blood 17

Qu'est-ce que le Tiers Etat? (Sieyès) 44
Queveedo, Juan 19
Quinet, Edgar 45

race(s) 2–6, 143
    Aryan 119
    Bible on 11–2, 28, 30–1, 34
    cephalic index and 108–10
    Chamberlain on 139–40
    Comte on 69
    creation of the idea of 7–8
    Darwin on 76
    destiny of 66
    diversity of 28
    eighteenth century conception of 30
    Europeans and non-Europeans 29
    England on 31
    Greece (ancient) on 9–11

    Galton on 82
    Gobineau on 60–5
    Günther on 141
    Hume on 34
    inequality of 117
    Kant on
    Le Bon on 89–94, 97–8
    Littré on 69
    Middle Ages on 13
    Montesquieu on 34
    nineteenth century conception of 62
    Nordic (Germanic) 138
    Renan on 69–70
    Rome (ancient) on 11–13
    seventeenth century conception of 29, 31
    sixteenth century conception of 27, 31
    Spencer on 78
    Tocqueville on 60, 67–8
    use in European languages 9
    Vacher de Lapouge on 104–10, 117
    Voltaire on 34
Race et milieu sociale (Vacher de Lapouge)
    105, 108, 117
racial degeneration 39, 63
Racial Geography of Europe, The (Rifley) 113
racial inequality 103
racial interpretation of history 61
racial miscenegation 3, 57
racial prejudice 34
racial war 42
racial classification
    Buffon on 38–9
    Cuvier on 39–40
    Gobineau on 57–72
    Linnaeus on 35–6
Raciology of the German People (Günther) 141
racism 9, 18
    Aryan 57, 139
    Nazi 135, 138
radical conservatives 1
Ranulf, Svend 99–100
reciprocal altruism 79
*Reflections sur la violence (Reflexions on
    Violence)* (Sorel) 4, 121–2, 124–5, 128, 130
Reflexions on the Revolution in France (Burke)
    51
religion 125–6
    African absence of 31

as a pillar of social order 55
Renan, Ernest 45, 69, 89
*Researches into the Physical History of
Mankind* (Courtet de l'Isle) 61
revolutionary violence 2, 4, 121–3, 135, 143
Revue International de Sociologie (journal) 116
Ribot, Théodule 89
Ripley, William Z. 113
Robespierre, Maximiliene 96
Rome (ancient), Romans 11–13, 44–5, 69
  Gobineau and 62,65
Roosevelt, Franklin Delano 87
Roger, Jacques 38
Rousseau, Jean Jacques 1, 28, 47, 50–2, 85
Rosenberg, Alfred 4, 120, 135, 142–3
Royer, Clement 88
Ruse, Michael 76–9
Russian Revolution 132

Sahlins, Marshall 80
Saint Petersburg Dialogues (Maistre) 52
Saint-Simon, Henri de 48
Salamanca, School of, 21
savagery, savages 31, 39
Saxons 43
Schumpeter, Joseph 87
Scythians 11
Sellière, Ernest 58
Semites 70
Sepúlveda, Ginés de 20, 23–5
Sergi, Giuseppe 113
Service, Elman R. 80
sexual selection 80
Shakespeare, William 30, 73
Shem (biblical figure) 11–2
Sièyes, Emmanuelle Joseph 44–5
Sighele, Scipio 85, 101
skull
  intelligence and 88
slavery
  Aristotle and 19
  Bible and 11–2
  Cuvier and 40
  Enlightenement and 34
  French revolution and 46
  Montesquieu and 34
  race and 10
  Spain and 24

Slavs 141–2
Snowden, Frank 11
social Darwinism 3, 73, 75–7, 79, 103, 105–6,
  135–8, 140
social psychology 87, 101
social revolution 122–4
social selectionism 105–8, 112–3, 117, 119
socialism 104, 107–8, 119, 121, 123, 126,
  131
society, societies 93
sociology 131–2
Sociology (Giddens) 57, 94
Sorel, Georges 3–5, 90, 99–100, 121–33, 135,
  143
Sorokin, Pitirim 101, 118
Spain, Spanish 2
  burning of Jews and Moors 26
  conquest of America by 18
  early concept of race in 8
  early state in 18
  exploitation of American Indians by 25
  Inquisition and 52–3
  medieval Jews and 14–5
  purity of blood 17
  sixteenth century discourse on race in
    17–26
  slavery in 24
Spencer, Herbert 76–80, 89, 137
Spencerism, Spencerianism 89, 106
Stael, Madame de 45
state racism 42
Sternhell, Zeev 87, 99, 119
Stoll, Otto 101–2
struggle for existence 79
Sublimis Deus (papal bull) 18
*Suggestion und Hypnotismus in der
  Völkerpsychologie (Stoll)* 101–2
Suicide (Durkheim) 131
survival of the fittest 80, 136
symbols 122
syndicalist movement 125, 127
Système de politique positive (Comte) 69
Systema Naturae (Linnaeus) 35

Tacitus 11
Taguieff, Pierre-André 89, 93, 107
Taine, Hypolitte 69–70, 85, 89
Talmon, Jacob L.47

Tarde, Gabriel 85, 119, 138
Thierry, Augustine 45
totalitarianism 4, 6, 143
  Calvinist Geneva and
  early modern France and 42
  Le Bon and 99
  Maistre and 47–56
  modern 100
  Rousseau and 47–8, 50
  Sorel and 121
Tocqueville, Alexis de 48, 58–60, 67–8, 142
Tours, Gregory of 43
Trotter, Wilfred 86
Turks 20
Tyson, Edward 28–9

Über Wahnideen in Völkerleben (Friedmann)
  102
UK
  see England
United States, US 123
  eugenics in 84
  race and the 67–8

Vacher de Lapouge, Georges 3–5, 83, 103–9,
  111–20, 135, 137–8, 140–1, 143
Valladolid Council 19, 23, 25–6
*Very Brief Account of the Destruction of the
  Indies* (Las Casas) 22
Vico, Giambattista 124–5

Victorian(s) 73, 75
  values 79
violence
  see revolutionary violence
Vitoria, Francisco de 20–2
Voegelin, Eric 11–2
Völker, Volkish 138, 140
Voltaire (Arouet, François-Marie) 28, 33–4, 44,
  51

Wagner, Richard 138, 142
Wallace, Alfred Russel 78
Weber, Max 101
Western Civilization 1–2, 5, 12
Western Europe 2
white race 63–4, 98
White Over Black (Jordan) 30
Williams, Eric 10
Wilson, Edmund O. 80
Winiarski, Ryszard 113
Woltmann, Ludwig 4, 104, 1117, 119, 137–8,
  141–2
women
  inferiority of 89, 91
Worms, Renée 116

yellow race 63–4
Young, Kimball 101

Zur Anthropologie der Badener (Ammon) 105